$7.50

ORGANIZATION DEVELOPMENT IN SCHOOLS

Edited by

Richard A. Schmuck, University of Oregon

Matthew B. Miles, Center for Policy Research, New York City

University Associates, Inc.
7596 Eads Avenue
La Jolla, California 92037

CONTENTS

PREFACE

We remain very much excited about this book and are optimistic that organization development consultation can help to turn our public schools around. Our own consulting experiences, plus systematic empirical evidence accumulated since the first printing of this volume five years ago, continue to suggest strongly that the techniques of organization development are a plausible and useful vehicle for humanizing schools. Although use of the techniques has really just begun, recent achievements have caused us to be excited about their possibilities for the future. There is a great need for a wider diffusion of organization development consultation in schools, and it is the aim of this book to deepen and extend that process.

The essential purposes of this book are to encourage wider diffusion of organization development in schools and to stimulate and strengthen scholarly research on it. Wider diffusion must, we believe, be accompanied by continuing research on organization development theories and techniques. The effects of training in organization development for schools must be scrutinized and evaluated with great care. Informal case studies and informed speculation are no substitute for thorough empirical research.

We believe that this book will interest people in a variety of professional roles. Those actively involved in the practice of organization development in school districts will of course take note. However, the book should also be of great interest to practitioners of organization development who work in psychology or sociology departments, professional schools of business and public administration, and private consulting firms. We hope that many of these practitioners will henceforth be encouraged to use their skills in educational settings as well.

In the field of professional education proper, this book is intended for five specific audiences: (1) educational administrators, department heads, unit leaders, and teachers concerned with enhancing the effectiveness of their schools; (2) school psychologists, curriculum specialists, and counselors who in one way or another must deal with systemic variables; (3) state department of education personnel concerned with improving the performance of local school districts; (4) specialists working in regional educational laboratories and professors of education involved in the redesign of pre-service and in-service training programs and materials for educators; and (5) educational researchers interested in schools as organizations and the dynamics of educational change.

Following an introductory chapter which deals with background, we present nine studies of organization development in schools. We have chosen recent studies that are based in theory, explicit about training techniques, and inclusive of evaluative research data. Before each chapter we have included brief comments on its most notable elements: its theory, technology, measurement methods, place in the literature, relationship to other studies, and unique features. The concluding chapter summarizes the work done and suggests areas for further investigation. Unsolved issues are usually most interesting, and our review of them, it is hoped, will give direction to the future of organization development in schools.

During the last five years a host of empirical studies on organization development in schools have been carried out. The Appendix to this volume provides an annotated bibliography of all the studies that have come to our attention since the fall of 1971. In the first printing, the Appendix contained a list of people who had participated as organization development trainers in school districts. We have replaced that list of resource people with the annotated bibliography of studies because we have been better able to keep track of the latter. In addition, several years ago the International Association of Applied Social Scientists was organized to accredit and certify organization development consultants, and we recommend that the reader refer to that membership for names of consultants to school districts.

RAS

MBM

1

IMPROVING SCHOOLS THROUGH ORGANIZATION DEVELOPMENT: AN OVERVIEW

Matthew B. Miles and Richard A. Schmuck

Schools are everywhere in need of improvement. In a society as dynamic as ours, that is almost axiomatic. The progressive reform efforts of the 30's and 40's, the post-Sputnik flurry of the late 50's, and the curriculum innovations of the 60's were all accompanied by unassailable rhetoric pointing out the exponential rate of change in society, the degree to which schools were lagging behind and in some cases even resisting needed transformations, and the massive need for school improvement.

Yet, despite its forcefulness, such rhetoric has remained largely unaccompanied by practical long-range strategies for actual improvement. Schools remain largely as they were, with new features—materials, teaching procedures, daily schedules, and personnel roles—in evidence only here and there. If anything, the depth of what we have come to call the American educational crisis perennially increases. As Silberman (1970) has pointed out, our expectations for the educational system have risen faster than our ability to fulfill them.

The underlying assumption of this book is that schools are primarily *organizations,* and that many if not most efforts at educational reform have collapsed or have been absorbed without effect precisely because of the limited attention given to the organizational context in which the reforms have been attempted. Any major innovation in curriculum or instructional technique implies a change in the "culture" of the school. The relationship between teachers and administrators, for example, is apt to change. Often the change affects not only the principal and his faculty but also the relationship between them and the nonprofessional staff and students. Consequently, authority relationships, communication networks, status groupings, and even friendship cliques are forced to change. In this process, the innovation itself often fails or is restructured (and so invalidated) to conform to the "old way" of doing things.

Real improvement in learning is determined not so much by the adoption of specific educational practices as by the modification of organizational conservatism (evidenced by self-contained classrooms, civil service examinations in large cities, the "tyranny of the schedule," and the practice of ability grouping, for example) and organizational pathology (school-community paranoia and mistrust, powerlessness and alienation in teachers, and repressive management of students' lives). As Miles (1965b, p.11) states:

It is time for us to recognize that successful efforts at planned change must take as a primary target the improvement of *organizational health*—the school system's ability not only to function effectively, but to develop and grow into a more fully functioning system. . .attention to organization health ought to be priority one for any administrator seriously concerned with innovativeness in today's educational environment.

Serious, workable strategies for improving organizational health have been used widely in industrial and governmental settings since the mid-1950's. In practice they have been categorized under the label "organization development" (OD). We are convinced, theoretically and empirically, that OD can provide a major contribution to school improvement. This book presents evidence documenting that belief, and is frankly aimed at encouraging the diffusion of OD approaches throughout American education. The case descriptions and empirical data we have included are, we hope, sufficiently explicit to provide a basis on which local administrators, boards of education, and the personnel of state departments of education can begin to initiate OD work in school districts. We believe that these findings will also be instructive and encouraging to both OD consultants and researchers on the process of educational change.

The Nature of Organization Development

Definition of OD

OD can be defined as a planned and sustained effort to apply behavioral science for system improvement, using reflexive, self-analytic methods. Let us examine each element of this definition in detail.

System Improvement. The emphasis of OD is on the system, rather than the individual, as the target of change. In this respect the approach differs from "sensitivity training" and "management development." "System" may mean either an entire organization or a subsystem such as an academic department or team of teachers. The emphasis, however, is always on improving both the ability of a *system* to cope and the relationships of the system with subsystems and with the environment. Individuals, of course, often gain insights and new attitudes during such improvement processes, but the primary concern of OD is with such matters as adequate organizational communication, the integration of individual and organizational goals, the development of a climate of trust in decision-making, and the effect of the reward system on morale.[1]

Reflexive, Self-Analytic Methods. OD involves system members themselves in the assessment, diagnosis, and transformation of their own organization. Rather than simply accepting diagnosis and prescription from an outside "technocratic" expert, organization members themselves, with the *aid* of outside consultants, examine current difficulties and their causes and participate actively in the reformulation of goals, the development of new group process skills, the redesign of structures and procedures for achieving the goals, the alteration of the working climate of the system, and the assessment of results.[2]

---

[1] For further explication of the distinction between changing the organization and changing the person, see Schmuck, Runkel, and Langmeyer (1969) and Burke and Schmidt (1970).

[2] Sensitivity training, human relations laboratory training, and similar approaches also in-

Planned and Sustained Effort. OD involves deliberately planned change, as contrasted with system "drifts." Unlike an innovative project or program, it is generally not limited to a specific period of time. To implement OD, an organizational subsystem (such as a Department of Organization Development) is created and charged with the specific responsibility for planning, managing, and evaluating the continuous process of organizational self-renewal. Members of such a subsystem act as inside change agents or OD development specialists (see Chapter 10) and usually link with outside consultants to carry out their mission. The essential concept is that some fraction of an organization's resources is devoted to continuous organizational maintenance, rebuilding, and expansion. Such a concept is familiar to managers in the field of plant and equipment maintenance but is much less widely known and accepted in the maintenance of the human organization.

Organizations are not easily or quickly transformed. The available evidence (see, e.g., Buchanan, 1967 and 1969) suggests that in large organizations two to three years of OD effort is typical before the completion of serious and self-sustaining change. In addition, it must be borne in mind that an organization is never transformed permanently. Instead, institutionalized, built-in OD functions must continually be involved in facing the dilemmas and vicissitudes of organizational renewal.

Applied Behavioral Science. OD relies strongly on concepts from the behavioral sciences: primarily social psychology but also psychology and sociology. Such concepts are used to diagnose an organization's problems, to equip organization members with a conceptual language for talking about phenomena they are facing; to redesign unsatisfactory structures and procedures, and to provide a basis for evaluation of OD interventions and processes.[3]

Historical Sources of OD

Efforts at organizational improvement have a long history, from the wisdom of the *I Ching* to the dispassionate advice of Niccolo Machiavelli to his prince.

---

volve a reflexive, self-analytic approach to the application of behavioral science. However, the primary purpose is the creation of change or improvement in *individual* behavior. See Golembiewski and Blumberg (1970) for a summary of recent work in these areas. It should be pointed out that training focused on the individual often does form part of an OD program (many OD practitioners began as human relations trainers), but such training occurs in the context of efforts at *organizational* change and does not primarily emphasize changing individual psyches. Furthermore, in OD training, group members are not strangers, as in the typical training laboratory, but interdependent members of the same system or interlocked systems.

[3] OD in schools is, of course, part of the larger domain of the social psychology of education. A reader who wishes more background in the corpus of behavioral science relevant to improvement of educational systems should examine Getzels' thorough review (1969), the comprehensive book of readings by Miles and Charters (1970), the analysis of the classroom group as the primary site and mediator of learning by Schmuck and Schmuck (1971), and any of three excellent recent texts (Backman and Secord, 1968; Guskin and Guskin, 1970; and Johnson, 1970).

Probably only after the Industrial Revolution and the rise of the "Protestant ethic," however, did efforts to conceptualize and improve the functioning of non-governmental organizations become explicit. During the first three decades of this century, the most typical organizational improvement activities centered around time and motion studies and the "scientific management" movement led by Frederick Taylor. The focus was primarily on production output at the lower levels of an organization; even Barnard's classic text, *The Functions of the Executive* (1938), which drew strong attention to the human functions in organizations, did not lead directly to the establishment of managerial training or development programs. Many consulting firms and a few internal consulting departments existed during this period; their approach was primarily "technocratic" (study and advice-giving) and did not encourage the self-analytic behavior discussed briefly above. It is of interest that the "scientific management" movement made strong inroads into the schools during this period as well. (See Callahan and Button, 1964.)

Beginning in 1947, a group of social psychologists and educators stimulated by Kurt Lewin began holding summer training conferences at Bethel, Maine, and formed the National Training Laboratories in Group Development (now the NTL Institute of Applied Behavioral Science). The field of human relations laboratory training, centering around the intensively self-analytic experience of the "T-group," developed rapidly. (See Miles, 1962, for an overview.) This training helped to spawn a large and helpful literature on planned change.[4]

The original T-group experiences were set up for groups of strangers meeting in a "cultural island" away from their homes and places of work. During the early 1950's, people involved in training and management development began to experiment with the use of T-groups in their own organizations. Programs of T-group training were launched in such settings as Republic Aviation, the American Red Cross, the Episcopal Church, and the West Virginia Pulp and Paper Company. One of the first experimental OD programs was developed at the Pasadena and China Lake Naval Ordnance Test Stations beginning in 1954 by Paul Buchanan, collaborating with Robert Tannenbaum, Charles Ferguson, and I. R. Weschler as outside change agents from UCLA. T-groups were first set up among school district personnel in the early 1950's in Seattle under the leadership of Donald Nylen.

In the late 1950's a major development occurred when the Esso Company, stimulated by applied behavioral scientists Paul Buchanan, Robert Blake, and Herbert Shepard, launched a large-scale program involving not only T-groups for "cousins" (persons drawn from different parts of the same organization) within Esso refineries, but also training in problem-solving for teams of superiors and subordinates to help them to be more open, trusting, and effective in their work, and "intergroup" labs for revealing, clarifying, and resolving conflicts between departments and divisions and between management and labor (Foundation for Research on Human Behavior, 1960).

---

[4] For a useful analytical discussion of various approaches to planned change, see Bennis (1961) and the variety of material included in Bennis, Benne, and Chin (1969)—especially the review of change strategies by Chin and Benne (pp. 32-59). A systematically constructed framework for processes of planned change appeared in Lippitt, Watson, and Westley (1958). We also commend to the reader Havelock's (1969) very comprehensive review and synthesis of 4000 studies on planned change. Miles's (1964) assembly of research, case studies, and theory in the domain of educational innovation is also relevant.

The experience of the Esso program, which involved the recruitment and active participation of more than fifty competent T-group trainers, proved crucial. A group of experienced and capable consultants was developed who had seen for themselves that intensive group methods could have powerful and useful effects upon organizational improvement. The Esso program was also instrumental in inducing a half-dozen faculty members of the influential Harvard Business School to experiment with laboratory training methods and thus to open the way for change in the graduate instruction of future managers and, later, OD specialists.

The movement labeled "OD" began spreading; various companies, including Union Carbide, IBM, Aerojet, Pacific Finance, Non-Linear Systems, Space Technology Laboratories (later TRW Systems), and Alcan, began establishing departments of organization development. The OD specialists in such departments, unlike their lower-power predecessors involved in management and supervisory training, had considerable influence and usually reported directly to top management. At this time most external OD consultants had membership in the National Training Laboratories and were on university faculties. However, non-university consultants began moving into the field: Richard Beckhard, for example, stimulated OD programs in such firms as the Hotel Corporation of America, Bankers Trust, and J. Lyons.

For its basic ideas OD has relied heavily on several seminal books. The classic Hawthorne studies by Elton Mayo, as reported by Roethlisberger and Dickson (1939) did a great deal to turn attention from time and motion analysis toward human factors. A fascinating study in overcoming resistance to organizational change (Coch and French, 1948) demonstrated the power of group discussion in changing organizational norms and productivity. Jacques (1952) provided a classic case study of consultation which influenced many who were to become OD practitioners.

Perhaps most crucially, McGregor (1961) showed managers and OD specialists a new vision of man in the organization. His set of assumptions, labeled "Theory Y," pictured man as inherently curious and capable of growth, of being trustworthy, and of taking initiative. This contrasted with the more traditional "Theory X," which viewed man as indolent, passive, self-protective, and requiring managerial control from above. Likert's (1961) empirical studies of organizational effectiveness demonstrated that, contrary to traditional expectations, "Theory Y" managers could and did obtain high productivity in a setting of high morale. Argyris's (1964) analyses of the ways in which traditionally structured organizations contributed to "psychological failure" were also influential, as was Bennis's explication (1963) of organizational change as a new and exciting arena for the application of behavioral science.

During the middle and late 1960's, OD techniques spread more widely, with economic support from companies interested in functional improvement. Governmental and additional non-profit agencies also began work. The first systematic testing of OD approaches in schools was begun by Miles (1963). Blake and Mouton (1968) developed a thorough, carefully packaged OD program and began distributing it all over the world. The program was set up to take place over a period of three to four years and centered around the "Grid" concept: a two-dimensional view of leadership and group behavior oriented toward both production and people.

Thorough research on the actual impact of OD on organizational effectiveness and productivity tended to lag behind practice. Buchanan (1969) provided a useful review of experience in laboratory training, including its use as a component in OD programs. His earlier (1967) analysis of successful and unsuccessful OD programs identified features such as the availability of new cognitive models to guide planning and goal-setting and the designing of successive action steps to link the initial point of change in the system with other persons, roles, and groups. Such case studies have been criticized as lacking in power to lead to general conclusions by Campbell and Dunnette (1968), who have reviewed available empirical studies of OD within a larger analysis of T-group effectiveness in managerial training and development.

The literature on OD is largely scattered through journals (for example, the *Journal of Applied Behavioral Science*) and technical reports. There are also a very few book-length treatments. For a useful overview of OD and its assumptions, see Bennis (1969). Leavitt (1965) has provided a thorough review of approaches, and Shepard (1965) presents a useful framework for thinking about change in interpersonal and intergroup relationships in organizational settings. Beckhard (1969) discusses specific OD programs as exemplars. For technical discussions of current OD methods, see Burke and Hornstein (in press), and Schmuck, Runkel, Derr, Martell, and Saturen (in press).

Studies showing clear impact of OD on the functioning of industrial organizations are few. (See, for example, Blake, Mouton, Barnes, and Greiner, 1964; Beckhard and Lake, in press; Seashore and Bowers, 1963 and 1970; and Marrow, Bowers, and Seashore, 1967). They are reviewed below. It should be pointed out that the reports of systematic empirical research on OD in schools provided in the present volume are a distinctly needed addition to the literature. On balance, industrial firms appear to have adopted OD more often on the basis of subjective impressions than on the basis of empirical evidence of success.

As OD departments and programs have proliferated (it is estimated that about 250 organizations now have substantial OD programs under way), the need for training OD consultants has mounted as well. University programs have been developed at Case Western Reserve University, UCLA, the Harvard School of Business, Massachusetts Institute of Technology, the State University of New York at Buffalo, the University of New Hampshire, and elsewhere. The NTL Institute of Applied Behavioral Science began offering annual intensive programs for the preparation of OD consultants in the summer of 1965. An "OD network" of skilled and interested persons, initiated by NTL, now numbers more than 375 members. A list of consultants experienced in the design and execution of OD programs for schools appears in Appendix 1 of this book. The extension of OD approaches into the domain of educational systems has proceeded vigorously since the mid-1960's and will be reviewed further below.

Certain themes prominent in the history of OD should be noted before moving on. Practical and experimental work on OD began as T-group leaders and organization-based trainers who had attended human relations laboratories explored the possibility of working intensively within organizations. Certain essential concepts served as support for this work. As an influential group of OD specialists began to develop, they stimulated one another to further invention and experimentation. Formal training in OD skills came later, as did empirical research. Financial support for OD proved crucial in attracting competent practitioners and in enabling substantial programs to be mounted.

We include the foregoing material on the history of OD not only for its general interest but also to indicate that, like any new "social technology," OD has roots and has developed in a real social context. Those interested in adopting OD approaches need to know something of its sources and the way in which to judge the background and credentials of those purporting to offer this new service.

How OD Works

A typical sequence of events in the initiation and development of an OD program is as follows:

1. Middle or top management of an organization becomes interested in OD and feels that the organization has problems which can be met through training. Initial interest is often developed after a manager's personal attendance at a T-group laboratory.

2. Management invites an outside OD consultant to visit the organization.

3. After the consultant's entry and contact with a variety of organization roles and groups, the organization works out a contract with the consultant specifying the nature of the projected relationship and its goals and general procedures.

4. The consultant, working with insiders, collects data about the organization via interviews, questionnaires, and observations.

5. These data form the basis of a joint diagnosis of the points of difficulty in the organization and, if appropriate, between the organization and its environment. Goals for change are explicitly identified.

6. A first "intervention" (usually an intensive meeting involving several key roles, a group, or more than one group) is planned. The data collected earlier are often fed back and discussed. Exercises for training in communication skills or group functioning are often used as constructive vehicles for discussing the data. (For a delineation of the range of interventions employed, see below.)

7. The intervention is evaluated following a new collection of data. Often the future success of the effort depends on the degree to which key figures have been "freed up" to be more open, concerned, and creative about organizational improvement.

8. Subsequent steps in intervention are planned on the basis of these data, and the process continues.

The usual primary effect of the early stages of an OD training program is to change the "culture" of the organization: it becomes more open, trusting, collaborative, self-analytical, and inclined to take risks. As a program proceeds, structural changes become more typical as outcomes; reorganizations, the development of new roles and groups, and new forms of work-flow are planned and set into motion. Typical additional steps in the OD program which occur at this later stage are as follows:

9. The OD function itself becomes institutionalized within the organization. An OD department or group is formed and takes central responsibility for continuing the OD process, drawing on outside resources as needed.

Figure 1-1   The OD Cube: A Scheme for Classifying OD Interventions

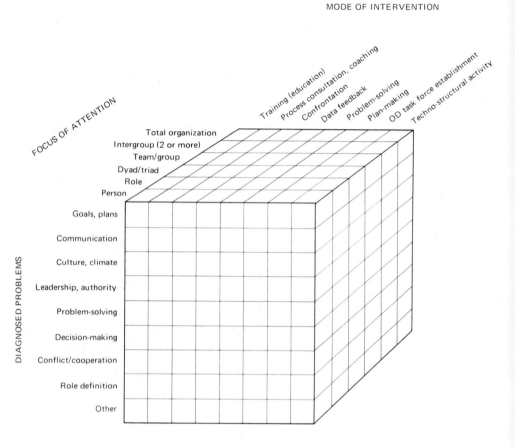

MODE OF INTERVENTION

10. The internal OD specialists become increasingly professionalized and responsible for their own development via such bodies as NTL and networks of other professionals. They may at times serve as outside change agents to other organizations.

Technology of OD

The OD cube in Figure 1-1 displays the typical interventions employed in OD training. At the left are the *problems diagnosed* by the inside/outside change team; they may include difficulties in goal-setting and planning, communication, climate, and other matters. These problems may occur either in *existing* units, or in such *new* units as those created during the start-up phase of a new organization, those developed during the course of mergers with or acquisitions of other organizations, and those emerging during the course of the major reorganization of a firm. For clarity, the three additional "cubes" for start-ups, mergers and reorganizations are not shown here. The interventions used in such new systems often differ substantially from those used in existing systems.

The diagonal edge of the cube identifies the *focus of attention* of the forthcoming intervention. The intervention may be focused essentially on a change in persons (individuals), in roles, in dyads or triads (two- or three-person groups), in work teams, in the relations between two or more groups, or in the organization as a whole. OD training most frequently focuses on key roles, teams, relationships between groups, and the total organization.

The modes of intervention which can be employed are as follows:

1. Training or education: procedures involving direct teaching or experience-based learning. Such technologies as lectures, exercises, simulations, and T-groups are examples.

2. Process consultation: watching and aiding on-going processes and coaching to improve them.

3. Confrontation: bringing together units of the organization (persons, roles, or groups) which have previously been in poor communication; usually accompanied by supporting data.

4. Data feedback: systematic collection of information, which is then reported back to appropriate organizational units as a base for diagnosis, problem-solving, and planning.

5. Problem-solving: meetings essentially focusing on problem identification, diagnosis, and solution invention and implementation.

6. Plan-making: activity focused primarily on planning and goal setting to replot the organization's future.

7. OD task force establishment: setting up ad hoc problem-solving groups or internal teams of specialists to ensure that the organization solves problems and carries out plans continuously.

8. Techno-structural activity: action which has as its prime focus the alteration of the organization's structure, work-flow, and means of accomplishing tasks.

These intervention modes flow into each other and are not mutually exclusive. They range roughly from "soft" (person-changing) to "hard" (task-oriented or structure-changing) in emphasis. A strong OD program will typically involve all eight components at one time or another.

Any particular OD intervention can be classified according to problem, focus of attention, and mode of intervention. For example, an intervention might be aimed at increasing problem-solving and decision-making skills in an existing team—a plant manager and his seven subordinate division heads, for example. Its mode might be process consultation: the outside change agent watches the group work and provides feedback from time to time on their process *(how* they are proceeding, who is and is not listened to, whether the boss's word always holds sway, etc.). For another example, an intervention might focus on the entire faculty of a new junior high school to increase its ability to solve problems. The modes of the intervention could be training in communication skills, followed by training in problem-solving and then process consultation during real-life problem-solving at faculty meetings.

As the latter example shows, the OD process is further complicated by the fact that most training interventions sequence various modes in unique ways. As one considers the complexities of OD design, the number of combinations involving all three of these dimensions becomes very large. Research as yet tells us little about optimal sequencing of interventions directed toward specific targets and problems over a period of years, but such strategic planning is the central stock-in-trade of the OD specialist.

Effects of OD

What do OD interventions like those described above accomplish over a period of time? Here we shall review briefly the rather scanty evidence available from quantitative data rather than impressionistic case studies.[5] These data are based on well-designed studies, usually including controls, and deal with efforts to change and improve a *system* rather than individual attitudes or beliefs.[6]

"Cousin" Training. Some OD efforts involve working with persons from within the same organization, but drawn from different organizational families or departments. Buchanan and Brunstetter (1959) found that, three to seven months after such "cousin" group sessions, those managers who had participated perceived greater improvement in the departmental functions which they supervised than did those in a control division.

Boyd and Ellis (1962) found that 65 percent of thirty-four managers who attended laboratory training in a large public utility organization were seen by their working associates as improved in such behaviors as sensitivity, openness, and role flexibility, while only 34 percent of a control group were thus seen. Valiquet (1968), using the same measures, found rates of 73 percent for thirty-four managers and 20 percent for controls. The largest experimental-control differences were found in new behaviors involving increased interdependence with others, insight into self and role, role flexibility, risk-taking, sensitivity to others' feelings, and acceptance of others. Underwood (1965), studying fifteen supervisors, found that their job associates, in comparison with the associates of controls, reported two and a half times as many changes in job-related behavior (including negative changes). Blake and Mouton (1966) showed that thirty-three managers and twenty-three union members from the same plant who attended

[5] Case studies of OD interventions and longer-term efforts are reasonably plentiful but provide primarily descriptive, exploratory evidence. See, for example, Beckhard (1966); Buchanan (1965a); Crockett (1970); Croft (1970); Davis (1967); Dayal and Thomas (1968); Dyer et al. (1970); Foundation for Research on Human Behavior (1960); Greiner (1967); Kuriloff and Atkins (1966); Winn (1966); and Zand, Miles, and Lytle (1970).

[6] For reviews of the impact of laboratory training on individuals and its linkage to in-dividual behavior in organizations, see Buchanan (1965b, 1969) and Campbell and Dunnette (1968).

one-week Grid seminars changed their attitudes toward desired managerial styles: e.g., managers endorsed a "9,9" style (strong production and people orientation) more fully. Both managers and union members were more likely to reject a "1,9" style (low people orientation, high production orientation). Union members showed a slight increase in preference for "9,1" (stronger production than people orientation). An item analysis showed that managers shifted style preferences on 19 percent of the items, while union members did so on 11 percent.

However, in none of these studies was it unequivocally shown that *system* changes had occurred as a result of the intervention, though the interventions had presumably been aiming at such improvements. Buchanan (undated) in discussing such consequences of cousin group training as increased openness, moderation of extreme behavior, increased skills (e.g., listening and encouraging participation), and the increased importance given to emotional factors in work relations, points out:

> While these outcomes are quite compatible with the goals of laboratory training, it is easy to see that such changes, even if of great magnitude and even if attained by a sizeable proportion of the members of an organization. . .would not, without further planned improvement effort, be likely to result in major changes in the functioning of the organization.
>
> . . .Such skepticism rests on the fact that an employee at any level is part of a complex, interdependent field of forces and thus any attempted change in the behavior of the individual is likely to engender forces which impede and eventually counteract the change attempt.

Team Training. A solution to this problem, of course, is to use integral subsystems or groups of the organization as the target of OD efforts. Team training is an intervention dealing with the members of an existent group composed of a superior and his subordinates on one or two levels. Harrison (1962) found that the members of a managerial team, after training, described each other in more "human," emotional terms, but did not describe other associates who had not attended the training in this way.

Friedlander (1967) found that managers attending team training (four teams) reported that their participation, personal involvement, mutual influence, and problem-solving effectiveness had increased more than those of managers in a comparison group (eight teams) without training. A more detailed follow-up (Friedlander, 1968) showed that the team which had had the most extended pre- and post-training contact with the outside trainer showed the most change.

Morton and Wight (1964), in a study of three organizational training laboratories, compared members of six teams with those of six cousin groups; the team-trained managers reported more events in areas involving improved team functioning. Team-trained managers were more likely to report resistance *outside* their teams; cousin-trained managers saw resistance more *within* their usual working groups.

Using the same data, Morton (1965) reported that of 396 critical incidents reported three months after training by ninety-seven participants, 35 percent were related to strictly personal gains, 18 percent were related to difficulty in applying new concepts learned in the laboratory, and the remaining 47 percent were related to improved working relationships, improved organizational climate, and conflict reduction.

Zenger (1969) studied the effects of two years of team training on a sales organization consisting of a six-man top team plus related subordinate teams. He found improvements in sales, income of sales agents, and company standing. He concluded that these changes were accompanied by improved perceptions of self, superior, the work group, and the organization.

Zand, Steele, and Zalkind (1969) studied the effects of cousin laboratories followed by team training. For most managers, attitudes immediately after the cousin laboratories changed in the direction of *less* trust, openness, giving and receiving of help, etc. Zand and his associates suggest this was the result of the managers' application of stricter judgment standards, but it is possible that things really did get worse.

Zand and his associates did show that managers who had been actively involved in the cousin labs were also actively involved in team development work later. However, one year later, although the managers said there had been an increase in the ability to face conflict and in willingness to ask for help, their subordinates said these factors had *not* changed. The program did not appear to change the managers' management philosophy, which was already oriented toward the "Theory Y" or collaborative side. (For a perceptive critique of this study and discussion of the problems of meaningful research on OD, see Berkowitz, 1969.)

Intergroup Improvement. Some interventions involve clarifying relationships and conflicts between work groups of an organization. Golembiewski and Blumberg (1967, 1968, and 1969) report data showing that such an intervention improved the attitudes of the members of nine groups toward other groups (e.g., perception of need and willingness to collaborate). In addition, this effect was substantially stronger in those three groups which had been more intensively involved or represented in the intervention design. A follow-up study seven months later suggested that the changes had been maintained in spite of much subsequent organizational stress. However, the data are very incompletely reported, and it is difficult to place strong confidence in the findings.

Blake, Mouton, and Sloma (1965) describe a vivid case study of intergroup "therapy" during a union-management dispute. Improved conflict management and realistic collaboration were claimed as the outcomes, but no quantitative information was supplied to support the conclusion.

Comprehensive Strategies. In the field of non-educational organizations, we are aware of only three studies *systematically* assessing the effects of a comprehensive OD strategy which employed several types of intervention over a period of several years.

Blake, Mouton, Barnes, and Greiner (1964) assessed the effect of a Grid OD program run by line managers within a petroleum refining organization of 4000 employees over a one-year period. Profits increased approximately 78 percent over the preceding three-year average; 14 percent of this increase was attributed to procedural improvements flowing from the Grid program, and 30 percent was due to manpower reduction, which had also been an effect of the program. The participants reported a 23 percent improvement in work group performance, a 31 percent increase in meetings, a 52 percent increase in transfers, more frequent promotion of younger line managers, improved working relationships, and more success in solving organizational problems. Managers reported that they had moved toward the "9,9" style (oriented toward both productivity and individual satisfaction). They were also seen as more effective by their subordinates. Greiner (1967) stressed, however, that the improvements might have come as much from environmental pressure and management's commitment to organizational improvement as from the OD program itself.

Beckhard and Lake (in press) studied the effects of an intensive OD intervention aimed at developing a team approach to management in a large banking organization. Over the 1963-1964 period of intervention, the division worked with most intensively (in comparison with control divisions) improved productivity, reduced turnover and absenteeism, developed better internal communication and greater structural inventiveness, and improved problem-solving capacities. Data from superiors of the managers most closely affected by the intervention (primarily team training and problem-solving) indicated that intergroup conflicts were reduced and that more problem-oriented and productive work was being accomplished. The subordinates of the same managers reported that they had more frequent access to their superiors, whom they saw as more egalitarian, less closely supervising (a key variable found by Likert to correlate with productivity), more open to suggestion, and influential with their own superiors. The changes described were in general shown to be maintained when studied four years later in 1968—in part because the OD effort had been extended throughout more divisions of the bank.

Marrow, Bowers, and Seashore (1967) studied the processes and outcomes of a planned change effort aimed at applying Likert's ideas on participative management to a garment manufacturing firm in poor financial condition, with traditionally authoritarian management. (It is of some interest to note that the firm had just been acquired by the Harwood Company, whose head, Alfred Marrow, had long been committed to active and successful experimentation with participative methods within his firm.)

The change program occupied the 1962-1964 period. Seashore and Bowers (1970) also collected four-year follow-up data in 1969; their very readable review of the study and its results shows that the two-year increases in employee satisfaction, motivation, and performance, the profitability of the firm, and its assumption of "the characteristics of an adaptive, self-controlling, participative system" were essentially maintained four years later. Most job attitude indicators (such as the degree to which employees felt their work was satisfying) and task orientation indicators (such as the degree to which employees felt the company was quick to improve methods) had been maintained or improved. Management style was clearly seen to have moved in a participative direction, and the influence, goal emphasis, and work facilitation of supervisors was seen by workers to have increased. Seashore and Bowers speculate that the durability of the changes may have stemmed from any of three sources: structural changes which served to "lock in" the new participative norms; the legitimization of continued organizational self-awareness and self-study; and the inherently attractive character of life in a participative system.

This review of quantitatively based studies of OD suggests that its claims are not unwarranted. Though the studies are meager and do have many faults (see Campbell and Dunnette, 1968, for acerb criticism), they are plausible and are supported by case study testimony as well. OD can accomplish its hopes of creating self-renewing systems reflective of "Theory Y" if there is clear commitment from top management and a sufficient investment of time and energy in OD work.

School Improvement

Jacob Getzels once asked, "How can the schools be improved?" and then answered his own question: "In almost every conceivable way known to man." Since the range of change approaches that have been employed historically is truly enormous, one could infer either (1) that school districts are stubbornly resistant to improvement efforts or (2) that those wishing to change schools have more often than not been well-meaning but naive. This is not the place to review school improvement efforts in depth. (See Miles, 1964, pp. 18-29, for a listing and analysis of strategies in use in America during the 1950's and 60's; and see Cremin, 1961, for a historical overview of the period 1876-1957). We believe that school improvement efforts generally have failed because they have been piecemeal. They have not focused on the systemic features of schools that enhance or retard innovative efforts.

School Improvement Approaches

Many strategies of school improvement focus on *structural* changes of various kinds. Legislation to require special schooling for retarded children, the elimination of one-room schools, age-grading, the creation of new roles such as teacher aide, and the design of new subsystems such as teaching teams and the multi-unit school all involve structures, with official power as a base for change.

Another approach to school improvement might be called *curricular,* in that it focuses primarily on the procedures, materials, and equipment of the immediate classroom learning setting. Examples include the creation of new comprehensive curricula (e.g., PSSC Physics, developed by the Physical Science Study Committee), new textbooks, programmed instruction manuals and machines, self-teaching film loops in eight millimeter cassette film projectors, exercises for "affective education," overhead projectors as a means of accompanying lectures, training packages for achievement motivation, and "contract teaching," in which a desired final mark and the amount of work required are agreed on by student and teacher ahead of time.

Another category of strategies for school improvement can be termed *role-shaping.* It is built on the assumption that persons occupying roles such as teacher, administrator, board member, student, or parent need to be educated or changed in some way to bring about more effective performance of existing role behaviors or adequate performance of new behaviors. Examples are interaction analysis and feedback; micro-teaching and video tape playback; in-service education workshops; sensitivity training groups involving teachers, parents, administrators and students; experimental pre-service education designs; simulation exercises in decision-making for school principals; parent education workshops; and training of students in conflict escalation and management.

Finally, some strategies for improving schools take a *holistic* approach, usually involving the creation of a new or innovative educational system which avoids the constraints of the existing one. Such an approach usually involves structural, curricular, and role-shaping substrategies, all integrated into a grand design for a new learning environment. Examples include campus laboratory schools, "house plans" or subschools within larger schools, pilot programs of all sorts, and, currently, "free" schools set up outside of formal educational systems.

Ways of Classifying School Improvement Approaches

It may be useful to examine briefly some dimensions of strategies used to improve schools.

The first three categories above (structural, curricular, and role-shaping) closely parallel three general approaches to organizational change described by Leavitt (1965): structural, technical, and "people-changing." Other conceptualizations have been developed that parallel and overlap these.

Chin and Benne (1969), in an especially thorough review of strategies for improvement, argue that planned change can be characterized as being essentially rational (e.g., research, consultation, Utopia creation, and personnel replacement), normative-re-educative (e.g., improvement of problem-solving skills and personal growth enhancement) or power-coercive (e.g., nonviolence, legislation, or change in elites). Sieber (1968) suggests a similar classification of change strategies involving rational appeals (e.g., the usual "dissemination" strategy), the development of cooperation (e.g., two-way communication between expert and client), or the exercise of power (e.g., change via fiat, compliance, or legislation). He suggests that a "status occupant" approach, recognizing that the parties to an educational change find themselves linked in a network of interdependent statuses, may be most effective.

Miles (1964) offers a strategic classification based on the stage of pre-adoption behavior involved (design of the innovation, creation of awareness of and interest in its existence, evaluation, and local trial), whether the initiative rests inside or outside the local district, and whether existing structures or new structures are used to "carry" the strategy. Finally, Havelock (1969) suggests that strategies may involve focus on: rational processes of decision-making based on information (the research, development and diffusion approach), the social interaction among potential adopters in status systems (e.g., superintendents who are more respected become interested in and try out innovations faster), or the problem-solving processes that go on as an adopter struggles with his difficulties in carrying out an educational program. He proposes a "linkage" model in which expert resources are brought into conjunction, by linking roles or groups, with the needs and demands of local school districts.

OD as an Improvement Strategy

OD in schools can be described according to the overlapping rubrics presented above. For Leavitt, OD is essentially a people-changing strategy. Chin and Benne would classify it similarly as "normative-re-educative," in that the focus tends to be on altering norms, role relationships, and "climate," especially in early stages of the intervention. Sieber would view OD as a cooperation strategy.

OD's emphasis on problem-solving and the self-analytic examination of the structure and processes of the school organization would probably lead Havelock to classify it as a problem-solving strategy. Sieber's view of status occupants as examining and reinforcing the changes that take place in a network of connected roles and Havelock's social interaction and linkage strategies also are applicable to OD. During later stages, as the capability of the organization for self-transformation mounts, Leavitt's category of structure-changing applies.

Finally, in terms of Miles' categories, OD involves initiative taken both inside and outside the district, plus the creation of a new structure (an OD steering group or department, internal specialists, etc.) within the old structure to manage all phases of pre-adoption behavior.

In general, OD approaches do *not* assume that merely rational or information-diffusing approaches to educational improvement will work. OD is not primarily a rational strategy, as defined by Chin and Benne, Sieber, and Havelock; neither would these authors classify it as a power-oriented approach. OD strategies tend to work along power-equalizing lines rather than toward the exercise of coercive or arbitrary power. Finally, OD approaches emphasize interaction among organizational members as they use the help of experts to improve the ability of their own system to produce innovations. The increased adoption of specific valid innovations, however, is only one index of an effective OD program; such a program should primarily affect such basic "organizational health" dimensions as goal focus, communication adequacy, competence-based power, resource utilization, cohesiveness, morale, autonomy, adaptation, and general problem-solving adequacy (Miles, 1965a, 1965b).

Special Features of Schools

The assumption of many OD practitioners has been that schools are not seriously different from other complex organizations. Thus it has been believed that training strategies used in industrial OD programs may be used in schools with little change of theory and technology. Yet we believe that there are differences in schools that make a difference in OD training.

One of us (Miles, 1967) has suggested, for instance, that schools, more than industrial organizations, suffer from ambiguity and diversity of goals. Such goal diffuseness has often resulted in conflict between a school and its community environment and in difficulties in measuring goal attainment. Moreover, schools are "low-interdependent" systems in which roles are minimally differentiated from each other, barely integrated, and carried out "invisibly"—i.e., outside the range of colleague support and sanction. In addition, schools, unlike industrial organizations, are "domesticated" organizations that are especially vulnerable to short-run demands from their environments. Being largely in a noncompetitive position, they tend (1) to underinvest in research and development, and (2) to respond non-adaptively (defensively and laggingly) to long-run changes in their cultural, social, and intellectual environments.

Sieber (1968) stresses vulnerability, which he defines as the probability of being subjected to pressures incompatible with one's goals, without the capacity to resist. He comments that this characteristic of schools encourages subjugation to the environment, discrepancies between school goals and environmental demands, and inadequate provision of financial resources. He further comments on the low level of autonomy and the weak knowledge base of school personnel, referred to as quasi-professionalism, and suggests that this feature promotes status insecurity, ritualistic use of procedures, and scanty communication among staff members. Sieber also mentions goal diffuseness and believes that it reinforces the effects of vulnerability and quasi-professionalism. Finally, he suggests that the formal coordination and control structures of a school tend to induce pressures toward the "processing of cohorts"—the cohorts being batches of students—rather than individualizing of teaching and learning, and toward the watering down of innovations.

Characteristics such as these not only suggest some goals for OD in schools (e.g., development of fuller, more open, and more direct communication, and development of teams that are genuinely interdependent) but also suggest the kinds of resistance to the very idea of OD that may be expected from professional educators. Blumberg and Schmuck (in press) have addressed themselves explicitly to this issue. They, like Miles and Sieber, comment on the isolated, individuated character of the teacher's role, which encourages an "acollaborative" stance. The typical principal's preoccupation over effective individual contact with each teacher is reinforced by the low level of organizational complexity of the school (usually only two or three hierarchical levels). Thus, teachers and administrators alike tend to deal with each other on a one-to-one informal basis, avoiding questions of overall coordination, collaborative work, change, and development.

Blumberg and Schmuck also suggest, with only limited empirical support, that schools tend to hire and retain people with dependent, submissive attitudes who have a difficult time in situations requiring the exercise of influence, collaborative decision-making, and open, frank problem-solving. Such situations, naturally, are characteristic of OD training programs. Moreover, time restrictions flowing from the custodial responsibility for children make it difficult for schools to become actively and seriously involved with OD efforts. Finally, they suggest that university-based change agents, such as those involved with OD, often have low credibility and legitimacy in the eyes of school personnel.

This analysis may be viewed as gloomy; the properties of schools cited appear to make the likelihood of serious improvement small. We do not think so. These properties do account in part for the low rates of change characteristic in education, but they also provide clearly defined change goals and "leverage points" for OD entry. For example, it has been our experience that many teachers, because of their individuated roles (characterized by a low level of interdependence), often feel isolated, alienated, and lonely. OD interventions which increase interdependence and sharing among teachers often liberate a good deal of energy, lift morale, and make the school an exciting place in which to work. Moreover, the empirical work reported in this book gives us confidence that OD can be effective and productive in schools, helping them to correct or transcend the problems they face because of their special systemic properties. The reader can make that judgment for himself as he proceeds through these studies.

Improvement in the Last Decade

In spite of the diversity of school improvement strategies which have been employed since the explosion of interest in educational innovation during the late 1950's, the net effect has not been substantial. An Educational Testing Service report (Silberman, 1970), summarizing 186 studies of educational achievement in the 1950's and 1960's, did show, on the average, that a 20 percent improvement had taken place. However, as Silberman points out, there is a pervasive sense of educational crisis. Most large cities have experienced serious conflict over racial integration, community control, and educational quality. Sixty percent of the school principals sampled in 1969 reported having faced significant student protests. The fact that Stephens (1967) was able to find no significant differences in school outcome as a function of varied teaching methods employed in a wide range of studies suggests that the 20 percent increment may have been due primarily to the widespread exposure of children to television. (It has been suggested that, on a yearly basis, television contact hours now generally exceed school contact hours.)[7]

Current difficulties with the schools cannot, of course, be separated from the general malaise of American society. Peter Marin (1970), head of a "free school," writes:

We try. We open the classroom a bit and loosen the bonds. Students use a teacher's first name, or roam the small room, or choose their own texts. It is all very nice; better, of course, than nothing at all. But what has it got to do with the needs of the young?We try again. We devise new models, new programs, new plans. We innovate and renovate, and beneath it all our schemes always contain the same vacancies, the same smells of death, as the schools. One speaks to planners, designers, teachers, and administrators; one hears about schedules and modules and curricular innovation—new systems. It is always "materials" and "technique," the chronic American technological vice, the cure that murders as it saves. It is all so smug, so progressively right—and yet so useless, so far off the track. One knows there is something else altogether: a way of feeling, access to the soul, a way of speaking and embracing, that lies at the heart of all yearning or wisdom or real revolution. It is that, precisely, that has been left out. It is something the planners cannot remember: the living tissue of community. Without it, of course, we shrivel and die, but who can speak convincingly about that to those who have never felt it?

Students, teachers, and administrators are part of American life: a life replete with alienation and lack of supportive community, pervasive racism, political polarization, violence, apathy, repression, the steady continuance of war and harried preparation for war, and the threat of ecological collapse. In the face of all this—fully documented and visible daily to everyone through mass media—it seems ridiculous to suppose that minor tinkering or the issuance of replacement parts for our school districts will create competence in coping with the appalling social demands we are facing.

Can OD for schools create such competence? Can it breathe the "living tissue of community" back into our young as they meet together in the classrooms? Can it make teaching a humanized activity? Such claims are unsupported, but it appears more likely than not that OD can create, in schools, the sense of community Marin speaks of, a new feeling of autonomy, more willingness to take risks, a more open attitude toward the frightening realities of our world, and an increased loosening and "informalization" of the dead bureaucratic structures with which so many of our schools are afflicted. Students, teachers and administrators working in such schools may be able to establish a more meaningful base from which to explore themselves and the world as it is, more awareness of themselves as controlling their own fate (the single most important variable in predicting school achievement, in the Coleman report),[8] and more competence at the sort of self-initiated learning that can serve them for the rest of their lives.

We believe that OD is worth a serious and concentrated try; it may do more

---

[7] The clear gains shown in studies of children viewing "Sesame Street" provide some backing for this possibility.

[8] Coleman, in his massive study, *Equality of Educational Opportunity* (1966), found that "sense of control over the environment" showed more relation to achievement at the sixth, ninth, and twelfth grade levels than all family variables put together, and more than all school variables put together. A similar variable, "internal locus of control," was found by Forward and Williams (1970) to predict militancy in young blacks; those high on this variable are more likely to react actively to change the repressive and discriminatory systems blocking their aspirations.

to make healthy educative environments in schools than any specific innovation we might think of. The target, then, is the school as a social system—a living interpersonal culture. As an organization, can it learn, with the aid of special resources and new technologies in training, how to become more self-renewing, how to gain greater contact with its environment, and how to become more responsive to the desires and interests of its members? Can schools become more like communities for growing their members than like machines for processing them?

We believe that the approaches to educational improvement which have been taken over the past decade have been less than effective because: (1) they mainly gave substantial weight to "rational" processes of innovation adoption; (2) they took a narrow, overly technical view of the problem, assuming that the best strategy was to develop "teacher-proof" packages and diffuse them widely; (3) they took the systemic properties of local school districts largely as "given" and not as subject to substantial change and improvement efforts; and (4) most crucially of all, they ignored (except in rhetoric) the necessity to create self-renewing, vital, and growing educational organizations as the primary base for learning and living.

History of OD in Schools

As we indicated earlier, the Seattle schools were the first to use T-groups, during the mid-1950's. In 1961, the National Training Laboratories began offering annual T-group laboratories specially designed for educators. Neither of these involved OD.

It was not until the early 1960's that the first systematic effort to carry out and conduct research on OD methods in school districts was launched, by Miles (1963). His three-year Project on Organization Development in Schools at Teachers College, Columbia University, involved collaboration with two school districts, near New York and Pittsburgh respectively. The interventions tested included data feedback, problem-solving workshops, and the training of teams through process consultation. The studies were reported in Miles et al. (1966), McElvaney and Miles (1969, reported in Chapter 6 of this volume), Miles et al. (1969), and Benedict et al. (1967).

In the early 1960's NTL took active leadership in stimulating educational OD through the Core Committee on Education, led by Dorothy Mial. It took initiative in proposing and seeking funding for the COPED project (see below) and in 1966 concurrently developed an educational intern program for OD specialists and educational training consultants which is still in operation.

Beginning in the fall of 1965, a group of university-based specialists and researchers carried out a large-scale OD project labeled COPED (Cooperative Project for Educational Development). Teams based in the Boston area (Boston University and Lesley College) and the New York area (Teachers College, Columbia University; Yeshiva University; and Newark State College) and at the University of Wisconsin, the University of Chicago, and the University of Michigan collaborated through a consortium on the conceptualization,[9] planning, and initiation of a well-studied effort to bring about self-renewing processes in twenty-three school districts. A jointly used instrument package was

---

[9] See the series of working papers in Watson (1967a, 1967b).

designed to test outcomes in all districts. The approaches varied considerably from district to district and area to area. For example, the Michigan teams concentrated primarily on the training of teachers and principals as internal change agents to aid other teachers and administrators via in-service education in problem-solving and in the effective, innovative use of research. The Boston team tested a similar strategy, plus a "saturation" intervention with heavy use of outside consultants. The New York team emphasized survey data feedback as a basis for building effective top administrative teams through process consultation. The Chicago project emphasized process consultation and the creation of an internal change management group. This approach was also studied by the Wisconsin team.[10] Chapter 8 of this book describes subsequent work carried out by the Wisconsin group.

COPED did not produce any studies of the impact of organization change efforts, because funding was terminated during the first year of active OD intervention. Since quantitative data were collected in the twenty-three districts on a wide variety of variables (norms, morale, goals, problem-solving, communication patterns, innovativeness, and others) the research carried out focused on interrelationships among these variables at a single point in time rather than on the impact of change efforts. These findings (COPED, 1970, Volume I) tended to confirm the general position we suggested earlier: that school district and building-level innovativeness is a function of organizational variables such as the degree of leadership-sharing and personal support provided by the principal, the adequacy of problem-solving procedures in faculty meetings, the perception of the reward system as favoring creativity, the degree of trust among colleagues, and the amount of teacher initiation of innovative proposals. No relationships, on the other hand, were found between innovativeness and per-pupil expenditure.

The interested reader may also wish to examine the eleven case studies of change efforts (COPED, 1970, Volume II), as unusually thorough and useful accounts of the way in which outside change agents collaborated with insiders in the first year of OD work. These studies discuss processes of entry, contract formation, data collection, diagnosis, feedback, and other beginning interventions. The cases described in Chapter 8 of this book used the COPED instrument package, but the University of Wisconsin effort was funded through other sources, so that studies of effects could be carried out.

Although because of funding termination COPED did not produce the OD impact studies hoped for, the net products of the project were several. It was successful in producing clearer conceptualizations and strategies for OD in schools, useful research instruments appropriate for assessing school organizations, and a great amount of practical experience for both university personnel interested in the study of OD in schools and a growing core of school- and university-based OD practitioners.

A study which developed as an offshoot of COPED was Manno's (1969), on an experimental intervention aimed at increasing teacher innovativeness; it might be termed a "mini-OD" project. Working in nine schools, Manno found that teachers who participated with their principals in a series of programmed ex-

---

[10] Cooperative Project for Educational Development (COPED) (1968) contains accounts of specific interventions and training materials. COPED (1970) includes research, case studies, the complete instrument package, and a diagnostic kit of instruments for local school district use.

ercises helping them to share and discuss their own innovative practices (1) learned more about each other's innovations, (2) felt more friendly toward other teachers, and (3) innovated slightly more—all in comparison with both a control group who discussed practices for reporting to parents about student perform- ance and a non-discussing control group. The intervention (six one-and-a-half hour sessions) was not successful, however, in changing norms regulating in- novativeness, which returned to their previous level two months later.

During 1967, three educational OD projects began which took an intensive approach to the training of individuals as such.

Rogers (1969) has described the assumptions and initial approach to the Immaculate Heart School district which includes a college and twenty-five as- sociated schools (three secondary, twenty-two elementary) in Los Angeles. Es- sentially, the strategy (planned by Western Behavioral Sciences Institute and later the Center for Studies of the Person) involved students, faculty, and administrators meeting in intensive weekend encounter groups, plus the develop- ment of internal "facilitators" to enable a larger and larger proportion of organization members to participate in such groups. The primary target of change was seen as the person rather than subsystems or the organization as a whole. Preliminary experience with the project (Rogers, 1969, pp. 330-42) sug- gested that the personal impact of the group experience was useful, especially in close personal relationships, but had little or no influence on organizational structure and functioning. As the project proceeded, the Immaculate Heart com- munity, according to an external evaluation team's report (Shaevitz and Barr, 1970), tended to become more and more polarized regarding encounter groups themselves as an instrument of change. During the project's second year the use of an outside team from TRW Systems, focusing on organizational problem- solving, seemed to aid movement toward improved functioning (e.g., increased student influence and participation, more requests for and provision of help, and more acceptance of individuality).

A second person-oriented project was begun at about the same time in Brevard County, Florida. A series of nine one-week T-group meetings, including teachers, students, and parents from a single high school, was conducted. How- ever, the faculty and students became severely polarized; pre- and post-project data using the COPED package showed a net *drop* in measures of such items as goal clarity, communication adequacy, and trust.[11] The program was terminated by administrative action.

A third project, the Adult-Youth encounter groups begun in 1967 in the East Williston, New York, school district, is continuing, though school and com- munity polarization has beset it as well. (See Chapter 7.)

Though the data are primarily anecdotal, we think it likely that programs solely oriented to personal growth as such, and not linked to organizational problem-solving, do not typically result in self-renewing school districts, for two reasons. First, as Katz and Kahn (1966, p. 391) point out:

The essential weakness of the individual approach is the psychological fallacy of con- centrating upon individuals without regard to the role relationships that constitute the social system of which they are a part. The assumption has been that, since the organization is made up of individuals, we can change the organization by changing its members. This is not

[11] Dale G. Lake (personal communication).

so much an illogical proposition as it is an oversimplification which neglects the inter-relationships of people in an organizational structure and fails to point to the aspects of individual behavior which need to be changed.

Secondly, the intensive climate of the T-group or encounter group creates strong personal bonds and genuine psychological intimacy among group members. Group members are often vague and inarticulate about expressing what has "happened," and since the groups do not have organizational "output" there is little visible task-oriented product. Thus, characteristically, "in-group" and "out-group" phenomena develop; the existing affective relationships of the system are disturbed; and those persons for whom close personal encounter is threatening—whether or not they have been participating in the local groups—tend to form coalitions in opposition to the menace of the open expression of feeling.

These last comments are speculative, but they seem plausible to us. Polarization tends to appear much less frequently in projects which have a clear organizational thrust, such as those reported in this volume. We do not wish to deny the importance of personal growth and development in OD projects; all of our own successful projects have had a strong personal development component. But interventions which are solely oriented toward the individual do not, we believe, alter social systems—and may block their growth.

In this review of past work with schools, we have not included the studies published in the present volume, which—to our knowledge—are the only empirical studies showing clear impact on schools. Until the preparation of this volume, well-designed quantitative studies of OD efforts in school districts have been meager indeed. The available data from COPED do suggest that crucial dependent variables such as innovativeness are correlated with organizational variables (e.g., trust level) which are known to be responsive to OD efforts in non-educational systems. The work we report indicates that OD efforts can achieve predicted results in changing such variables. In short, OD does work in schools and can make a difference in the life and learning of adults and children.

Current Work on OD in Schools

Currently, the most active center doing research and development on OD in schools is the Program on Strategies of Organizational Change of the Center for the Advanced Study of Educational Administration at the University of Oregon. Its work began in 1967 when Richard Schmuck and Philip Runkel commenced the program. Their initial project, reported in Chapter 3 of this volume, was the basis for the paper honored in 1969 as the outstanding work of that year delineating a connection between behavioral science theory and the practice of organizational improvement. As such, it won the Douglas McGregor Memorial Award and was the first report on an OD project in schools to do so. (See Schmuck and Runkel, 1970, for more complete delineation of the project.)

Next the Oregon group launched an OD project with the Kent school district near Seattle. Schmuck and Runkel, aided by nine graduate students, first started training personnel in 1968 and carried on training until 1970. The major objective was to develop a special team in the school district that would be able to replace the Oregon consultants. The group of internal OD trainers became known as organizational specialists. This project is described in detail in Chapter 10.

The work at Oregon continues. Its present emphasis is on OD for multi-unit schools with differentiated staffing and teaching teams and on the establishment of teams of organizational specialists in several districts, especially those in large urban centers.

Two other centers, each with professional staffs of fifteen to twenty members, are actively involved with educational OD. The Educational Change Team at the School of Education, University of Michigan, has been testing the use of power- and conflict-oriented change strategies, as well as the use of students as change advocates, since 1967. Chapter 9 reviews the conceptual base for their work and provides illustrations.

The Program in Humanistic Education (see Chapter 7), at the State University of New York at Albany, began work in 1970 with such educational systems as state education departments, community colleges, regional clusters of districts, and local school districts.

Informed estimates are hard to come by, but it seems likely that no more than a handful of school districts today have an administrator, department, or small formal group explicitly devoting time to OD. Examples of such districts are South Brunswick, New Jersey; Quincy, Massachusetts; Louisville, Kentucky; Kent, Washington; and Portland, Oregon.

It is worthwhile noting that the examples of school OD projects now in existence were mostly initiated by researchers who invited school districts to collaborate. In contrast, most industrial OD programs were initiated from within as organization-based trainers requested collaboration from outside experts. We hope that the studies reported in this book will encourage schoolmen to take such initiative. We need more strongly owned OD programs, and careful study of their processes and outcomes.

References

Argyris, C. 1964. *Integrating the individual and the organization.* New York: Wiley.

Backman, C. W. and Secord, P. F. 1968. *A social psychological view of education.* New York: Harcourt, Brace and World.

Barnard, C. I. 1938. *The functions of the executive.* Cambridge, Massachusetts: Harvard University Press.

Beckhard, R. 1966. An organization improvement program in a decentralized organization. *Journal of Applied Behavioral Science* 2:3-26.

_____. 1969. *Organization development: strategies and models.* Reading, Massachusetts: Addison-Wesley.

_____, and Lake, D. G. In press. Short and long-range effects of a team development effort. In *Strategies of social intervention: a behavioral science analysis,* eds. H. A. Hornstein, B. A. Benedict, W. W. Burke, R. Lewicki, and M. G. Hornstein. New York: Free Press.

Benedict, B. A.; Calder, P. H.; Callahan, D. M.; Hornstein, H. A.; and Miles, M. B. 1967. The clinical experimental method of assessing organizational change efforts. *Journal of Applied Behavioral Science* 3:347-80.

Bennis, W. G. 1961. A typology of change processes. In *The planning of change: readings in the applied behavioral sciences,* eds. W. G. Bennis, K. D. Benne, and R. Chin. New York: Holt, Rinehart and Winston. Pp. 154-156.

_____. 1963. A new role for the behavioral sciences: effecting organizational change. *Administrative Science Quarterly* 8:125-65.

_____. 1969. *Organization development: its nature, origins and prospects.* Reading, Massachusetts: Addison-Wesley.

_____; Benne, K. D.; and Chin, R. 1969. *The planning of change* (2nd ed.). New York: Holt, Rinehart and Winston.

Berkowitz, N. 1969. Audiences and their implications for evaluation research. *Journal of Applied Behavioral Science* 5:411-27.

Blake, R. R., and Mouton, J. S. 1966. Some effects of managerial Grid seminar training on union and management attitudes toward supervision. *Journal of Applied Behavioral Science* 2:387-400.

_____. 1968. *Corporate excellence through Grid organization development: a systems approach.* Houston, Texas: Gulf Publishing Company.

_____; Barnes, L. B.; and Greiner, L. L. 1964. Breakthrough in organization development. *Harvard Business Review* 42:133-55.

_____; and Sloma, R. L. 1965. The union-management intergroup laboratory: strategy for resolving intergroup conflict. *Journal of Applied Behavioral Science* 1:25-57.

Blumberg, A., and Schmuck, R. A. In press. Barriers to training in organizational development for schools. *Educational Technology.*

Boyd, J. B., and Ellis, J. D. 1962. *Findings of research into senior management seminars.* Toronto: Hydro-Electric Power Commission of Ontario.

Buchanan, P. C. 1965a. *Organizational development following major retrenchment.* New York: Yeshiva University. Mimeographed.

_____. 1965b. *Evaluating the effectiveness of laboratory training in industry. Explorations in human relations training and research, Report No. 1.* Washington, D.C.: National Training Laboratories. [Also in *Studies in personnel and industrial psychology* (rev. ed.), ed. E. A. Fleishman, 1967. Homewood, Illinois: Dorsey.]

_____. 1967. Crucial issues in organization development. In *Change in school systems,* ed. G. Watson. Washington, D.C.: NTL Institute for Applied Behavioral Science.

_____. 1969. Laboratory training and organization development. *Administrative Science Quarterly* 14:466-80.

_____. Undated. *Sensitivity, or laboratory, training in industry.* New York: Yeshiva University. Mimeographed.

_____, and Brunstetter, P. H. 1959. A research approach to management development: II. *Journal of the American Society of Training Directors* 13:18-27.

Burke, W. W., and Hornstein, H. A. In press. *The social technology of organization development.* New York: Van Nostrand Reinhold.

_____, and Schmidt, W. H. 1970. Primary target for change: the manager or the organization? In *Organizational frontiers and human values,* ed. W. H. Schmidt. Belmont, California: Wadsworth.

Callahan, R. E., and Button, H. W. 1964. Historical change of the role of the man in the organization, 1865-1950. In *Behavioral science and educational administration,* ed. D. E. Griffiths. Sixty-Third Yearbook (Part II), National Society for the Study of Education. Chicago: University of Chicago Press.

Campbell, J. P., and Dunnette, M. D. 1968. Effectiveness of T-group experiences in managerial training and development. *Psychological Bulletin* 70:73-104.

Chin, R., and Benne, K. D. 1969. General strategies for effecting changes in human systems. In *The planning of change* (2nd ed.), eds. W. G. Bennis, K. D. Benne, and R. Chin. New York: Holt, Rinehart and Winston. Pp. 32-59.

Coch, L., and French, J. R. P., Jr. 1948. Overcoming resistance to change. *Human Relations.* 1:512-32.

Coleman, J. S. 1966. *Equality of educational opportunity.* Washington, D.C.: U.S. Government Printing Office, Catalog No. FS 5.238:38001.

Cooperative Project for Educational Development (COPED). 1968. Final Report, Project No. OE 6-10-205. Grant No. 3-6-062802-1527. Washington, D.C.: United States Office of Education.

Cooperative Project for Educational Development (COPED). 1970. Final Report, COPED Data Analysis Project. Project No. 8-0069. Grant No. OEG-3-8-080069-0043

(010). Washington, D.C.: U.S. Office of Education. (Vol. I, *Research outcomes.* Vol. II, *Case studies.* Vol. III, *Diagnosing the professional climate of your school.* Appendix, *Instruments and code manual.*)

Cremin, L. A. 1961. *The transformation of the school: progressivism in American education, 1876-1957.* New York: Knopf.

Crockett, W. J. 1970. Team building—one approach to organizational development. *Journal of Applied Behavioral Science* 6:291-306.

Croft, J. C. 1970. Organization development for Thornlea: a communication package and some results. *Journal of Applied Behavioral Science* 6:93-114.

Davis, S. 1967. An organic problem-solving method of organizational change. *Journal of Applied Behavioral Science* 3:3-21.

Dayal, I., and Thomas, J. M. 1968. Operation KPE: developing a new organization. *Journal of Applied Behavioral Science* 4:473-512.

Dyer, W. G.; Maddocks, R. F.; Moffitt, J. W.; and Underwood, W. J. 1970. A laboratory-consultation model for organizational change. *Journal of Applied Behavioral Science* 6:211-31.

Forward, J., and Williams, J. 1970. Internal-external control and black militancy. *Journal of Social Issues* 26:75-92.

Foundation for Research on Human Behavior. 1960. *An action research program for organization improvement.* Ann Arbor, Michigan: The Foundation for Research on Human Behavior.

Friedlander, F. 1967. The impact of organizational training laboratories upon the effectiveness and interaction of ongoing work groups. *Personnel Psychology* 20:289-308.

———. 1968. A comparative study of consulting processes and group development. *Journal of Applied Behavioral Science* 4:377-99.

Getzels, J. W. 1969. A social psychology of education. In *The Handbook of Social Psychology* (2nd ed.), Vol. 5, eds. G. Lindzey and E. Aronson. Reading, Massachusetts: Addison-Wesley. Pp. 459-537.

Golembiewski, R. T., and Blumberg, A. 1967. Confrontation as a training design in complex organizations: attitudinal changes in a diversified population of managers. *Journal of Applied Behavioral Science* 3:525-55.

———. 1968. The laboratory approach to organizational change: a confrontation design. *Academy of Management Journal* 11:199-210.

———. 1969. Persistence of attitude changes induced by a confrontation design: a research note. *Academy of Management Journal* 12:309-17.

———, eds. 1970. *Sensitivity training and the laboratory approach: readings about concepts and applications.* Itasca, Illinois: F. E. Peacock.

Greiner, L. L. 1967. Antecedents of planned organizational change. *Journal of Applied Behavioral Science* 3:51-86.

Guskin, A. E., and Guskin, S. L. 1970. *A social psychology of education.* Reading, Massachusetts: Addison-Wesley.

Harrison, R. 1962. Impact of the laboratory on perceptions of others by the experimental group. In *Interpersonal competence and organizational effectiveness,* ed. C. Argyris. Homewood, Illinois: Irwin.

Havelock, R.; Guskin, A.; Frohman, M.; Havelock, M.; Hill, M.; and Huber, J. 1969. *Planning for innovation through dissemination and utilization of knowledge.* Ann Arbor, Michigan: Institute for Social Research, University of Michigan.

Jacques, E. 1952. *The changing culture of a factory.* New York: Holt, Rinehart and Winston.

Johnson, D. W. 1970. *The social psychology of education.* New York: Holt, Rinehart and Winston.

Katz, D., and Kahn, R. 1966. *The social psychology of organizations.* New York: Wiley.

Kuriloff, A., and Atkins, S. 1966. T-group for a work team. *Journal of Applied Behavioral Science* 2:63-93.

Leavitt, H. J. 1965. Applied organizational change in industry: structural, technological and humanistic approaches. In *Handbook of organizations,* ed. J. G. March. Chicago: Rand McNally. Pp. 1144-1170.

Likert, R. L. 1961. *New patterns of management.* New York: McGraw-Hill.

Lippitt, R.; Watson, J.; and Westley, B. 1958. *The dynamics of planned change.* New York: Harcourt, Brace and World.

Manno, A. O. Group interaction as a means of inducing innovative teaching in elementary schools. Unpublished. Ed. D. dissertation, Teachers College, Columbia University. (Abstracted in COPED, 1970, Vol. I.)

Marin, P. 1970. Children of the apocalypse. *Saturday Review,* Sept. 19, 1970, pp. 71-73, 89.

Marrow, A. J.; Bowers, D. G.; and Seashore, S. E. *Management by participation.* New York: Harper and Row.

McElvaney, C. T., and Miles, M. B. 1969. The school psychologist and organizational improvement. In *Professional school psychology,* Vol. 3, eds. M. G. Gottsegen and G. B. Gottsegen. New York: Grune and Stratton. Pp. 20-50.

McGregor, D. M. 1961. *The human side of enterprise.* New York: McGraw-Hill.

Miles, M. B. 1962. Human relations training: current status. In *Issues in training,* ed. L. P. Bradford. Washington, D.C.: National Training Laboratories.

_____ . 1963. *Organizational development in schools: the effects of alternate strategies of change.* New York: Horace Mann-Lincoln Institute of School Experimentation, Teachers College, Columbia University. Mimeographed research proposal.

_____ , ed. 1964. *Innovation in education.* New York: Teachers College Press.

_____ . 1965a. Education and innovation: the organization as context. In *Change perspectives in educational administration,* eds. M. G. Abbott and J. T. Lowell. Auburn, Alabama: Eleventh Career Development Seminar on Change Perspectives. Pp. 54-72.

_____ . 1965b. Planned change and organizational health: figure and ground. In *Change processes in the public schools,* ed. R. O. Carlson, et al. Eugene, Oregon: Center for the Advanced Study of Educational Administration. Pp. 11-36.

_____ . 1967. Some properties of schools as social systems. In *Change in school systems,* ed. G. Watson. Washington: National Training Laboratories. Pp. 1-29.

_____ ; Calder, P. H.; Hornstein, H. A.; Callahan, D. M.; and Schiavo, R. S. 1966. Data feedback and organizational change in a school system. Paper read at American Sociological Association meetings, 1966.

_____ , and Charters, W. W., Jr. 1970. *Learning in social settings: new readings in the social psychology of education.* Boston: Allyn and Bacon.

_____ ; Hornstein, H. A.; Callahan, D. M.; Calder, P. H.; and Schiavo, R. S. 1969. The consequences of survey feedback: theory and evaluation. In *The planning of change* (2nd ed.), eds. W. G. Bennis, K. D. Benne, and R. Chin. New York: Holt, Rinehart and Winston. Pp. 457-468.

Morton, R. B. 1965. The organizational training laboratory: some individual and organizational effects. *Advanced Management Journal.* 30:58-67.

_____ , and Wight, A. 1964. A critical incidents evaluation of an organizational training laboratory. Working paper, Aerojet General Corporation.

Roethlisberger, F. J., and Dickson, W. J. 1939. *Management and the worker.* Cambridge, Massachusetts: Harvard University Press.

Rogers, C. R. 1969. *Freedom to learn.* Columbus, Ohio: Charles E. Merrill.

Schmuck, R. A. and Runkel, P. J. 1970. *Organizational training for a school faculty.* Eugene, Oregon: Center for the Advanced Study of Educational Administration.

_____ ; Runkel, P. J.; Derr, C. B.; Martel, R.; and Saturen, S. In press. *Handbook for organization development in schools.* Eugene, Oregon: Center for the Advanced Study of Educational Administration.

_____ ; Runkel, P. J.; and Langmeyer, D. 1969. Improving organizational problem-solving in a school faculty. *Journal of Applied Behavioral Science.* 5:455-82.

_____ , and Schmuck, P. A. 1971. *Group processes in the classroom.* Dubuque, Iowa: Wm. C. Brown.

Seashore, S., and Bowers, D. 1963. *Changing the structure and functioning of an organization: report of a field experiment.* Ann Arbor, Michigan: Institute for Social Research. Monograph No. 33.

_____ . 1970. Durability of organizational change. *American Psychologist* 25:227-33.

Shaevitz, M. H., and Barr, D. J. 1970. Encounter groups in a small college: a case study. La Jolla, California: University of California at San Diego. Mimeographed.

Shepard, H.A. 1965. Changing interpersonal and intergroup relationships in organizations. In *Handbook of organizations,* ed. J. G. March. Chicago: Rand McNally. Pp. 1115-1143.

Sieber, S. D. 1968. Organizational influences on innovative roles. In *Knowledge production and utilization in educational administration,* eds. T. L. Eidell and J. M. Kitchel.

Eugene, Oregon: Center for the Advanced Study of Educational Administration. Pp. 120-142.

Silberman, C. E. 1970. *Crisis in the classroom: the remaking of American education.* New York: Random House.

Stephens, J. M. 1967. *The process of schooling.* New York: Holt, Rinehart and Winston.

Underwood, W. J. 1965. Evaluation of laboratory method training. *Training Directors Journal* 19:34-40.

Valiquet, M. I. 1968. Individual change in a management development program. *Journal of Applied Behavioral Science* 4:313-25.

Watson, G., ed. 1967a. *Change in school systems.* Washington, D.C.: National Training Laboratories.

_____, ed. 1967b. *Concepts for social change.* Washington, D.C.: National Training Laboratories.

Winn, A. 1966. Social change in industry: from insight to implementation. *Journal of Applied Behavioral Science* 2:170-85.

Zand, D. E.; Miles, M. B.; and Lytle, W. O., Jr. 1970. Development of a collateral problem-solving organization through use of a temporary system. New York: Graduate School of Business Administration, New York University.

_____; Miles, M. B.; and Lytle, W. O., Jr. In preparation. Enlarging organizational choice through use of a temporary problem-solving system. In *Organizational development: theory and practice,* ed. D. E. Zand.

_____; Steele, F. I.; and Zalkind, S. S. 1969. The impact of an organizational development program on perceptions of interpersonal, group and organizational functioning. *Journal of Applied Behavioral Science* 5:393-410.

Zenger, J. P. 1969. As cited in D. G. Lake, M. R. Ritvo, and G. M. St. L. O'Brien, Applying behavioral science: current projects. *Journal of Applied Behavioral Science* 5:384-5.

2

IMPROVING CLASSROOM GROUP PROCESSES*

Richard A. Schmuck

Interpersonal relations in the classroom do have an impact on academic performance. A student's learning can be influenced by his feelings about himself in relation to his teacher and peers. His personal growth as a student depends to a large measure on the emotional climate of his classroom group.

This chapter describes how teachers can learn to change their teaching to improve classroom group processes. The projects show that teachers who become more cohesive among themselves, and who have opportunity for behavioral practice and feedback, do change their classroom behavior. The projects also show that "insight," as such, is not enough. Learning from consultants about new teaching behavior does change verbalizations and even the attitudes of teachers, but it does not change the emotional climate of the classes they are teaching.

Although the first two projects bear most directly on what to do to help teachers change, the third project is most closely related to organization development. It sets the stage for Chapters 3 to 10 by showing that teachers who have a successful organization development experience also try to improve the group processes in their classrooms. A more complete analysis of this OD training is given in Chapter 3.

Training for organization development, if successful, should improve the working relationships, efficiency, and creativity of the adult staff of a school. But in the end successful OD training must be judged by how much it helps students. If there is no benefit in the classroom, why prepare teachers and administrators to work more efficiently together?

Classroom group processes affect not only students' attitudes but their academic performance. It is possible for teachers to modify these group processes constructively if they are trained to do so. This chapter describes and systematically evaluates two action research interventions designed to help teachers improve the informal group processes in their classrooms: a teacher development laboratory and classroom mental health consultation.

---

* This chapter is an adaptation of Richard A. Schmuck, "Helping Teachers Improve Classroom Group Processes," in the *Journal of Applied Behavioral Science,* Vol. 4, No. 4, 1968. It has also appeared in Matthew B. Miles and W. W. Charters, Jr., *Learning in Social Settings* (Boston: Allyn and Bacon, Inc., 1970).

A third intervention, an organization development laboratory, is also offered as a means for effecting improvement in classroom group processes within a school. It is this sort of organizational training that sets the stage for the rest of this volume.

The Problem: Teacher Influence

Classroom groups, like other groups, have both formal and informal aspects. The formal aspects have to do with ways in which various members work toward carrying out the official or specified goals of the group. In the classroom, for instance, one formal feature is the way in which any child performs the role of academic student as defined by the teacher, school district, and adult community at large.

The informal aspects of a group involve the manner in which each member relates to other members as persons. In the classroom, an informal aspect is the way affection, or students' friendship for one another, is distributed. Such informal features often have an important bearing on the formal aspects. Many of them, such as friendship and willingness to help one another, are positive in effect and can enhance classroom group processes.

Such informal features can also affect a student's self-esteem, attitudes toward schoolwork, and academic achievement. In previous studies (Schmuck, 1962, 1963, and 1966), we showed that classroom groups with diffuse patterns of friendship and influence, as compared with those having more hierarchical patterns, possessed greater cohesiveness and more supportive norms for learning. Most students in these diffuse groups perceived themselves as having high group status, while in the hierarchical groups only students who actually had high status perceived themselves as having it. Students who perceived themselves as having high peer status tended to have higher self-esteem and more positive attitudes toward schoolwork, and were applying their intellectual abilities more effectively than others. Academic performance was shown to be conditioned by a student's self-concept, which was in turn partly influenced by his friendships and influence relations with his classmates.

Other studies have shown that teachers can influence classroom group processes. Flanders and Havumaki (1960) showed that a teacher's support and constructive praise were likely to increase a student's sociometric position among his classmates. In contrived classroom settings teachers interacted with and praised only students seated in odd-numbered seats, while in comparison groups all students were encouraged to speak and the teacher's praise was directed to the whole class. In the former situation the students in the odd-numbered seats later received more sociometric choices than students in the even-numbered seats. In the comparison classrooms, the difference between sociometric choices of students in the odd- and even-numbered seats was insignificant: the peer choices were spread more evenly, indicating greater general acceptance.

In another study (Schmuck and Van Egmond, 1965), the results of a multistage analysis indicated that when the variables—familial social class, perceived parental attitudes toward school, perceived peer status, and satisfaction with the teacher—were compared for their relative relationships to academic performance, pupils' satisfactions with the teacher and performance were associated when the effects of the other three variables were held constant. The results indicated that the teacher, especially as a social-emotional leader, had an effect on the academic performance of both boys and girls which was independent, to a significant degree, of the effects of parents and peers.

Further research indicated that teachers of more cohesive classroom groups attended to and talked with a larger variety of students per hour than teachers of less cohesive groups (Schmuck, 1966). Many teachers with less positive classroom group processes tended to call on fewer students for participation and seemed to neglect especially the slower, less involved students. Teachers with more supportive peer groups tended to reward students for helpful behavior with specific statements and to control behavioral disturbances with general, group-oriented statements. Teachers working in less positive climates tended to reward individuals less often and to reprimand them publicly more often for breaking classroom rules. All of these results indicate that teachers can and do influence classroom group processes. The three action research interventions described below illuminate how teachers might be helped to create classroom group processes which are psychologically more supportive.

Project 1: Teacher Development Laboratory

In establishing Project 1 we assumed that for classroom changes to be viable and effective, teachers need to learn more than theories, facts, and specific innovative practices and techniques. Teachers must integrate theories, facts, and techniques into their value systems, emotional styles, and role conceptions. Sensitivity training and role-playing experiences accompanied by a scientific problem-solving orientation were hypothesized to facilitate such a re-education process. These experiences are intended to encourage a teacher's search for alternative ways of teaching, to stimulate him to try out new ideas, and to encourage him to collect feedback from colleagues and students on the new practices.

Seven core training activities were carried out: (1) sensitivity training and related human relations laboratory experiences, (2) didactic discussions on basic research about classroom group processes, (3) problem-solving techniques for improving group processes, (4) analyses of diagnostic data from the teachers' own classrooms, (5) discussions about useful classroom practices developed by other teachers, (6) role-play tryouts of new classroom practices, and (7) follow-up discussions during the school year.

Twenty teachers participated in all of these activities and formed Laboratory Group A. Twenty other teachers participated in all the activities except (1) and (6), sensitivity training, related human relations laboratory experiences, and role-play tryouts, and formed Seminar Group B. Ten additional teachers, who received no special treatment, formed Control Group C.

This project began in the spring of 1965, when a brochure announcing a four-week summer laboratory for upper elementary teachers went to twelve school districts in metropolitan Detroit. The selection of school districts was accomplished by sampling broadly across social classes and racial and ethnic groups. Chief school officers in all districts agreed to inform their upper elementary teachers of the program. More than seventy-five teachers applied. Twenty teachers were placed in Laboratory Group A and an additional twenty in Seminar Group B. The ten teachers in Control Group C were selected later from other schools in the same school district. The final selection of the entire sample was based on principles of demographic heterogeneity of students within the experimental categories and demographic similarity among the categories. All three categories of teachers, therefore, had students with a full range of social characteristics, but the groups themselves were quite similar.

For Laboratory Group A the training period lasted six months, from July to December 1965. Seminar Group B met from September to December. There was no training for Control Group C. The program for Group A began with a daily six-hour intensive laboratory during the four weeks of July, and was followed up with feedback discussions with individual teachers and bimonthly discussion sessions from September to December. The program for Group B consisted of weekly seminar meetings and individual conferences.

Laboratory for Group A

The first week of the four-week laboratory consisted almost entirely of general human relations training. The T-group, focusing on personal sensitivity, was the core of this program (Bradford, Gibb, and Benne, 1964). Twenty teachers were divided randomly into two T-groups that met separately for two-hour periods twice daily; the remainder of each day was taken up by theory presentations, discussions, and skill exercises. While a skilled trainer was present in each group to maximize learning, the teachers created a group with their own concepts and in their own ways. Through this semistructured process, some of the teachers learned how groups are formed, and others became aware of the significant events in group development and of the kinds of functions they personally perform in groups. Many participants realized that their manner of speaking and relating to others could be just as important as the content of their communication.

Theory presentations, discussions, and skill exercises supplemented these T-groups. Theoretical short lectures and discussions dealt with such topics as "Roles Persons Play in Groups," "Communication and Feedback," and "Personal Styles in Groups." Often skill exercises were based on these theory sessions. For instance, the discussion on communication and feedback was followed by a skill exercise in which the teachers gave feedback to one another in small groups and, at the same time, were required to indicate that they were "hearing" by paraphrasing what another had just said. In another combination session of theory and skill training, the teachers privately completed the Edwards Personal Preference Inventory, received their own scores on ten psychological needs, were informed of what the scores meant conceptually, and then role-played how such need patterns would be expressed behaviorally in the classroom.

During the second week T-groups continued to meet, but only once each day, as the laboratory's discussions centered on the classroom as a human relations setting. Three categories of information, listed below, were presented during the second week:

1. Some basic research on classroom group processes was presented to the teachers.

2. A problem-solving scheme was presented. It included these stages:

   a. Identifying classroom group problems

   b. Diagnosing classroom problems

   c. Developing a plan of action

   d. Trying out the plan

   e. Getting feedback and making an evaluation (Schmuck, Chesler, and Lippitt, 1966)

3. The process of classroom diagnosis, the second stage of the problem-solving scheme, was explored in depth. The discussion included the following topics:

   a. Assessing the classroom learning climate

   b. Social relations in the classroom

   c. Peer group norms

   d. Student-teacher interaction

   e. Outside influences on students' learning

   f. Parental influences on school adjustment

   g. The student's self-concept

   h. Students' attitudes toward school and teachers (Fox, Luszki, and Schmuck, 1966).

Pairs or trios of teachers took one of these diagnostic topics and were responsible for teaching the entire workshop group how to use questionnaires and other measurement tools associated with that topic. The trio working on teacher-student interaction received special instructions in Flanders' Interaction Analysis and used this procedure for collecting data on the instructional styles used by the other teachers as they taught the various diagnostic techniques. When the other teachers had completed their instruction, this group reported on the interaction by giving feedback to all of the instructional teams on how they behaved according to the observation categories. Discussions on diagnosis were completed by the end of the second week.

Next, the teachers were asked to skim through a booklet containing other teachers' practices and to decide tentatively on some practices they would like to use in order to improve classroom group processes or, more specifically, to solve classroom peer-relations problems (Kaufman, Schmuck, and Lippitt, 1963). The teachers' techniques, devices, and special procedures included in this booklet were examined for their soundness by skilled teachers, educational administrators, and social psychologists. A few examples of procedures drawn from the booklet are:

Development of a classroom group government to assist in social relations management. Early in the year the class votes for a Rules Committee which sets up a Bill of Rights for all students and presents it to the rest of the group for discussion and approval. A Judiciary Committee is constituted to enforce the rules and serves for four weeks. Every day a member of the Judiciary Committee puts a schedule of the day's activities on the board, including the name of the committee member who will be responsible for supervision of behavior during each period. The Judiciary Committee and the class officers meet to arrange the class seating plans and rearrange them as necessary. Every month four students who have not been on the Judiciary Committee are elected to serve. This method is followed until all students have taken part.

Formation and clarification of peer group behavior standards. The teacher divides the class into small subgroups for discussion of behavioral standards. The groups are initially led by sociometrically high students who have been given some preliminary leadership training. Each subgroup reports its findings orally to the class, the whole class identifies the standards they like best, and these become classroom rules. These subgroups meet once every week. Each student receives some leadership training and a chance to lead a group.

Role-playing to increase understanding of group behavior. The teacher asks the class to create a play and the class discusses what the content of the play should be. The class is advised to choose a plot familiar to all and including at least one group relations problem. The play is written, actors are chosen, and the play is enacted. Discussion takes place on applications of the play to life together in this classroom. Human relations in the classroom peer group in general are discussed.

Teaching human relations skills. Short class meetings are held three times each week concerning human relations topics. Some of the class discussions are taped to be played back later and evaluated by the students. The students also are encouraged to express their opinions by answering questions such as "What did you like about today?" and "What do you like (or not like) about our school?" When problems are identified, role-playing situations are set up and enacted. The students suggest alternative ways of behaving during the role-plays and discuss the meaning of role-plays for their classroom group relations.

On Monday and Tuesday of the third week the T-groups discussed the teachers' perceptions of the classroom practices presented in the booklet. Each teacher was asked to develop at least one practice that he wished to try out as a way of improving classroom group processes. On those same days, several two-hour sessions were held on the rationale for role playing and some ways of using this technique (Chesler and Fox, 1966). One session was also held on the procedure for collecting feedback from students. From Wednesday of the third week to Wednesday of the fourth and final week, each teacher spent one hour simulating part of his chosen practice in a role-play enactment, using the other teachers in roles as students or as outside observers.

During the last two days of the laboratory the teachers made specific plans to implement these new classroom procedures during the school year. Lewin's field of forces analysis was presented so that each teacher could estimate the restraining forces that would deter him from following through with the plan (Coch and French, 1948). After considerable thought was given to implementing the plan, each teacher conferred with a staff member about his plan. This conference took the place of a final examination and was tape-recorded. A schedule was set up for playing the tape early in the fall at a similar conference as a reminder and motivational device for supporting tryouts of the plan.

From September until December of 1965, the teachers continued to be involved in the program. Early in September, data were collected on the quality of group processes in all classrooms. Some data were immediately presented to the teachers. Next the teachers listened to their tape recordings with a person from our staff and made more realistic plans based on the new data and their summer plans. Bimonthly group discussions were held during which the teachers discussed the strong and weak points of their teaching experiences. Attempts were made to support the teachers' efforts to follow through on their plans and to help the teachers to engage continuously in the problem-solving process. The program of training for Laboratory Group A ended with an informal gathering one week before winter vacation.

Seminar for Group B

Group B met weekly from September to December 1965. The members were initially presented the same problem-solving sequence used by Group A. They learned about the uses of diagnostic tools and received group process data from their classrooms for analysis. Basic research findings about classroom group processes also were presented to them, and they read about the classroom practices of other teachers and discussed those which they wanted to try. The principal activities omitted from the Seminar for Group B were sensitivity training and role-playing.

Results of Project 1

Early in the fall, during the school year, and again late in the spring, students completed self-report questionnaires on classroom group processes and their attitudes toward peers, school, self, and teacher. Teachers in Groups A and B kept diaries relating to their planned attempts at improving group processes. Every teacher was also observed for an hour's duration three or four times during the school year. Data were collected on teachers in Group C only during the spring. The assumption made was that Group C classes, in which no interventions were tried, would more nearly reflect the fall than the spring patterns of classes in Groups A and B.

An overview of the results indicates that the Laboratory Group A teachers and students made more positive changes in their group processes than those in Seminar Group B and that both Groups A and B were more improved at the end of the school year than Control Group C.

Perhaps the most obvious difference between teachers in Groups A and B was in their group cohesiveness. The *esprit de corps* in Group A was extremely positive, while almost none existed in Group B. Group A teachers telephoned one another twenty-five times about professional matters, while only two such calls were reported by Group B teachers. Fifteen of the twenty teachers in Group A visited socially during the school year; only three from Group B met informally. Numerous instances of sharing classroom teaching ideas occurred in Group A, while the teachers in Group B talked about their practices only during seminar time. Group A teachers talked more about their classrooms before and after class and during coffee breaks. Group A initiated a party at the end of the laboratory, and many members indicated strong desires to continue or at least to keep in touch. Group B teachers showed more interest in receiving college credit than in one another.

These differences would not be very significant in themselves if they were not accompanied by changes in classroom practices. Evidence from diaries and observations indicated that the Group A teachers were much more innovative than the Group B teachers. Teachers in Group A produced more elaborate plans of action and attempted more practices for improving group processes than the Group B teachers. Group B teachers typically tried one or two practices during the year to improve group processes, while teachers in Group A tried from five to seventeen different procedures with their students. Indeed, the enthusiasm of two teachers was discussed by several students critically when they wrote on their questionnaires that they wished their teacher would keep one grouping procedure for at least two weeks instead of the usual one week. Even though some similar criticisms were aimed at other Group A teachers by their students, these represented a minor percentage of student response.

The most sharply emphasized goal of Group A teachers was to increase openness in classroom communication among peers and between students and the teacher. Communication was encouraged by such activities as summarizing data from student questionnaires and discussing their meanings, role-playing in difficult classroom situations, discussing critical statements placed in a suggestion box, discussing thoughts about what makes for a "good" or "bad" day in class, and reviewing how the class had been proceeding by holding once-weekly evaluations and review-discussions. Group B teachers used a few of these practices but tried fewer per teacher and continued using them for shorter durations.

The most widespread interest, shown by fifteen of the twenty Group A teachers, was in increasing student participation levels in deciding on classroom regulations and procedures. In seven Group A classrooms, student governments were formed and functioned successfully throughout most of the year. Teachers with such governments attempted to increase the diffusion of influence in the peer group by encouraging all students to take part at some point in the classroom government.

We also collected "before and after" self-report questionnaires from the students in Group A and B classrooms in the fall and spring of the school year. Students in Group C completed questionnaires only in the spring. Averages from the fall measure taken on students in Groups A and B were used as estimates of the "before" data in Group C.

In general, the questions centered on the students' perceptions of their influence and friendship status in the classroom group and the extent to which they supported one another and felt a part of the group. Students were asked to estimate whether they saw themselves in the highest part (quarter) of the class, the second highest part, the third part, or the lowest part. The questions were these: (1) *Influence*—"Compared with others in the class, how often can you get others to do what you want them to do?" and (2) *Friendship*—"Where would you place yourself on the basis of how much the others in the class like you?" Improved group relations would be indicated by the students' feeling that they were more influential and had more friends in the spring as compared with the fall.

Furthermore, we asked students to describe, through a symbolic drawing, the friendship structure of the classroom group as they saw it. Students were presented the five rectangles, as shown in Figure 2-1. Each rectangle represents a different group pattern. Students selected the rectangle that best represented their view of the peer group, or drew their own version in the blank rectangle. About 40 percent of the students drew their own picture of the group. Each

Figure 2-1   The Classroom Group (A Method for Measuring Friendship Structure)

If you were to think about this class as a group, which one of these drawings would most nearly resemble your class?

Pretend that each circle stands for a person in this class. Circles that are close together stand for people who are friends. (Check the one most like your class.)

Place an "X" within the circle that stands for your position in the group.

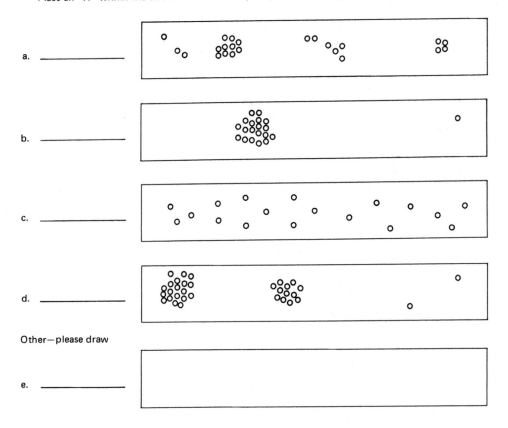

Other—please draw

student also was asked to place an "X" within one circle that would stand for his own position in the group.

We defined a friendship group as more than two circles in a cluster and compared the average number of these perceived to exist in the class early and late in the school year. We also categorized the position in which a student felt himself to be within the group, during fall and spring by using these four categories: (1) at the center of a larger group, defined as more than four circles; (2) at the periphery of a large group; (3) in a smaller group, defined as four or fewer circles; and (4) alone or isolated. Finally, as a means of getting some idea of the supportive nature of the group, especially with regard to academic matters, we asked a series of questions about the frequency of supportive behavior in the classroom. One such question was: The students in this class help one another with their schoolwork (a) almost always, (b) usually, (c) seldom, or (d) almost never.

The data on perceived influence clearly supported the hypothesis that the Laboratory for Group A would result in greater benefits than the Seminar for Group B, and that both would show gains over the Control Group C. The data on friendship were not so clear but did suggest the same pattern. Results shown in Table 2-1, on the perceived influence status of each student early and late in

Table 2-1   Student Perceptions of Influence Status in Their Classroom Groups, Early and Late

		Laboratory Group A				Seminar Group B				Control Group C			
	Perceived Influence Statuses	Fall		Spring		Fall		Spring		Est. Fall		Spring	
		No.	%	No.	%	No.	%	No.	%	No.	%	No.	%
High	Highest part	55	10	28	5	45	9	44	9	31	10	29	9
	Second part	236	43	309	56	168	35	154	32	126	39	113	35
	Third part	106	37	155	28	187	39	202	42	124	38	120	37
Low	Lowest part	55	10	60	11	80	17	80	17	42	13	61	19

chi-square = 48.90   df = 3 $p < .005$ chi-square = 2.39   df = 3   p = NS   chi-square = 10.16   df = 3 $p < .025$

the school year, indicated the positive significance of the laboratory experience for the Group A classrooms. The percentage of students with Group A teachers who perceived themselves as high (above the median) in peer group influence increased significantly from 53 to 61 percent during the school year. Students in Group B, on the other hand, showed no significant change from fall to spring on perceived influence. In the Control Group C classes, the results were that the students became significantly more negative in their perceptions of influence. While 49 percent viewed themselves as high in influence during the fall, only 44 percent perceived that they were high in the spring.

Results in Table 2-2 indicated that positive gains in perceived friendship status were made in all three categories of classrooms during the school year. Comparisons of the chi-square totals as well as the percentages indicated that the positive gains made in Laboratory Group A were greater than those made in either Seminar Group B or Control Group C. Fifty-seven percent of the students in Group A classrooms viewed themselves as much liked early in the year. This number increased to 77 percent in the spring: an increase of 20 percent. Percentage increases in Groups B and C were significantly positive also, but were only half as great as the increase in Group A. We conclude that in most classrooms students tended to perceive that they were liked by more people in the spring than in the fall, but the laboratory teachers appear to have increased this positive trend even more than the others.

Additional data indicating changes in classroom friendship patterns are summarized in Tables 2-3 and 2-4. In general, these data also supported our expectation that the laboratory would have positive benefit for Group A classroom groups. Results in Table 2-3 showed that gains in the number of friendship groups perceived by the students to exist in the class were made in all three

Table 2-2 Student Perceptions of Friendship Status in Their Classroom Groups, Early and Late

Perceived Friendship Statuses		Laboratory Group A				Seminar Group B				Control Group C			
		Fall		Spring		Fall		Spring		Est. Fall		Spring	
		No.	%	No.	%	No.	%	No.	%	No.	%	No.	%
High	Highest part	79	14	99	18	101	21	91	19	56	17	58	18
	Second part	237	43	326	59	221	46	278	58	143	44	171	53
	Third part	171	31	105	19	106	22	72	15	87	27	55	17
Low	Lowest part	65	12	22	4	52	11	39	8	37	12	39	12

chi-square = 92.39   chi-square = 29.84   chi-square = 17.37
df = 3   df = 3   df = 3
$p < .005$ $p < .005$ $p < .005$

Table 2-3 Student Perceptions of Number of Classroom Friendship Groups, Early and Late

Number of Friendship Groups	Laboratory Group A				Seminar Group B				Control Group C			
	Fall		Spring		Fall		Spring		Est. Fall		Spring	
	No.	%	No	%	No.	%	No.	%	No.	%	No.	%
0 or 1	157	30	89	17	143	31	83	18	97	31	70	22
2	100	19	68	13	78	17	83	18	57	18	73	23
3	22	4	37	7	41	9	37	8	20	6	16	5
4 or more	245	47	330	63	199	43	258	56	143	45	158	50

chi-square = 69.17   chi-square = 43.37   chi-square = 14.38
df = 3   df = 3   df = 3
$p < .005$ $p < .005$ $p < .005$

Table 2-4 Student Perceptions of Own Position in a Classroom Friendship Group, Early and Late

Own Position in Friendship Group	Laboratory Group A				Seminar Group B				Control Group C			
	Fall		Spring		Fall		Spring		Est. Fall		Spring	
	No.	%	No.	%	No.	%	No.	%	No.	%	No.	%
At center of large group	96	20	120	25	48	16	51	17	55	18	81	27
At periphery of large group	120	25	97	20	72	24	66	22	74	25	66	22
In small group	158	33	245	51	151	50	155	51	119	40	117	39
Alone	106	22	18	4	31	10	30	10	52	17	36	12

chi-square = 131.35   chi-square = 0.81   chi-square = 18.10
df = 3   df = 3   df = 3
$p < .005$ p = NS $p < .005$

categories. As in Table 2-2, comparisons of the chi-square totals as well as the percentages in Table 2-3 indicated that the positive gains were greatest for teachers in Laboratory Group A. Whereas 51 percent of the students in Group A classes saw three, four, or more friendship groups during the fall, 70 percent perceived that same number during the spring. Increases in Group B (52 percent to 64 percent) and Group C (51 percent to 55 percent), though statistically significant, were not so great.

The results shown in Table 2-4 emphasized the success of the laboratory even more than those in Table 2-3. Here significant changes occurred in the extent to which students viewed themselves as being an integral part of either large (four or more persons) or small (three or fewer persons) friendship groups in the class. Fifty-three percent of the Group A students saw themselves at the center of a large or small group during the fall. This increased to 76 percent by the spring. The comparable increase in Control Group C classes was from 58 percent to 66 percent, representing a minor increment compared with that of the laboratory classes. No significant change was made during the year in the Seminar Group B classroom groups on perception of friendship group position.

Finally, the data in Table 2-5 indicated that the students in both the Group A and Group B classrooms increased during the school year in the degree to which they were helpful to one another with their schoolwork. A comparison between Groups A and B indicated that Group A classes made greater gains in helpfulness. For instance, in the fall 45 percent of Group A students reported "almost always" or "usually" helping one another, while in the spring, 58 percent reported this: a gain of 13 percent. Group B, on the other hand, increased from 49 percent to 57 percent: an increase of only 8 percent. Students in the Group C classroom groups showed no difference from fall to spring in helpfulness.

Table 2-5 Students' Perceptions of How Often They Help One Another With Schoolwork, Early and Late

How Often They Help One Another	Laboratory Group A				Seminar Group B				Control Group C			
	Fall		Spring		Fall		Spring		Est. Fall		Spring	
	No.	%	No.	%	No.	%	No.	%	No.	%	No.	%
Almost always	56	11	86	17	71	15	71	15	42	13	48	15
Usually	172	34	206	41	162	34	200	42	110	34	107	33
Seldom	187	37	171	34	157	33	162	34	113	35	120	37
Almost never	92	18	44	8	85	18	42	9	58	18	48	15

	chi-square = 49.19	chi-square = 30.81	chi-square = 3.09
	df = 3	df = 3	df = 3
	$p < .005$	$p < .005$	p = NS

Project 2: Classroom Mental Health Consultation

In Project 2 skilled psychological consultants attempted to increase teachers' capabilities for coping with group processes in the classroom. Our hypothesis was that through problem-oriented discussions with mental health specialists teachers would develop a better understanding of the social-emotional aspects of classroom groups and greater skill in handling them (Edelmann and Schmuck, 1967). Consultation sessions centered on the relationships of consultants to teachers, teachers to teachers, and teachers to students. Since the project was carried out in metropolitan Philadelphia, some attention was given to increasing teachers' facilities for working with groups of students from disadvantaged families.

Six highly trained consultants—two psychiatrists, two clinical psychologists, and two social workers—were employed for the project. The bias of the consultants was psychodynamic and interdisciplinary. Only the social workers, however, had had professional experience in public schools. The consultants were assigned one to a school for half a day each week for fifteen weeks. Three consultants worked in schools with mostly middle class children, while the others worked in schools with culturally disadvantaged youngsters. Forty upper elementary teachers received consultation. Three consultants worked with groups of six teachers each; the other consultants worked with five, eight, and nine teachers, respectively.

Two additional schools, one middle class and one lower class, were included for comparison purposes. The twenty upper elementary teachers in these two schools received no consultation.

The consultants received special training prior to and concurrent with their work with the teachers in the schools. Drs. Eli Bower (Hollister and Bower, 1967) and Ruth Newman (Newman, 1967) were responsible for much of this training. They discussed their respective approaches to school consultation and guided the six specialists through problematic situations that would arise during the consultations.

This project began during the fall of 1966 when pre-data were collected; consultation took place during the fall and winter months, and final data were collected in May 1967, three months after the consultations were completed. The consultants spent two hours each week in group discussions with the teachers. They also visited classrooms to make observations, which would often culminate in individual conferences. The project plans called for both the group discussions and the individual conferences to center on teachers' own reactions to the classroom groups and especially to problem incidents involving several students. The consultants were to emphasize the development of trust in the group and to open up new pathways of behavior and new understanding of the changes desired, but only after some trust had developed. Finally, they were to explore in depth how teachers might interact with students having interpersonal relations problems, low self-esteem, marked disinterest in learning, or recurrent daydreams and inattention.

Consultation Sessions

The consultants wrote historical accounts of every meeting with teachers, whether in group discussions or individual conferences. Along with these detailed descriptions, the consultants were asked to jot down at the close of each session any problems they were having in establishing themselves as helpful and to specify any changes they saw in the schools—especially changes in the teachers with whom they were consulting.

Analyses of the consultants' reports indicated that certain recurrent themes appeared during the fifteen weeks. During the first several sessions, classroom group problems were viewed as resulting from forces outside the control of the teachers. The teachers primarily ventilated their antagonistic feelings toward the "impersonal and unhelpful central office," the "authoritarian principal," the "incompetent counselor," the "uninterested parents," or the "intransigent students." These parties were seen as limiting the level of effectiveness that could be expected of the teachers. Some teachers felt that membership in the consultation group was involuntary: that the group had been organized in reality by a school counselor, parental group, or the principal. Others needed reassurance that the principal or central office personnel would not be involved directly in the consultation groups.

After the teachers had a chance to voice these feelings in a supportive atmosphere (without sanction by the consultants, however) they were more likely to discuss problems present in their classrooms and to see themselves and their students as jointly involved in them. As classroom group or individual problems were brought up for discussion, the teachers looked to the consultants for the solutions. They expected the consultants to recommend concrete actions that could be taken to solve the problem. At times they expected the consultants to advise the principal or central office administrators that certain students perceived as mentally unhealthy should be removed formally from the regular classroom and placed in special education classes. The consultants generally took the view that they could only help teachers find their own answers, that these answers would most likely involve the teachers' changing their own classroom behavior, and that as consultants they did not have the authority to remove youngsters from classes.

Toward the end of the fifteen week period, the teachers talked more about their own insecurities, doubts, and lacks in knowledge and skill. During this phase the teachers turned more to one another for sharing ideas on handling classroom group problems. They offered to meet with one another at other times during the week to share teaching practices. The consultants' role became less prominent as the teachers conversed more freely and openly about their own classroom problems.

Results of Project 2

The consultants generally agreed that significant and positive changes occurred in many teachers as a consequence of the consultations. Perhaps the most striking change was in teachers' asking one another for help. Early in the year, many teachers reported that they were ashamed to ask for one another's assistance. The teachers were generally discouraged or indifferent about staff relations. But after the consultations many teachers had formed a strong group feeling, possessed a new sense of challenge and interest, and were using one another outside the sessions to talk over problems, trade materials, and respond to new ideas. Some teachers who had decided during the fall to give up teaching changed their minds as they noted how much support they felt from their colleagues.

The teachers also became more flexible in examination of their standards and attitudes, and became able to accept a somewhat greater variety of student behaviors. One consultant noted that his teachers showed more interest in and ability to deal with individual differences. Another commented that at the start a number of teachers had perceived some of their students as "disturbed," but that during the course of consultations the teachers began to see these students more as energetic, restless, and child-like than as disturbed. According to one consultant, some classroom problems seemed to disappear as the teachers' behavior toward these children changed.

Some teachers were seen to reach a stage in which they could examine their own behavior as a factor in creating undesirable behavior in their students. Other teachers spoke less judgmentally of students and parents at the end of the consultation and instead were more likely to explore their own relationships to their students. Some began to sort out their own needs from those of the students, while others noted publicly that "problem students" often ceased being problems when a teacher extended special help and affection and arranged for some success.

Early during the fall and again late in the spring, four self-report questionnaires were collected from the total group of sixty teachers. Three teachers' questionnaires focused on perceptual variables, measuring conceptions about self as teacher, ways of categorizing students, and conceptions of positive mental health in the classroom. Two skilled raters who had no contact with the consultants scored the results of these three questionnaires without knowing whether the teachers being rated were in the consultation or comparison groups. Their initial ratings were in high agreement (generally above 90 percent) but they continued to score items about which they disagreed until they achieved 100 percent agreement.

The fourth questionnaire queried teachers on how they might handle a variety of problematic situations in the classroom. Each consultant scored all of these protocols. The consultants did not know what teachers or schools they were scoring, nor did they know whether they were scoring the fall or the spring data. Scores of plus, zero, minus, or question mark were used. A plus meant that the situation was handled effectively. A score of minus meant that the consultant viewed the teacher's response as ineffective. A zero meant that the consultant was unable to make a judgment because the verbal content required a nonverbal response or context. A question mark meant that the response was unclear and therefore could not be coded. In the analysis of these data, we required that four or more of the consultants agree before giving the response a plus, minus, or zero score. When only three or fewer consultants agreed, we scored the item with a question mark. The consultants did not see any results of the four questionnaires until after the consultations were completed.

In measuring the teachers' self-concepts, we asked them to write down ten phrases which described themselves as teachers. Then they were asked to go back and place a double plus sign by each characteristic they considered very positive, a single plus sign by each one they considered somewhat positive, a negative sign if they thought it somewhat negative, and a double negative sign if they considered it very negative.

We anticipated that the consultations would lead the teachers to more balanced views of themselves *as teachers*. We thought that those teachers who viewed themselves in the fall as quite negative and insecure would gain a greater sense of competence and self-esteem from the consultation. On the other hand, we considered that those who saw themselves as solely positive and effective in the fall would begin to uncover some areas within themselves that required some improvement. Thus the raters judged as more positive those self-concept patterns which became more balanced (containing both positive and negative attributes) or which changed from more negative to more positive. Conversely, the raters judged as more negative those patterns which remained predominantly negative or defensively positive.

In the questionnaire on categorizing the students, teachers were given a set of cards with the names of all students (one to a card) and the following instructions:

In your mind, there are probably many ways in which the students can be seen as similar to and different from one another. Place these cards in piles in as many different ways as might occur in your thinking. Each time you place the cards into piles, you should have some main idea in mind and a descriptive title for each pile.

For instance, in your mind, you might divide the class into boys and girls. Then you would sort the cards into two piles; the main idea is "sex difference" and the descriptive titles of the piles are "boys" and "girls." Another division which might occur could be color of hair. Then "color of hair" would be the main idea, and "blondes," "brunettes," and "redheads" could be the descriptive titles.

In this questionnaire we expected that the teachers would show evidence of having developed in several ways as a result of consultation. For one thing, we assumed that at the end of the school year teachers who had had consultation would use more main ideas relating to emotional factors, attitudes, motivations, and interpersonal relations. We expected more categories on topics such as anxiety, security, self-esteem, attitudes toward school, and peer relations. Further, we expected that teachers who had received consultation would increase the number of differentiations that they made under the main categories. We felt that the consultation would facilitate a more sophisticated and differentiated view of the students. We expected that the teachers might see their students more in terms of the students' feelings but also increasingly as being different from one another.

The third questionnaire was aimed at measuring the teachers' cognitive structures concerning "mental health" in the classroom. Each teacher was to express his ideas concerning good mental health practices and conditions in the classroom according to the following directions:

Let us suppose that the following situation occurs. A visiting teacher from a foreign country engages you in conversation about school practices in this country. Assume that your visitor knows very little about American teaching practices. He wants to know what you consider to be good mental health practices and conditions in the classroom. What sorts of things would you include in a list which he could refer to as he tries to learn about classroom mental health?

Using these cards which have been provided, write one word, phrase, or sentence on each card which describes good classroom mental health practices or conditions. Use as few or as many cards as you need. A total of twenty-five cards is supplied.

In order to ensure that the foreign visitor has understood you, try to organize the items you listed on the cards. Do this in the following way. Lay out in front of you all the cards you used in listing mental health practices and conditions. Look them over to see whether they fall into some broad, natural groupings. If they do, arrange them into such groups. Now look at your groups to see whether these can be broken into subgroups. If they can, separate the cards accordingly. It is also possible that these subgroups can be broken down still further.

The range of groupings included physical properties of the room and school, physical properties of teachers or students, intellectual skills, personality characteristics (including attitudes and motives), interpersonal relations, group social relations, and group climate and cohesiveness. We expected that after the consultation the teachers would emphasize students' attitudes, feelings, and motives, as well as classroom interpersonal relations and group climate. Although physical characteristics might be included, we viewed these as less central to effective classroom group processes. We further considered that the mental health categories would have more detailed subgroupings and that the teachers would relate these more directly to the students in their class.

The fourth questionnaire, titled "Classroom Situations," was made up of forty-four situations which were taken from actual classrooms and presented in the form of dialogues. The teachers received these directions:

Pretend you are the teacher in each situation (even if you have not met such a situation or would not have allowed it to develop). When the dialogue closes, write the exact words or nonverbal responses you would use at that point.

Data collected from the teachers generally indicated positive and significant changes during the school year in their perceptions of self as teachers, their cognitions of mental health categories, and their views on how to work with problematic classroom situations. The data on categorizing students did not change greatly during the year. These data are summarized in Table 2-6. Fisher's

Table 2-6 Summary of Teachers' Perceptions of Self, Students, and Classroom Processes by Group, Fall and Spring

Evaluations in Spring Compared with Fall	Self-Concept				Categorizing Students				Mental Health Categories				Classroom Situations			
	Consultation Group		Comparison Group		Consultation Group		Comparison Group		Consultation Group		Comparison Group		Consultation Group		Comparison Group	
	No.	%	No.	%	No.	%	No.	%	No.	%	No.	%	No.	%	No.	%
More positive	14	35	2	10	5	12	0	0	15	38	0	0	19	48	3	15
No change	24	60	16	80	35	88	20	100	24	60	20	100	14	35	13	65
More negative	2	5	2	10	0	0	0	0	1	2	0	0	7	17	4	20

Probabilities from Fisher's Exact Test	$p < .01$				$p = NS$				$p < .01$				$p < .01$			

Exact Test, applied because of the very small sample, requires a two-by-two contingency table, and thus for purposes of this statistical analysis the data labeled "more negative" were dropped. In each case, except for the data on categorizing students, results of Fisher's Exact Test showed probabilities less than .01 (Hays, 1963). We can assume that these data indicate significant changes and therefore that the consultations altered many teachers' cognitions related to successful teaching.

The students also were asked to complete four questionnaires in the fall and spring. One questionnaire measured students' perceptions concerning the informal group processes in the class. Each student answered twelve questions on how he saw others in the class behaving with one of four answers: almost always, usually, seldom, or almost never. Some of the items were: "Help one another with their schoolwork," "Laugh when someone misbehaves," and "Work well with one another." The second questionnaire measured attitudes toward school and self-esteem with incomplete sentence stems. Examples of items used to measure the former were: "Studying is _____," "Homework is _____," "Learning out of books is _____." Self-esteem was measured with stems such as "When I look at other boys and girls and then look at myself, I feel _____," "When I look in the mirror, I _____," and "My teacher thinks I am _____." The third questionnaire presented sociometric questions on friendship and helping relations, asking students to choose the four other students in the class whom they liked the most and the four who were most helpful to other students. They also estimated their own status in the group on being liked and helpful. The fourth questionnaire dealt with students' attitudes about academic work and school in general. The students were asked about such things as how hard they saw themselves working, whether the teacher really understood them, and whether the students helped one another.

An overview of the results indicated that positive and significant changes did *not* occur in the consultation classes. The students' attitudes toward school and self did not improve in either the consultation or the comparison groups. The informal group processes appear to have remained about the same throughout the year, except for some evidence that helpfulness increased in the consultation groups.

The overall results do, however, obscure some positive changes that occurred in a few classrooms. Out of the 40 consultation classes, six showed distinct improvement and these, interestingly, were all within two schools. In these six classes, the friendship and helpfulness patterns became more diffuse over the course of the year. Moreover, significant changes occurred in the positive self-esteem of many of these students. In contrast with this, no changes whatsoever occurred in the students' attitudes toward school.

It appears that the cognitive and attitudinal changes which occurred in the teachers were *not* also accompanied by behavioral changes that made a difference in their classrooms. The teachers grew in their intellectual awarenesses about interpersonal relations in the classroom and in their willingness to explore new ways of handling them, but they did not in fact make major shifts in their classroom behavior. Any behavior changes that did occur, as reported by the consultants, were probably short-term and motivated out of desires to please the consultants. The group processes in the classrooms, by and large, remained unaffected by the consultations.

Project 3: Organization Development Laboratory

In Project 3, we did not attempt to influence directly the teachers' capabilities for working more effectively with classroom group processes. Rather we assumed that the social relations of a school set the stage for classroom innovation and that more effective organizational processes would support teacher innovativeness and performance in the classroom (Lippitt, Barakat, Chesler, Dennerell, Flanders, Worden, and Schmuck, 1967). Some aspects of effective school processes that we assumed to be related to classroom innovativeness and productivity were the interpersonal relations and feelings, communication patterns, and group norms of the staff.

This project was aimed at improving school organizational processes so that classroom innovations might be made more easily. The project employed an organizational training program to help a junior high school faculty to become more aware, open, analytic, and skillful about its interpersonal relationships, communication patterns, behavior norms, decision-making processes, and group problem-solving skills.

Procedures of Project 3

A six-day laboratory was held in 1967 before the beginning of school and involved the entire faculty (except for two members with illness in their families), including the head custodian, head cook, and administrative secretary—making a total group of fifty-four participants. The laboratory staff was composed of five trainers. The laboratory was designed to help the staff discuss its interpersonal relations, identify and explore its communicative problems, and move toward tentative working solutions through group problem-solving. Several follow-up training sessions were scheduled during the 1967-68 school year. Details of the training events are delineated in Chapter 3 of this volume and in Schmuck and Runkel (1970).

Results of Project 3

Faculty members were asked to complete several self-report questionnaires just prior to or during the laboratory sessions. These were designed to measure the school's organizational climate, reactions to staff meetings, staff communication patterns, and perceptions about the principal. The research evaluation also called for some interviews and observations to be collected during the school year, as well as completion of the same self-report questionnaires again in the spring. All the measures, whether they were questionnaires, interviews, or observations, were designed originally to center only on organizational processes. They did not include questions about classroom innovations.

We learned only inadvertently that the teachers were making use of experiences from the laboratory in their classrooms. The first signs came immediately after the laboratory when a one-page questionnaire was filled out by all faculty members on their reactions to the laboratory. Even though no question about classroom applications of the workshop was asked, seven teachers mentioned plans to make use of some laboratory experiences in their classrooms.

A second indication came in some of the essays about the laboratory written by twenty-one teachers. (All workshop participants had the opportunity of receiving two hours of university credit for active participation. However, twenty-one teachers desired three credit hours and so were required to prepare an essay on their laboratory experiences.) Their assignment was to write about any changes, positive or negative, in the school's operation which they considered attributable to the laboratory. They were asked to complete the essay no later than six weeks after the end of the laboratory. Most papers came in about one month after it closed. Primarily we expected to receive analyses of the school's organizational functioning. Many of the faculty members, however, wrote extended reviews of the ways in which the laboratory had positively influenced their classroom performances. Some were quite specific about having used, with their students, some of the group formations, techniques, and processes employed during the laboratory.

Finally, a third sign of classroom application came about six weeks after the laboratory closed when we visited the school to interview staff members about the faculty's organizational processes. Again, even though during the interview no question was formally asked about classroom innovations, fifteen teachers mentioned using new group processes in their classrooms. With these unanticipated data, we added one question for the next round of interviews: "Has the laboratory experience influenced your classroom teaching in any ways? If yes, in what ways?" Of the twenty teachers who were interviewed on the second round, nineteen answered yes to the question.

The teachers' comments on the ways in which the laboratory had influenced their teaching fell into three categories. Some teachers mentioned only a very general outcome, such as "a change in my general approach to students," "a better atmosphere in my classroom," or "more attention to the feelings of the students." Another small group of teachers commented on specific attitude changes, such as "I am more comfortable this year," "I am sensitive to students' feedback," or "I am more relaxed in letting the students discuss things." Eleven of the nineteen teachers provided answers fitting into a third category. They mentioned specific group procedures that they were actually using in their classrooms, such as "small groups for projects," "nonverbal exercises to depict feelings about the subject matter being studied," " 'theatre in the round' or 'fishbowl' formations for having students observe one another," "a paraphrasing exercise to point out how poor classroom communications are," "the problem-solving sequence and techniques in social studies classes to learn more about social problems," and "small groups for giving and receiving feedback about how the class is going." As far as we know, none of these practices was used by these teachers before the organization development laboratory.

Discussion and Conclusions

The three interventions discussed above helped teachers, directly or indirectly, to work toward improving classroom group processes.

The organization development laboratory for a school staff, described in the section on Project 3, set the stage unexpectedly for staff members' attention to classroom group processes by encouraging them to experiment with innovative group procedures in the school organization. Training activities carried out during the laboratory presented group forms, techniques, and procedures that could be used just as appropriately in the classroom as at staff meetings. The laboratory was a living example of McLuhan's dictum that "the medium is the message" (McLuhan, 1964). A majority of the teachers tried new group processes in their classrooms that were directly patterned after their organizational laboratory experiences.

In Project 2, regular discussions about classroom group processes with psychological consultants helped improve teachers' perceptions of themselves as teachers, their cognitions of mental health categories, and their views on how to work with problematic classroom situations. However, these cognitive and attitudinal changes were not accompanied by behavioral changes in the classroom. This is not surprising, since verbal learning is quite different from skill learning. People do not learn to play baseball, to dance, or to give speeches by reading books or through discussions. Nor should a teacher be expected to improve the complex skills of classroom instruction through mere discussion. Discussions on classroom group problems, students' psychodynamics, and different approaches to teaching can be expected to assist a teacher to think, talk, or write more intelligently about the issues, but actual behavioral tryouts and experiences are necessary before new skills are used easily in the classroom.

A teaching development laboratory which included problem-solving techniques, sensitivity training, and role-play tryouts did lead to behavioral changes in the classroom. The sensitivity training and related human relations activities seemed to challenge teachers' cognitions of interpersonal relations, to lead teachers to introspect on their effects on others, to encourage teachers to explore their values about teaching, and to develop colleague norms of support and helpfulness. The problem-solving procedures helped teachers think more systematically about new patterns of classroom behavior, and the role-play tryouts helped build psychological connections among new cognitions, attitudes, and behaviors.

Taken together, these interventions can fit well into integrated action programs that might be employed by school districts for improving classroom group processes. Two integrated programs of different durations can be mentioned here.

One would take place over an eighteen-month period. It would commence with an organization development laboratory during the latter part of August, just prior to the beginning of the school year. Following this, teachers would be asked to volunteer for a program of consultation and training in classroom group processes. A psychological consultant, skilled in interpersonal relations theory and classroom processes, would work with them two hours each week for the entire academic year. Then, during the following summer, a teacher development laboratory would take place. Follow-up discussions could be scheduled during the fall semester to help the teachers follow through on trying out new procedures and to reinforce continuously any insights or new skills developed during the previous year.

Another, shorter program, lasting for only about six months, would be launched with an organization development laboratory just two weeks before school begins. Since many school districts now grant some days prior to the schools' opening for in-service training, it might be possible to extend those days into a week and to spend that week in a teacher development laboratory. This two-week, back-to-back laboratory program would facilitate the translation of group processes found to be useful during the organizational laboratory into classroom innovations during the teacher development laboratory. Then, during the fall semester, follow-up discussions could be led by psychological consultants who would emphasize the problem-solving process and give support to teachers trying to implement their plans.

Many other action designs might be developed using these three basic inter-

ventions as the elements. We hope that behavioral scientists and educators will
collaborate in trying some of them.

_____

References

Bradford, L., Gibb, J., and Benne, K. 1964. *T-group theory and laboratory method.*
    New York: Wiley.

Chesler, M., and Fox, R. 1966. *Role-playing methods in the classroom.* Chicago: Science
    Research Associates.

Coch, L., and French, J. R. P., Jr. 1948. Overcoming resistance to change. *Human Relations,*
    1:512-32.

Edelmann, A., and Schmuck, R. 1967. *Pilot study in exploring the use of mental health
    consultants to teachers of socially maladjusted pupils in regular classes.* Un-
    published report. Philadelphia: Mental Health Association of Southeastern
    Pennsylvania.

Flanders, N., and Havumaki, S. 1960: The effect of teacher-pupil contacts involving praise
    on the sociometric choices of students. *Journal of Educational Psychology*
    51:65-68.

Fox, R., Luszki, Margaret, and Schmuck, R. 1966. *Diagnosing classroom learning environ-
    ments.* Chicago: Science Research Associates.

Hays, W. 1963. *Statistics for psychologists.* New York: Holt, Rinehart, and Winston.
    Pp. 598-601.

Hollister, W., and Bower, E., eds. 1967. *Behavioral science frontiers in education.* New
    York: Wiley.

Kaufman, M., Schmuck, R., and Lippitt, R. 1963. *Creative practices developed by teachers
    for improving classroom atmospheres.* Document No. 14, Inter-Center Program on
    Children, Youth, and Family Life. Ann Arbor, Michigan: Institute for Social
    Research.

Lippitt, R., Barakat, H., Chesler, M., Dennerell, D., Flanders, Mary, Worden, O., and
    Schmuck, R. 1967. The teacher as innovator, seeker and sharer of new practices.
    In R. Miller, ed., *Perspectives on educational change.* New York: Appleton-
    Century-Crofts. Pp. 307-324.

McLuhan, M. 1964. *Understanding media.* New York: McGraw-Hill.

Newman, Ruth. 1967. *Psychological consultation in the schools.* New York: Basic Books.

Schmuck, R. 1962. Sociometric status and utilization of academic abilities. *Merrill-Palmer
    Quarterly* 8:165-72.

____. 1963. Some relationships of peer liking patterns in the classroom to pupil attitudes
    and achievement. *School Review* 71:337-58.

____. 1966. Some aspects of classroom social climate. *Psychology in the Schools* 3:59-65.

____; Chesler, M., and Lippitt, R. 1966. *Problem solving to improve classroom learning.*
    Chicago: Science Research Associates.

____, and Runkel, P. 1970. *Organizational training for a school faculty.* Eugene, Oregon:
    University of Oregon, Center for the Advanced Study of Educational
    Administration.

____, and Van Egmond, E. 1965. Sex differences in the relationships of interpersonal
    perceptions to academic performance. *Psychology in the Schools* 2:32-40.

3

USING GROUP PROBLEM-SOLVING PROCEDURES*

Richard A. Schmuck, Philip Runkel, and Daniel Langmeyer

Projects 1 and 2 in Chapter 2 are examples of imaginative and effective efforts at training teachers in new classroom behaviors. Most in-service workshops— although not so successful as these—are similarly aimed at developing new behaviors in individuals instead of attempting to develop new organizational characteristics. The ensuing strategy often is to use this newly trained group as an entering wedge to bring about further change in a school.

In contrast, the intervention discussed in Chapter 3 was not piecemeal. The training events were designed not to have their primary effects on clusters of individuals, but on the actual intact faculty as a working group. Transfer to the school world was enhanced by having the entire staff at the training events. Even when training involved interpersonal exercises and group games which were not like patterns played out during the school day, staff members still behaved and acted in clear view of their colleagues. Their behavior was visible and open for discussion.

This total approach paid off. The results revealed that communication, norms, and problem-solving can be improved in a school through OD training with the entire staff. Indeed, the project exceeded its expectations; it produced more systematic data concerning favorable outcomes than had any previous project of organization development in schools. Effects of the training may even have reached the students, but the researchers did not collect data directly from classrooms.

Like many organizations with traditional modes of operation, schools are suffering stresses to which their customary practices seem ill-adapted. When faced with massive changes in the community, there are at least two strategies a school can adopt. One is for the school to remodel itself into a form maximally adapted to the new demands of the community, e.g., the middle school, the campus school, the unitized school, or the community school. The other strategy is to build new norms and procedures that enable the school constantly to monitor

* This chapter was adapted from Richard Schmuck, Philip Runkel and Daniel Langmeyer, 1969, "Improving organizational problem solving in a school faculty," *Journal of Applied Behavioral Science*, Vol. 5, No. 4. As such it received the 1969 Douglas McGregor Memorial Award. It has also been incorporated in a longer volume: Richard Schmuck and Philip Runkel, 1970, *Organizational training for a school faculty* (Eugene, Oregon: University of Oregon, Center for the Advanced Study of Educational Administration).

the changing community, to compare the results of its own reactions with what it would accept as movement toward its goals, and to establish new forms whenever the movement toward the goals falls below a given criterion. The latter strategy we call "flexible organizational problem-solving." John Gardner (1963) has called it *"self-renewal,"* and Walter Buckley (1967) has referred to it as "morphogenesis." The purpose of this project was to improve the capability of a school for group problem-solving.

From the point of view of research, our purpose was to test whether improved group problem-solving could be produced in a school faculty by training in interpersonal communication skills when the group processes to be altered and the methods of doing so were consistent with McGregor's thinking (1967). We assumed, along with McGregor, that functions within organizations are "carried" through interpersonal interactions and that the heightening of abilities for group problem-solving must commence with new norms for interpersonal openness and helpfulness. In seeking a lever with which to change group norms, we adopted McGregor's strategy (1967, pp.13-14):

... to provide opportunities for members of the organization to obtain intrinsic rewards from contributions to the success of the enterprise. ... The task is to provide an appropriate environment—one that will permit and encourage employees to seek intrinsic rewards *at work.*

We attempted to do this by inviting the faculty to state the frustrations they encountered in the school and to practice a sequence of problem-solving steps to reduce these frustrations. This activity led to reduced frustration and to the satisfaction of knowing that others valued the contribution one had made to outcomes highly desired by the faculty. It also facilitated changes in organizational norms by requiring staff members to behave in new ways in the actual work-group while others observed the new behavior and by allowing staff members to see that their colleagues actually accepted the new patterns of behavior in the school setting.

In designing this intervention, we made strong use of the laboratory method (Bradford, Gibb, and Benne, 1964). The training often called for conscious observation of the group processes of the faculty. The design required the actual practice of new behaviors before using them in daily work. Although the design made use of the school as its own laboratory, we made use of laboratory groups in ways very different from those associated with sensitivity training or the T-group. Personal development was not our target. We did not attempt to improve the interpersonal functioning of individuals directly; when this occurred, it was incidental. Our targets were the faculty as a whole and several subgroups within it. We sought to increase the effectiveness of groups as task-oriented entities. We tried to teach subgroups within the school and the faculty as a whole to function more effectively as working bodies carrying out specific tasks in that particular job setting. This strategy of training was supported by a recent review of research by Campbell and Dunnette (1968) on the transfer of skills from T-groups to organizations. They found that a T-group, as ordinarily conducted with focus on individual growth in a setting away from the job and without guided application to work-a-day tasks, has had little effect on organization development.

In comparison to other efforts at bringing about more effective organizational functioning in schools, our intervention contained a unique combination of three features. First, our training took place with actual groups from the school we sought to affect. Next, we carried on training with the entire staff of the school, including secretaries, the head cook, and the head custodian as well as all the faculty and administrators. Finally, during the training, especially in its early parts, we rotated sizes and memberships of subgroups so that every pair of staff members interacted with each other in more than one kind of group.

Training Goals

The major training goals were developed out of a conception of flexible organizational problem-solving. We hoped that the faculty of our experimental school would establish a continuing series of activities for improving its own communication; we held this to be a minimum necessity. Further, we hoped that participation at faculty meetings as well as the initiation of attempts at influence would spread to more and more members of the faculty. We strove to help the faculty to increase its discussions about interpersonal or inter-role problems and to continue making conscious use of a sequential problem-solving technique. We hoped that the teachers would show increased initiative in solving problems they were having with those in higher echelons and that the initiator of an idea would test his idea more frequently than previously with a lower-echelon subgroup before carrying it to the administration. For us the most significant goals had to do with structural and instructional changes in the school. We hoped that the staff would invent some new organizational forms within their school or at least borrow some from our training that would help them to confront problems continuously. Finally, we wanted the teachers to find some uses for the new forms and methods from the training that would have effects on their classroom instruction.

We supplemented these broad goals with more specific ones when designing the initial training events that centered on interpersonal skills and systematic problem-solving. We hoped first to build increased openness and ease of interpersonal communication among the faculty by training them in skills of paraphrasing, describing behavior, describing their own feelings, and checking perception. We hoped that through skillful and constructive openness with one another that the staff would develop an increased confidence that communication could have worthwhile outcomes. We hoped to increase skills in giving information to others about their behavior and in receiving information about their own behavior. After increasing communication skills, we hoped to stimulate skill development in using a systematic problem-solving procedure and in helping colleagues to enunciate ideas clearly that might develop into practical plans for solving organizational problems.

Interventions

We assumed that the faculty of our experimental school would be likely to attempt new interpersonal procedures if it could first practice them away from the immediate demands of the school day. At the same time, we assumed that transfer of the training to everyday work at school would be maximized if the faculty expected to continue problem-solving activities on their own after each training event and if the training design called for additional training some weeks and months following the first event. Within this general framework for transfer of organizational training, we made several other assumptions.

We felt that communication could be improved, that feelings of solidarity could be increased, and that power differences could be clarified if virtually every pair of persons on the faculty were brought into face-to-face interaction during the initial training period. Next, we thought that the initial input during training should pose a discrepancy between the ideal and actual performances of the faculty. Out of confrontations with discrepancies would come problem-solving. We felt that applications to the work of the school building would be maximized if the faculty dealt with real organizational problems even during the first week of training. Furthermore, we thought that training in a series of overlapping small groups would help individuals to use the skills learned in one group in each of the next training groups, and subsequently to transfer the accumulated skills to groups in which they worked ordinarily. Finally we assumed that the transfer of the communication and problem-solving skills to the school would be facilitated if the faculty members conceptualized the possible applications of the skills and made plans to try them out in the real school setting.

The training commenced with a six-day laboratory in late Auguest of 1967. Staff members present included almost the entire building staff other than students. There were fifty-four trainees: all of the administrators, all but two of the faculty, and the head cook, head custodian, and head secretary. The first two days were spent in group exercises designed to increase awareness of interpersonal and organizational processes; e.g., the NASA Trip-to-the-Moon exercise, the five-square puzzle, and the hollow-square puzzle. Although these exercises were game-like, they demonstrated the importance of clear and effective communication for accomplishing a task collaboratively. After each exercise, small groups discussed ways in which the experience was similar to or different from what usually happened in their relations with one another in the school. All staff members then came together to pool their experiences and to analyze their relationships as a faculty. Each small group chose its own way to report what it had experienced. Openness and the giving and receiving of feedback about perceptions of real organizational processes in the school were supported by the trainers. Brief but specific training was given in clear communication, overcoming difficulties in listening, and skills in describing another's behavior. A couple of nonverbal exercises augmented this practice.

The faculty devoted the last four days to a problem-solving sequence, working on real issues that were thwarting the organizational functioning of the school. After a morning of discussion and decisions, which also served as practice in the skills of decision-making, three problems emerged as the most significant:

1. Insufficient role clarity, especially in the roles of principal, vice-principal, counselors, and area (departmental) coordinators.

2. Failure to draw upon staff resources, especially between academic areas but also within subject matter specialities.

3. Low staff involvement and low participation at meetings of committees, areas, and the full faculty.

Three groups were formed, each to work through a problem-solving sequence directed toward one of these problems. Each group followed a procedure having five steps: (1) identifying the problem through behavioral description, (2) diagnostic force-field analysis, (3) brainstorming to find actions likely to reduce restraining forces, (4) designing a concrete plan of action, and (5) trying out the plan behaviorally through a simulated activity involving the entire staff.

Each of the three groups carried through its sequence of steps substantially on its own. The trainers served as facilitators, rarely provided substantive suggestions, and never pressed for results. The group concerned with clarifying roles reasoned that an ambiguous role often served as a defense and that a first step must be to increase trust among the faculty. Accordingly, they carried out four nonverbal exercises to increase trust among the faculty. The group on using staff resources set up eight subgroups, each of which was to pretend to be a junior high faculty meeting a crisis due to lack of texts; each group then developed curricula drawing upon the others' resources. The group on low staff involvement arranged for three groups to have discussions on role clarification, staff resources, and staff involvement. During the discussions, the more loquacious members were asked one after another to stop participating, until there were only two members left. Discussions were then held in each group on feelings toward involvement at meetings of the staff.

The first week of the training culminated with a discussion to clarify the resources of the staff. Staff members described their own strengths and those of their colleagues. Finally they discussed what their school could be like if all the strengths of the faculty were used.

During the early fall, we interviewed all faculty members and observed a number of committees and subject-area groups in order to determine what uses they were making of the first week of training. The data indicated that problems still unresolved were communicative misunderstandings, role overload, and capabilities for group problem-solving.

The second intervention for training with the entire staff was held for one and a half days in December. In this session we attempted to increase the effectiveness of the area coordinators as communication links between teachers and administrators, to increase the problem-solving skills of the area groups and the principal's advisory committee, to help the faculty explore ways of reducing role overload, and to increase effective communication between service personnel and the rest of the staff. Training activities included communication exercises, problem-solving techniques, decision-making procedures, and skill development in group observation and feedback. On the first day, area (departmental) groups applied problem-solving techniques to their own communication difficulties and received feedback on their methods of work from observing area groups. Problems raised in area groups were brought the next day to a meeting of the Principal's Advisory Committee held before the rest of the staff. The staff observed the Advisory Committee, participated in specially designed ways, and later gave feedback on how effectively the committee had worked and how accurately members had represented them.

The third training intervention also lasted one and a half days and took place in February. The main objective was to take stock of how the staff had progressed since the workshop in solving the problems of using resources, of role clarity, and of staff participation, and to revivify any lagging skills. A group discussion of each problem-area was held. Each teacher was left free to work in the group considering the problem that most interested him. Each group discussed the positive and negative outcomes associated with its problem. For example, in the group discussing staff participation, the question was: "In what ways has staff participation improved and where has it failed to improve?" The group wrote out examples of improvement, lack of change, and regression in staff participation. The groups then focused on the negative instances and tried to think of ways to eliminate them by modifying organizational processes in the school. Faculty members continued with this activity in small groups during the spring without our presence.

Organizational Changes

One source of evidence for the effects of the training came in the form of concrete, observable changes in the behavior of faculty and administration in our experimental school. These data were taken primarily from spontaneous events that were later reported to us and corroborated by the parties involved or by disinterested observers. These actions were not directly a part of our planned training events and therefore constituted movements in the direction of increased flexible organizational problem-solving.

About three months after the first week of training, a sample of the faculty was interviewed and also asked to write essays on the effects of the training. From these data, we discovered that at least nineteen teachers were applying techniques learned in the organizational training sessions to improve the group processes in their classrooms. Application typically involved such group procedures as "using small groups for projects," "using nonverbal exercises to depict feelings about the subject matter being studied," "using theatre-in-the-round or fishbowl formations for having students observe one another," "using a paraphrasing exercise to point out how poor classroom communications are," "using the problem-solving sequence and techniques in social studies classes to learn more about social problems," and "using small groups for giving and receiving feedback about how the class is going." As far as we know, none of these practices was used by these teachers before the training.

Previous to our intervention, a group of eight teachers, called the Teach Group, was granted freedom to alter schedules, classroom groupings, assignment of teachers to classes, and other logistics decisions in an attempt to maximize their educational impact on a selected group of students. The Teach Group, made up mostly of area coordinators, received many negative reactions from other staff members. They were envied and misunderstood, and were often engaged in conflict with others. Their innovative ideas were more often resisted than emulated. However, the organizational training program seemed to ameliorate the distrust, and the end of the year saw the Teach Group's type of collaboration extended to twice as many teachers. At the same time, two other teachers decided to form a team of two to gain some of the advantages of mutual stimulation and the sharing of resources.

The Principal's Advisory Committee, made up of administrators and area coordinators, become a more powerful force in the school. It ceased to be merely advisory and became a representative senate with decision-making prerogatives. During the training event in December, this group delineated and accepted their roles as representatives of their areas and as gatherers of information for the upper-echelon administrators. Later, an actual occurrence lent credence to the power of the advisory committee. Members of the mathematics area decided that they were under-represented on the committee because their area coordinator held responsibilities in the district as a curriculum consultant. They petitioned the principal through the advisory committee for a new area coordinator and one was chosen. The primary criterion for selecting the person to fill the position seemed to be his recent improvements in interpersonal and group skills. Later in the school year, the advisory committee requested two other training events to help them clarify their role in the decision-making structure of the school.

A number of other events indicated that the quality of relationships on the staff improved because of the intervention. For instance, only two teachers initiated resignations from the staff at the end of the school year, giving the school a turnover rate of only 3 percent. Comparative rates in other junior high schools in the same district ranged from 10 to 16 percent. Several times during the year, faculty meetings were initiated by faculty members other than the principal. Such initiations ran counter to tradition, but nevertheless those meetings went very smoothly, with strong participation from many.

During the spring of 1968, faculty members initiated a meeting to discuss the possibility of having another group-process laboratory before the next school year. Faculty members first discussed the idea in area groups and later asked to meet as a total staff to present recommendations to the advisory committee. The laboratory or workshop was to have two goals: (1) to introduce new faculty members into this group-oriented staff and (2) to give teachers new skills to use with their classroom groups. The workshop actually took place, without our active participation, in August 1968.

The principal's interpersonal relationships with staff members were noticeably improved, and he became very excited about improving even more his own leadership skills. He requested funds to attend an Educator's Laboratory sponsored by National Training Laboratories: Institute for Applied Behavioral Science and was granted them. Later he served as an assistant trainer in a laboratory and performed with great effectiveness. During the summer of 1968, six members of the faculty planned to go to a laboratory in group processes and eventually did go at their own expense.

Perhaps the most dramatic changes after the intervention occurred in the school district. First, a new job was created at our experimental school: vice-principal for curriculum, to act as consultant on interpersonal relationships to task groups within the staff. The role also called for providing liaison between groups, providing logistic support for curricular efforts, transmitting to upper echelons in the district the proposals for curricular development originating at the school, and serving as a liaison with other junior high schools in the district concerning innovations in curriculum. This new vice-principal was asked by the Superintendent of Schools to maintain a log of his activities and to develop a job description for possible use in other schools. This was done, and the school board granted funds for this position in several other junior highs. The first vice-principal for curriculum has been asked to aid the other new vice-principals in learning the new role. Other schools in the district have requested funds for organization development training in their schools and the introduction of the facilitator role as a vice-principalship.

Comparisons with Other Schools

The previous section contains descriptions of directly observable outcomes reflecting commitments to action within the school. This section reports comparisons of data taken from questionnaires administered early and late during the 1967-68 school year at the experimental school with data from six junior high schools in the New York City area and four junior high schools near the Seattle area. None of the New York or Seattle schools was engaged in our kind of organizational training. In their demographic characteristics, too, they met some of the requirements for a control group.

The data for comparing our school with the New York schools came from two questionnaires: one dealing with the faculty's feelings about the principal's behavior and the other dealing with the faculty's feelings about staff meetings. The data for comparing the experimental school with the Seattle schools came from questions concerning innovations adopted, readiness to communicate about interpersonal relations, and readiness to use and share the resources of other staff members.

The Principal

The questionnaire used to measure the faculty's feelings about the principal contained twenty-four items; all twenty-four items were originally developed by Gross and Herriott to measure the "Executive Professional Leadership" (EPL) of elementary school principals.

The facet of educational leadership studied by EPL deals with the principal's efforts to improve the quality of performance of his staff. Gross and Herriott (1965) found EPL to be related to the morale of the staff, the professional performance of teachers, and learning accomplished by students. Hilfiker (1969) used the same instrument and found that both EPL scores and social support scores were related to school systems' innovativeness. Because of these findings we felt that the items in this questionnaire were reasonable indicators of the direction which the interaction of faculty and principal would take if our training of the faculty approached its goals.

EPL was measured by asking teachers to what extend their principal engaged in activities such as the following:

Makes teachers' meetings a valuable educational activity.
Treats teachers as professional workers.
Has constructive suggestions to offer teachers in dealing with their problems.

A principal's managerial support was measured by responses about items such as the following:

Makes a teacher's life difficult because of his administrative ineptitude.
Runs conferences and meetings in a disorganized fashion.
Has the relevant facts before making important decisions.

A principal's social support was measured by responses to items such as the following:

Rubs people the wrong way.
Makes those who work with him feel inferior to him.
Displays integrity in his behavior.

To compare the teachers' responses to this questionnaire at the experimental school with the responses at the six junior high schools near New York City, we performed a series of chi-square analyses. For every item and every school, we let the pretest results be the estimate of expected proportions against which to test the proportions obtained at the post-test—the proportions, that is, of teachers responding in one of six proffered categories in the EPL questionnaire. A summary of the analyses appears in Table 3-1, where the schools near New York are labelled A through F.

Table 3-1 Numbers of Items Showing Significant Changes (p < .10) Among Those in the Questionnaire on the Principal

		Schools					
	Experimental	A	B	C	D	E	F
Positive change	18	1	2	0	0	5	9
No significant change	6	19	17	12	13	19	11
Negative change	0	4	5	12	11	0	4

The results leave little doubt that the faculty of the experimental school changed its perceptions of the principal much more than did any of the other school staffs. At the experimental school, the teachers changed significantly (p < .10) on eighteen of the twenty-four items; more importantly, every one of these eighteen changes was in the positive and supportive direction. By contrast, in no other school except School F did the teachers change on more than half of the items. Furthermore, in Schools A, B, C, and D more of the changes were in a negative direction, indicating that the principal was being viewed less in accord with the EPL ideal at the end of the school year than in the previous fall. The staffs of schools E and F changed more positively than negatively, but on far fewer items than at the experimental school.

Specifically, the teachers at our school were reporting that their principal was easier to get along with, made better decisions, helped them more in their own problem-solving, improved faculty meetings and conferences, and treated them more as professionals after our training had been completed than before. Staffs at junior high schools in the New York City area not undergoing organizational training did not report similar changes in their principals' behavior.

Staff Meetings

We were concerned about staff and committee meetings because they are important formal arenas in which communication and group problem-solving can occur. Our early conversations with the staff at our experimental school revealed that low participation at staff meetings was viewed as an acute problem. We hoped that improvements in the conduct of meetings would occur as a result of the organizational training. To measure such change, we used a questionnaire to measure educators' responses to the meetings in their schools developed by the COPED instrument committee and reworded in minor ways by us. The questionnaire contains thirty-seven items and has yielded excellent reliability. The total score and subscale scores from this instrument have been found to be related to a school district's innovativeness (Hilfiker, 1969).

The thirty-seven items describe specific behaviors; teachers are asked to rate each in one of six categories of frequency of occurrence at staff meetings. The following are sample items from the instrument:

When a problem comes up in a meeting, it is thoroughly explored until everyone understands what the problem is.
People come to the meeting not knowing what is to be presented or discussed.
People bring up extraneous or irrelevant matters.
Either before the meeting or at its beginning, any group member can easily get items on to the agenda.
People don't seem to care about the meeting or want to get involved in it.
People give their real feelings about what is happening during the meeting itself.
When a decision is made, it is clear who should carry it out and when.

In a manner identical to the questionnaire dealing with the principal, pretest responses for each item and from each school were used as expected frequencies for evaluating shifts in post-test data. Data about staff meetings were available from only three of the six comparison schools: A, C, and D. Table 3-2 summarizes the chi-square analyses applied to these data. Like the results on the

Table 3-2 Numbers of Items Showing Significant Changes ($p < .10$) Among Those in the Questionnaire on Staff Meetings

| | | Schools | | |
	Experimental	A	C	D
Positive change	21	3	2	6
No significant change	14	30	32	23
Negative change	2	4	3	8

changed perceptions of the principal, the results on staff meetings also show major differences between the changes at the experimental school and the changes at the comparison schools. Among the thirty-seven items, our school showed significant positive change in twenty-one, school A in three, school C in two, and school D in six. Changes at our school were almost entirely in the positive direction; among twenty-three significant changes ($p < .10$) only two were negative. In contrast, changes in the comparison schools were almost evenly balanced between positive and negative. The nature of the items on the questionnaire permitted us to conclude that members of the experimental school reported that they could now be more open, had improved the conduct of their meetings, dealt with problems more completely, had more commitment to the meetings and solutions emerging from meetings, and felt that meetings were more worthwhile after completing our organizational training.

Innovations

The experimental school and four junior high schools from two cities near Seattle were administered an instrument as part of a larger project. One of the questions in the instrument was:

How about recent changes that could have useful effects on your school? Have there been any innovations, any new ways of doing things, that began during the last year or two that you think could have helpful effects in the school? If so, please describe each very briefly below. If none, write "none."

Teachers' responses to this item were coded into fourteen categories according to the nature of the innovations they mentioned. For this report, however, we have gathered these categories into the four types shown in Table 3-3. "Packaged" innovations include curricular changes, the establishment of new jobs or duties, the acquisition of equipment, and the adoption of methods of evaluating programs. We described these as "packaged" because some tangible set of materials or instructions usually went along with the innovation such as teaching materials, specifications for a new job, TV equipment, or instructions for a bookkeeping method. Moreover, innovations under this heading can usually be put into effect by training *individuals*; it is not often necessary to establish delicate new role relations or new modes of group problem-solving for such innovations to be successful. Packaged innovations were mentioned more frequently in three of the schools near Seattle (labelled W through Z in Table 3-3) than in the experimental school.

Table 3-3   Numbers of Teachers Mentioning Four Types of Innovations

| | Schools | | | | | |
Type of Innovation Mentioned	Experimental Dec. '67 N = 46	W* N = 30	X* N = 30	Y* N = 34	Z* N = 44	Experimental May '68 N = 39
"Packaged" innovations: curriculum, new jobs, equipment, program evaluation	18	25	11	36	22	15
Innovations that are instrumental in achieving new forms of organization	9	0	3	1	1	16
New methods of problem-solving or new organizational structure	21	1	1	0	1	17
Nonspecific improvements and vague answers	6	0	0	0	0	6

*Note: Schools W, X, Y, and Z answered the questionnaires in January 1968.

Another cluster of innovations contained those instrumental in achieving new forms of organization and new methods of solving organizational problems. In this group we included relations between teachers and students, the sharing of power among the faculty, and changes in frequency or content of communication, as well as new training of any kind and new attitudes (without mention of accompanying organizational rearrangement). Although the total number of responses in these categories was generally low by comparison with the set of "packaged" innovations, mentions in the experimental school were more frequent than mentions in any of the other four junior high schools.

Innovations of primary importance to our training goals were (1) new methods of solving problems or making decisions and (2) new organizational structures such as committees, channels, and conference groups. Table 3-3 shows that teachers at the experimental school reported many more innovations in this area than the other junior high schools.

Norms About Interpersonal Communication

We asked the faculty at the experimental school and the faculties at the four junior high schools near Seattle to answer a set of seven questions about their readiness to talk about feelings. Three of the seven questions were:

Suppose a teacher (let's call him or her Teacher X) disagrees with something B says at a staff meeting. If teachers you know in your school were in Teacher X's place, what would most of them be likely to do? Would most of the teachers you know here seek out B to discuss the disagreement?

(　) Yes, I think most would do this.
(　) Maybe about half would do this.
(　) No; most would *not*.
(　) I don't know.

Suppose you are in a committee meeting with Teacher X and the other members begin to describe their personal feelings about what goes on in the school; Teacher X quickly suggests that the committee get back to the topic and keep the discussion objective and impersonal. How would you feel toward X?

(　) I would approve strongly.
(　) I would approve mildly or some.
(　) I wouldn't care one way or the other.
(　) I would disapprove mildly or some.
(　) I would disapprove strongly.

Suppose Teacher X feels hurt and "put down" by something another teacher has said to him. In Teacher X's place, would most of the teachers you know in your school be likely to avoid the other teacher?

(　) Yes, I think most would.
(　) Maybe about half would.
(　) No; most would *not*.
(　) I don't know.

Taking those respondents who did not skip the question or answer "I don't know," we analyzed the responses to these seven items. We found that the faculty at the experimental school contained more teachers who would (1) seek out another person with whom they had a disagreement, (2) tell another teacher when they had been hurt by the other teacher, (3) be less approving of a teacher who tried to cut off talking about feelings in a committee meeting, and (4) be more approving of a teacher who shared his own feelings at a faculty meeting than the faculties of the four schools near Seattle. There was no significant difference between the teachers at the experimental school and other teachers in their estimation of the proportion of teachers who would (5) keep a disagreement to themselves. (Most respondents in all schools felt that most teachers would do so.)

On the other hand, many more teachers in the schools near Seattle than in our school claimed that their fellow teachers (6) would *not* avoid another teacher and (7) would *not* tell their friends the other teacher was hard to get along with if the other teacher had hurt them or "put them down."

On balance, we believe these results indicate that after our intervention the faculty at the experimental school were more open than the faculties near Seattle in their interpersonal communications and were more willing to talk about their feelings.

Norms About Sharing Ideas and Helping Others

Along with items reflecting norms about interpersonal communication, twelve items in the questionnaire concerned a faculty's readiness to ask for help from other staff members and give help to them. Here are three examples:

Suppose Teacher X develops a particularly useful and effective method for teaching something. In Teacher X's place, would most of the teachers you know in your school describe it briefly at a faculty meeting and offer to meet with others who wanted to hear more about it?

( ) Yes I think most would do this.
( ) Maybe about half would do this.
( ) No; most would *not*.
( ) I don't know.

Suppose Teacher X develops a particularly useful and effective method for teaching something. If X were to describe the method briefly at a faculty meeting and offer to meet further with any who wanted to know more, how would you feel about it?

( ) I would approve strongly.
( ) I would approve mildly or some.
( ) I wouldn't care one way or the other.
( ) I would disapprove mildly or some.
( ) I would disapprove strongly.

Suppose Teacher X wants to improve his classroom effectiveness. If X asked another teacher to observe his teaching and then have a conference about it afterward, how would you feel toward X?

( ) I would approve strongly.
( ) I would approve mildly or some.
( ) I wouldn't care one way or the other.
( ) I would disapprove mildly or some.
( ) I would disapprove strongly.

The faculty at the experimental school reported that they would (1) expect other teachers to report useful and effective teaching methods at faculty meetings, (2) seek administrative support to disseminate these methods, and (3) approve teachers who engaged in such activities—all to a significantly greater degree than the faculties of the schools near Seattle. Several items concerned a teacher's attempts to improve his classroom effectiveness. The faculty at our school reported that (4, 5) teachers would ask others, including the principal, to observe their teaching and have a conference afterward, (6) would ask to observe a colleague's teaching to get new ideas, and (7, 8) would approve a teacher who did these things in significantly greater numbers than the faculties of the other schools. The remaining four items showed no significant differences. These results indicate that teachers at the experimental school were willing to share new ideas to a greater extent than in those schools where no organizational training had taken place. Furthermore, teachers at the experimental school were willing to take greater risks to improve their teaching effectiveness.

Lessons for Consultants

In this section, we will discuss what the consultant can learn from this project that will help him in designing interventions to improve the organizational functioning of school faculties.

Special Nature of This Intervention

The training events in our intervention were aimed at improving the organizational problem-solving of a school faculty. The feature that most sharply sets this intervention óff from other laboratory training events is that natural workgroups, not individuals, were trained to be more effective. The intervention attempted to influence ways in which the entire faculty or its subgroups carried out their job-related tasks in the context of the school. This was, in other words, a training intervention pointed toward organizational development, not personal development. At the same time, it is an inescapable truism that role occupants and trainees are people. It is only an abstraction, a way social scientists conceptualize things, to say that roles are different from the people in a particular organization. People sometimes invest so much of themselves in a role (and this is perhaps particularly true of educators) that strong emotional reactions enter into organizational change of any kind. But although the emotional reactions of people must always be considered in designing even *organization* development programs, our target remained fixed on roles and norms and their relationships. Organizational training as we conceive it aims at rearranging, strengthening, or in some way refurbishing the relationships among people in various positions in the school.

The Research Evaluation

From the point of view of research, we hoped to learn whether improved organizational problem-solving could be produced by carefully integrating training in communication and problem-solving skills within the context of the living school, beginning the training just prior to the opening of school and continuing intermittently for some months. We have interpreted the data to support the claim that a number of desirable outcomes were at least partly due to our intervention. Many teachers began using a greater variety of more effective group techniques in their classrooms. Collaborating subgroups of teachers increased in both strength and number. The Principal's Advisory Committee became more potent and more specifically representative. Faculty turnover decreased well below the rates at the other junior high schools in the district. Additional training in organization development during the summer following our intervention was initiated by the faculty, and a number of staff members, including the principal, sought training in communicative skills and group dynamics. The district established a new variety of vice-principal modeled after a role fashioned at the school following our intervention; the definition of the role included skills in group development and problem-solving.

These definite changes in organzational practice and structure were accompanied by changes in verbally expressed attitudes about the principal and staff meetings, changes in the nature of innovations which were reported within the school, and changes in the norms concerning interpersonal openness, sharing of influence, and use of staff resources. Furthermore, these changes were found in the school where we conducted our organizational training but not in other junior high schools.

Strengths of the Summer Workshop: Macro-Aspects

These outcomes indicate that improvements occurred in the school, and we believe that the summer workshop was crucial in heading the project in a productive direction. Aspects of the design for a training activity like this one can be divided into macro- and micro-aspects. Macro-aspects are the design's overall structure and outline, its sequence of parts, and the general forms through which the individual activities flow. Micro-aspects refer to the specific activities played out during any limited period. We feel confident in offering the following features as the most successful macro-aspects of the summer workshop.

Inclusion of All Members of the Faculty. Almost the entire staff was included in the training right from the beginning. This meant that everyone learned about the goals of this training at the same time, that all were in the same circumstances vis-a-vis coping with the training activities, and that it was easy to transfer what was learned during the week to the school situation because staff members could remind one another of what had happened at the workshop. The importance of having everyone attend was underscored later when the two members of the staff who could not attend created significant barriers to the staff's further development.

Even a few days' difference can create distance and set up barriers between the trained and untrained. Perhaps the main reason is that one can feel a threat when others (especially those in roles comparable to one's own or removed by only one hierarchical level) develop skills or procedures that they might "use on you."

The faculty of a not-too-large elementary school or junior high school has no more than three levels of hierarchy: administrators, teachers, and non-professional personnel. For many purposes, there are only two layers: the administrators, and the teachers and non-professional personnel. Such an organization is closer to a primary group than to a bureaucracy. In a primary group, where people relate to one another with more emotionality and in-dividuality than in a more formal bureaucracy, there is no reasonable or legitimate way in which some can be chosen for special training while others are left out.

Structured Skill Activities. The macro-design called for a sequence of training events that started with games and structured skill activities and moved to first steps in solving real organizational problems. This sequence appears to have worked well in two ways. First, we think that faculty members who attend a training event as a duty rather than voluntarily find their ways into new interpersonal modes more easily through structured skill exercises than through less structured experiences demanding more personal commitment (such as the traditional T-group). The skill exercises were chosen because each one, in microcosm, demonstrated organizational issues reminiscent of role relationships in the school. An unstructured T-group probably would have led into considerations of particular interpersonal relationships within the staff; these, we believe, would have set the stage for personal development orientation and consequently would have led away from a focus on organizational problems. Second, the results of the exercise led rather naturally into "back home" problem-solving and seemed to set the stage for increasing role clarity, using staff resources further, and increasing staff participation at meetings. Unstructured activities probably would have led into work on relationships between certain persons and led away from our goals of working at the organizational level.

Rotation of Subgroup Membership. The macro-design called for staff members to rotate through groups of different size and composition during the first few days. This was done to increase the potential network of workable relationships on the staff and to decrease the possibility of an in-group, out-group pattern emerging. Another goal of such rotation was to increase staff members' identification with the staff as a whole so as to provide the motivation necessary to carry the project through the year. Rotating subgroup memberships appears to have increased the cohesiveness of the faculty.

Equal Treatment of All Ranks. The design was consciously contrived to reduce status differences on the staff. No member of the staff was singled out for special treatment. Rotating the staff through various groups brought teachers and administrators together as well as nonprofessional personnel, teachers, and administrators. The exercise emphasized that individuals should carry out tasks within groups and that one should attempt to do his best on a given task regardless of who happened to be in his group. Such an assumption brought staff members closer together—a prerequisite to achieving more openness and clearer communication.

Exemplification of New Organizational Forms in the Training. Group processes, new group forms, and procedures for problem-solving were introduced into the design with the assumption that the use of such procedures by staff members would lead to new organizational structures. New structures were expected to arise out of problem-solving and we believe that the macro-aspects of the design encouraged that to happen.

Strengths of the Summer Workshop: Micro-Aspects

Several micro-aspects of the design for the summer workshop warrant special attention because of their positive effects on the faculty.

The Fishbowl. The fishbowl arrangement, in which a group on the outside of a concentric circle observes a group working inside, became especially useful to this faculty. The arrangement used most often called for two or three empty chairs left in the inside area. Members of the outside group were invited to enter the inside when they chose to communicate something to the insiders. During the summer workshop, this pattern was used in the problem-solving phase late in the week. Later, in a follow-up session when the Principal's Advisory Committee met before the rest of the staff, the same group formation was used. We learned that the faculty spontaneously employed such a formation several times during the school year to increase communication flow and participation between groups.

Two-Way Communication. In several activities during the training we emphasized the importance of two-way communication. The impact on the faculty was great indeed, for it especially affected the shape of the area coordinator's role. Area coordinators were encouraged by their colleagues to serve as communication links between the Principal's Advisory Committee and the area groups. This was an instance when learning about new processes motivated structural change. The new structure was similar to the *link-pin* organizational structure described by Likert (1961). Likert's link-pin structure uses small face-to-face groups as multiple-path communication channels in themselves; work units are organized across hierarchical levels and members participate in group decisions at levels both above and below their own. In our school, the area coordinators were to represent their area colleagues on the Principal's Advisory Committee and to communicate actions of that advisory committee back to the members of their area.

Systematic Problem-Solving. Working through the problem-solving process step by step was another important micro-element. We returned to this problem-solving sequence many times. It became a convenient mnemonic device for staff members. They could easily keep the stages in mind and, in fact, made use of several of them spontaneously during the school year.

Strengths of Training During the School Year

Next, we wish to describe the things we believe went especially well during the remainder of the period of intervention. Five training activities stand out as crucial aspects of the training during the school year. One was the fishbowl technique which we have already mentioned. The other forms were as follows:

Interviews After Summer Training. The interviews brought our training staff psychologically closer to the faculty and gave us a number of key ideas for designing training events during the school year. We interviewed staff members during the hour set aside for them to prepare for their teaching. We interviewed some in groups and others individually. Where we seemed to get contradictory comments, we tried to probe for clarity or to go back to a person who had been previously interviewed to ask a few more questions. We tried to keep the interview process open to easy surveillance. All staff members knew that we were at the school on the day of the interviews, the interviews were held in accessible spots in the school such as the teachers' lounge, and staff members were invited to sit in or near while others were being interviewed.

Problem-Solving in Area Groups. During the first follow-up training session, we set up meetings of the area groups and asked them to carry out the problem-solving procedure. This simulation of a real meeting was a significant force in transferring learnings about problem-solving to new group procedures in the area groups during the school year.

Review of Progress Before the Departure of Trainers. A significant contribution to the total design occurred during the February follow-up session when the staff reviewed the extent of its progress toward solving its basic problems of role obscurity, low use of resources, and lack of participation at meetings. The session had three helpful effects: (a) it encouraged continuing discussion and collaborative problem-solving that had just begun to emerge; (b) it helped faculty members to recognize that they already had accomplished many positive things; and (c) it helped set the stage for a graceful departure of the training staff without also indicating that the project was over.

Final Unstructured Session. A significant event in the total design was the unstructured session, in the manner of a T-group, held for a complete day with the Principal's Advisory Committee. Members of the committee originated the session. Involvement on the part of most was very high and the results led to a strengthening of the group.

Weaknesses of the Summer Workshop

Certain features of our design were noticeably weak. We mention below some features we think could be bettered in another application.

Lack of Action Steps. First, we believe we should have encouraged the faculty at the end of the summer workshop to commit themselves to more specific and concrete action steps to be used in specific problem-solving processes at school. In essence, the problem-solving was learned as a process and used rather well later in the year, but more gains in terms of concrete action could have come from the problem-solving if the faculty had been enabled to use action steps started at the workshop as a springboard.

Dealing with Absent Persons. All but two staff members attended the summer workshop and they never were brought into the training psychologically. One attempt was made to bring one of the uninvolved people in by conducting a discussion about the workshop with that person together with three of her closest associates. There events of the workshop were interpreted to the person. Feelings at the meeting appeared to be supportive and positive. However, little improvement seemed to occur after that meeting. In retrospect, we feel that a session should have been designed in which the problem of informing those who were not present was dealt with openly and skillfully.

Information-Gathering Techniques. The problem-solving sequence lacked attention to concrete techniques for diagnosing organizational processes. The training could have included some diagnostic tools in the form of self-report questionnaires, brief but systematic interview schedules, and categories for observation that staff members could have used during the year to diagnose their own organization.

Weaknesses of Training During the School Year

Three things may have had adverse effects during the school year.

Demands on Personal Energy. Many teachers came to the training sessions after a difficult week of teaching. The training events constituted additional burdens for them. We are now considering ways of arranging training episodes within the context of the school day and are having some success with meetings held during free periods and at times when substitute teachers can be used. We are also making use of vacation time and the weeks just before and after the school year.

Changing Trainers. Only two members of our training staff remained throughout the project. At times, the faculty was not sure who were on our staff and who were not. Some of our own confusion probably resulted in faculty confusion.

Clarity of Expectations Among Trainers. Along with our own staffing difficulties, it should also be pointed out that our training plans often were not extensive and at points not sharply enough defined. This led to uneven performances, especially in subgroups within the faculty, when different trainers were involved. We tried to correct this by rotating trainers continually.

In conclusion, this project was salutary for a school faculty and contains valuable lessons for consultants or change agents. For us, it serves too as a preface to a series of forthcoming interventions in schools with different structures.

References

Bradford, L. P.; Gibb, J. R.; and Benne, K. D. 1964. *T-group theory and laboratory method.* New York: Wiley.

Buckley, W. *Sociology and modern systems theory.* 1967. Englewood Cliffs, New Jersey: Prentice-Hall.

Campbell, J. P., and Dunnette, M. D. 1968. Effectiveness of T-group experiences in managerial training and development. *Psychological Bulletin* 70:73-104.

Gardner, J. 1963. *Self-renewal: the individual and the innovative society.* New York: Harper and Row.

Gross, N. and Herriott, R. 1965. *Staff leadership in public schools.* New York: Wiley.

Hilfiker, L. R. 1969. *The relationship of school system innovativeness to selected dimensions of interpersonal behavior in eight school systems.* Technical Report No. 70. Madison, Wisconsin: Research and Development Center for Cognitive Learning.

Likert, R. *New patterns of management.* 1961. New York: McGraw-Hill.

McGregor, D. *The professional manager.* 1967. New York: McGraw-Hill.

Schmuck, R. A., and Runkel. 1970. *Organizational training for a school faculty.* Eugene, Oregon: University of Oregon, Center for the Advanced Study of Educational Administration.

Watson, G., ed. 1967. *Change in school systems.* Washington: National Training Laboratories, NEA.

4

CHANGING CLASSROOM INTERACTION THROUGH ORGANIZATION DEVELOPMENT*

Ronald C. Bigelow

As a consequence of the intervention described in Chapter 3, nineteen teachers reported that they were applying techniques learned in OD training to improve the group processes in their classrooms. Applications typically involved such procedures as using small groups for projects, using nonverbal exercises to depict feelings about the subject matter being studied, using a paraphrasing exercise to rectify poor classroom communications, and using small groups for giving and receiving feedback about how the class was going.

Unfortunately, the data of Chapter 3 were based on reports made by the teachers to the researchers and were open to considerable bias. Moreover, even if the teachers did try these unique practices there is no assurance that the students were affected.

The results of the project described in Chapter 4 are much more decisive. The data confirm the hypothesis that arose during the previous project: namely, effects of the training spill over into the relations between teachers and students in the classroom even when the training is not purposely designed to do so. Results indicate that after OD training teachers change their classroom behavior in expected ways and that the students develop more positive attitudes toward their peers. This last finding should not be minimized in importance. Previous research (Schmuck, 1963) indicated that positive relationships with classroom peers can enhance self-esteem and academic achievement.

As research on organization development in industry has progressed, much energy has been expended on attempting to determine the effects of training on subparts of the target organizations. Reviews of research on OD indicate that while training in industrial organizations may be useful for the individuals involved, utility for the individual may not be the same as utility for the subparts of the organization or the organization itself. Research on training in organization development for public schools has had more rewarding outcomes.

In Chapter 3, Schmuck, Runkel, and Langmeyer reported significant changes in the functioning of a junior high school as a consequence of OD training. These changes were in teachers' attitudes concerning the principal, staff meetings,

* This chapter was adapted from Ronald C. Bigelow, 1969, *The Effect of Organizational Development on Classroom Climate* (Eugene, Oregon: University of Oregon, Center for the Advanced Study of Educational Administration).

sharing ideas, helping others, and the redistribution of decision-making power. Several teachers reported transferring verbal skills and small-group techniques to their classrooms, which led to speculation on my part that the transfer of such techniques could have positive effects on classroom climate, thereby improving the students' academic achievement. Two phases of research were executed to answer two questions: (1) Do teachers transfer skills learned in organization development to their classrooms? and (2) If so, what effects do new teacher behaviors have on classroom climate?

Classroom Climate

Classroom climate is defined as the students' generalized attitudes toward their teacher and peers. Such attitudes are developed through a student's interaction with others in the class. As the student experiences interaction within the class, he learns what will happen in given learning situations; how his teacher and peers will act, and particularly how the teacher expects students to act. The student's perception of these actions and expectations develops within the context of his attitudes about his teacher and fellow students and in turn influences his attitudes toward the class. These attitudes color all aspects of the student's classroom behavior: his work, his spontaneity and initiative, his voluntary social contributions, and his involvement in group tasks.

The development of a classroom climate is closely related to the "integrative" and "dominative" behaviors of the teacher (Anderson, 1939; Anderson and Brewer, 1945; Anderson and Brewer, 1946; and Anderson, Brewer, Brewer, and Reed, 1946). Integrative behaviors are those that invite students to participate and to explore differences that may exist. Dominative behavior tends to reduce the free interplay of individual differences and to lead toward resistance or conformity in responding or adapting to others.

The difference between dominative and integrative behavior can be summarized as the difference between commands and requests. Anderson (1939) wrote:

Domination is characterized by a rigidity or inflexibility of purpose, by an unwillingness to admit the contribution of another's experience, desires, purposes or judgment in the determining of goals which concern others. . . .Domination is. . .antagonistic to a concept of growth. Domination is consistent with a concept of self-protection.

Both dominative and integrative behaviors are methods of responding to another person in a conflict situation. Domination moves the conflict toward a "win-lose" payoff. Integrative behavior tends toward a "best possible solution" for all parties involved in the conflict. According to Anderson (1939), integrative behavior is "not so much a pursuing of one's own unique purposes as attempting to discover and get satisfaction through common purposes."

Anderson found that the teacher, to a great degree, determined, by the use of dominative and integrative contacts, how students behaved toward one another. As the teachers he studied tended to be dominative, so did the students, and vice versa. Later research by Schmuck and Van Egmond (1965), Flanders (1959), and Flanders, Morrison, and Leland (1968) confirmed Anderson's findings. These studies indicated that the teacher was the social-emotional leader of his classroom group. The teacher determined the role the students could play in the classroom and provided a model for how students related to each other.

Flanders (1959) found that students in situations of high dominative teacher contacts experienced disruptive anxiety and had reduced ability to recall academic material studied. The students consistently disliked the dominative pattern. In classrooms with high integrative contacts, these tendencies were reversed. Cogan (1958) found that students with teachers who used high integrative patterns did more assigned and extra homework. Walberg and Anderson (1968) found very high relationships between classroom climate and achievement in the cognitive, affective, and behavioral areas.

The research on classroom climate consistently shows improved student academic achievement when integrative patterns and improved group relations exist. These findings demonstrate the importance of classroom climate and the teachers' role in establishing it. Teachers using integrative contacts tend to produce students with desirable attitudes and superior patterns of work and achievement.

Organization Development

Research in organizational functioning and employee effectiveness has demonstrated findings parallel to those on classroom climate. Employees working in an environment of trust who are made to feel an integral and important part of the organization, are managed according to relevant objectives, are involved in decision-making and problem-solving, and are rewarded for their contributions to their own development and the achievements of the organization have high levels of creativity and productivity. Their organizations are also more productive and better able to find solutions to problems and to adapt to changing conditions.

Organization development attempts to help an organization move toward modes of operation that produce the environment which employees and the organization itself need to achieve maximal effectiveness. As Schmuck, Runkel, and Langmeyer showed in Chapter 3, when organizational training is carried out optimally it results in flexible organizational problem-solving. At the employee level, communication channels are established that enable the problem-solving process to function effectively. Verbal communication skills are developed and decision-making by consensus is encouraged. Minority views and new solutions are considered and explored. The members and leadership of the organization move toward valuing "integrative" contacts and improved interpersonal relationships. My thesis in this chapter is that if these skills and attitudes from OD were transferred by teachers to the classroom, they would increase integrative contacts between the teacher and the students, resulting in improved classroom climate.

The Community Studied

The student population of the school district studied was 11,040. It was estimated that the total population of the district was 32,000 in 1968. The population of the county was 1,141,000 and the population of the state was 3,040,000. Though the number of people in the school district was not significant compared to the total population of the state, the district was experiencing an extremely rapid increase in population. In 1968 the school district had over 9,500 additional homes in some stage of planning or development. Predictions indicate that by 1971 well over 25,000 students will be in the district.

The district covers seventy-one square miles, which makes it geographically the second largest district in the state. The area was mainly agricultural but is now becoming more industrial. The remaining property is used for private dwellings and apartments. The industry of the area is generally oriented to defense work, particularly aircraft.

The district is confronted by the major problem of providing resources to deal adequately with the increased enrollment. Some double-shifting in the schools seems inevitable; however, building needs are generally being met. In order to meet new demands in its total instructional program, the district raised its program budget by 28.3 percent in one year (from $443.31 to $568.85 per student). Staff increases over the past three years have averaged about 18 percent.

Relationships Between Organization Development and Classroom Climate

The goals of the OD program reported in this study were specified by the training staff as follows:

1. Increased openness and ease of interpersonal relations

2. A feeling that clearer and more effective staff communication has been achieved

3. Increased willingness and skill in giving information about one's own behavior

4. Increased awareness of interpersonal processes when they are taking place

5. A widened and shared perception by members of the staff of some new varieties of organizational patterns

6. Skill in using a systematic problem-solving procedure

7. An increase of skill in sharing initiative; that is, skill in helping a colleague who has enunciated an idea to develop it into a practical plan for action

Beyond the organizational level of activity, one can consider effects on classrooms if these goals are applied to the classroom. Increased openness and ease of interpersonal relations and increased willingness and skill in giving information about one's own behavior, for example, would certainly have a positive effect on classroom climate. Students and teachers sharing their perceptions of classroom events and behavior in an open, constructive manner should move both the teacher and the student toward behavior that is desired by the students (Gage, Runkel, and Chatterjee, 1963). A widened and shared perception of some new varieties of classroom organization would be a logical outcome of this type of two-way communication between teacher and student.

Skills in problem-solving would aid the teacher and the student in defining classroom problems and finding solutions. This could work in concert with helping students to develop ideas into practical plans for action. These ideas might relate to student-initiated study, student council work, classroom organization, or indeed any problem area the students choose to confront.

All of these efforts would tend to increase both student participation in decision-making and also the level of integrative teacher contacts with students. This increased participation, involvement, and sharing of perceptions and feelings relate clearly to the characteristics of improved classroom climate (Schmuck and Schmuck, 1971).

Description of the Organization Development Project

The OD project was one facet of a program designed to include several schools and the administrative hierarchy of the entire school district. The program was carried out by the staff of the Center for the Advanced Study of Educational Administration at the University of Oregon. The first intervention, held in April 1968, was designed to prepare the administrative staff of the school district for the training events in individual departments and schools. The superintendent and his cabinet, the principals, and a selected group of teachers from the local professional organization attended this first training session. All of the principals attended a two-week human relations workshop during the summer of 1968. During September of 1968, the school district departments concerned with student personnel services, social work, counseling, and curriculum attended a three-day organization development laboratory. The superintendent of schools and his cabinet (directors and assistant superintendents) attended several organization development laboratories of varying lengths. On several occasions the participants requested that trainers attend their meetings to observe the group process and help them over the rough spots.

The training began by involving the upper echelons of the school district, on the assumption that the skills and enthusiasm of the formal leaders were critical to the success of such a project. This same assumption was made in the development of designs for the individual schools involved. The first appearance of the training staff in the school consisted of a single day of interviews with the principal, vice-principal, counselors, and teachers to determine the problems the professional staff of the building perceived to be affecting their performance most seriously. Interviews were carried out in small groups. Teachers were interviewed during their daily planning time. After the problems perceived by the staff were categorized and ranked in importance by the training team, one trainer returned to the building for a one-hour meeting with the total faculty. This meeting was held to determine whether the staff would agree with the final statement of the problems and their order of importance.

During January and the first part of February of 1969, two meetings were held, involving the principal, vice-principal, counselors, and the department heads of the school. This group as a whole was not a formal element of the school personnel structure, but was selected by the training staff and was referred to as "the cabinet." It should be noted that the role of department head in this school was not the role generally associated with that term. Generally department heads functioned as departmental clerks, with no teacher-supervision or evaluation functions. Some individuals in this role had exercised vigorous leadership, but the administration had specified that the position was not to be that of the classical "department head."

These cabinet meetings were scheduled to last two and one-half hours. Both meetings, however, lasted at least three and one-half hours. During these meetings, basic verbal communication skills were introduced and emphasized. Discussion during the meetings revolved around problems cabinet members were having in defining and filling their roles in the organization. There was also some discussion of relationships among cabinet members and between cabinet members and the principal. During the second meeting, each cabinet member brought a colleague from his department so as to begin involving more of the staff in the interaction.

Verbal communication skills and a group problem-solving sequence were introduced to the total staff during meetings held between mid-February and mid-March. These meetings were held during the school day, with a one-hour meeting following the end of the school day. The first day's groupings consisted of those teachers sharing common planning times during their planning periods. These meetings were fifty minutes long, and were used to introduce and provide practice in verbal communication skills. The meeting following the dismissal of school lasted one hour. The staff was asked to perform an exercise in one-way and two-way communication. This exercise was followed by a discussion of the differences between the two modes of communication.

The following four meetings involved departmental groups, working through a five-stage problem-solving sequence. The first three meetings were held during the school day. Teachers' classroom assignments were modified to free departmental members of classroom responsibilities during common periods. These periods were also fifty minutes in duration. Each day the staff came together again for one hour after dismissal of school. During these one-hour sessions, departmental groups were provided with opportunities to share their plans and to aid other groups in developing their plans.

The problem-solving sequence introduced to the staff consisted of the following five steps:

1. Definition of the problem.

2. Delineation of restraining and helping forces.

3. Selection of restraining forces to be confronted.

4. "Brainstorming" of potential ideas for the reduction of selected restraining forces and the selection of those ideas that seemed most viable.

5. Preparation of an action sequence and the planning of a tryout. (An action tryout consists of a role playing situation, during which the planning group presents their products to a second group for feedback and evaluation.)

These stages were introduced as the departmental groups progressed in the accomplishment of their tasks. Working in pairs, members of the training team aided the groups in maintaining focus on the task and sustaining clear communication. Communication skills were reinforced by the trainers. At no time did trainers mention the possibility of applying these skills in the classroom. However, most groups did discuss the potential of their classroom use.

The last meeting of the program was held in mid-March and was designed to be a culminating experience. This meeting was held on a Saturday and the total professional staff (forty-two members) were paid for their presence. The meeting lasted from 8:30 a.m. until 4:30 p.m., with lunch being served at the meeting site. The morning hours were used by the various departments to try out action plans derived during problem-solving. Departments were paired to provide aid and feedback for the group presenting. Most groups became very involved in their participation, and the feedback received by those presenting was seen as very helpful.

The afternoon was used to begin working the staff as a total group. Two departments presented topics for discussion to the total staff. Both problems were seen as school-wide in scope and elicited a great deal of discussion. In each case, decisions for staff action were achieved. The final thirty minutes of the afternoon were spent discussing the outcomes of the project and the teachers' feelings about its productivity. Several departments requested that members of the training staff return at a later date to aid them in a follow-up of the progress being made, and the training staff agreed. Most staff members of the school expressed the opinion that the meetings had been productive but also expressed concern about whether or not the plans developed would be implemented. Several indicated that they felt that the continuation of the plans was their responsibility, and that they "shouldn't need any crutches."

Research Evaluation

Two instruments were used in this study. Interaction Analysis according to Flanders (1960) was used to determine any changes in classroom interaction patterns and teachers' verbal behavior. The second instrument was a student perception survey called "Classroom Life," developed by Schmuck (1968). This instrument was used to determine any changes in students' attitudes toward the class in general, the teacher, and the other students in the class.

Both instruments were administered before and after the OD training. Fifteen teachers (representing about one third of each school's staff) in the organization development school and a corresponding control school were used in the study. All were junior high school teachers of science, mathematics, social studies, or English. Teachers who participated were selected at random from the two schools.

Teachers sampled for participation in both the OD school group and control group recorded six twenty-minute tapes of classroom sessions before and after the training program. Pre-recordings were made in early December, and post-recordings were made in late March. Tape recordings were then analyzed with Flanders's Interaction Analysis by disinterested observers. Thirteen teachers in each school returned completely usable tapes. Those not returning tapes indicated tape recorder failure and microphone difficulties as the reason.

The two junior high schools used in this study contained grades 7, 8, and 9. Each school had an enrollment of approximately 680 students. The principals of both schools had been involved in all facets of the district-wide organizational training. The OD school enjoyed newer physical facilities and was located in a suburban area; the control school was located near one of the main business areas.

Results from Flanders's Interaction Analysis

Flanders's Interaction Analysis (FIA) was used to achieve an answer to the first question: Do teachers transfer skills learned in OD to the classroom? FIA is a method of examining the verbal exchanges between members of a class, particularly between the teacher and the students. The system uses ten categories of statements, each category having a number from one to ten (See Figure 4-1). A coder listens to the classroom interaction and records a category

Figure 4-1 Categories for Flanders's Interaction Analysis

TEACHER TALK	**INDIRECT INFLUENCE**	1.* ACCEPTS FEELING: accepts and clarifies feelings of the students in a nonthreatening manner. Feelings may be positive or negative. Predicting or recalling feelings are included.
		2. PRAISES OR ENCOURAGES: praises or encourages student action or behavior. Jokes that release tension, not at the expense of another individual; nodding head or saying, "um hm?" or "go on" are included.
		3. ACCEPTS OR USES IDEAS OF STUDENT: clarifying, building, or developing ideas suggested by student. As teacher brings more of his own ideas into play, shifts to category five.
		4. ASKS QUESTIONS: asking question about content or procedure with intent that student answer.
	DIRECT INFLUENCE	5. LECTURING: giving facts or opinions about content or procedure; expressing his own ideas; asking rhetorical questions.
		6. GIVING DIRECTIONS: directions, commands, or orders to which student is expected to comply.
		7. CRITICIZING OR JUSTIFYING AUTHORITY: statements intended to change student behavior from nonacceptable to acceptable pattern; bawling someone out; stating why teacher is doing what he is doing; extreme self-reference.
STUDENT TALK		8. RESPONSE: student makes a predictable response to teacher. Teacher initiates the contact or solicits student statement and sets limits to what student says.
		9. INITIATION: talk by students which they initiate. Unpredictable statements in response to teacher. Shift from 8 to 9 as student introduces own ideas.
		10. SILENCE OR CONFUSION: pauses, short periods of silence and periods of confusion in which communication cannot be understood by observer.

*There is NO scale implied by these numbers. Each number is classificatory: it designates a particular kind of communication event. To write these numbers down during observation is to enumerate, not to judge a position on a scale.

number every three seconds. The number recorded indicates the category in use. This provides a sample of verbal events as they occur.

Categories numbered 1 through 7 indicate statements by the teacher. The first four are types of statements that tend to draw students into interaction. These are alternately described as "inclusive," "integrative," or "indirect." The categories numbered 5 through 7 are teachers' statements that tend to establish the teachers' control of the class, and are generally referred to as "exclusive," "dominative," or "direct" statements. Categories 8 and 9 indicate students' statements. Category 8 is a response to the teacher, while Category 9 indicates a self-initiated comment. Category 10 indicates silence or confusion. One can see from the distribution of categories that the system is designed for use in a "traditional" classroom context: that is, the teacher speaking to the class. It is a teacher-oriented system that is generally used in a teacher-centered classroom.

The number of coded tallies for each category gives the researcher information as to the verbal behavior of the teacher and the students. By comparing teacher "integrative" statements (categories 1, 2, 3, and 4) to the number of "dominative" statements (categories 5, 6, and 7), a ratio (the I/D ratio) can be derived which gives a measure of "teacher domination" in the classroom.

Data from the control school and the OD school provided impressive evidence that teacher verbal behavior had changed significantly in the hoped-for direction in the OD school. Statistical analysis of overall teacher patterns in the OD and control schools showed that teachers' verbal behavior changed significantly ($p. < .05$) in the predicted direction: toward more integrative patterns. Table 4-1 shows integrative/dominative (I/D) ratios for teachers in both groups, and the change that has occurred between, before and after measures. OD group teachers

Table 4-1 Summary of the Teachers' Integrative/Dominative Verbal Interaction Ratios in the OD and Control Groups

Teacher*	OD			Control		
	Before	After	Change	Before	After	Change
1	.428	.539	.111	.468	.482	.014
2	.467	.571	.104	.442	.443	.001
3	.423	.532	.109	.455	.459	.004
4	.441	.550	.109	.453	.466	.013
5	.455	.573	.118	.422	.427	.005
6	.452	.563	.111	.427	.425	−.002
7	.489	.575	.086	.438	.430	−.008
8	.417	.531	.114	.427	.477	.005
9	.439	.554	.115	.421	.424	.003
10	.472	.549	.077	.498	.477	−.021
11	.418	.533	.115	.451	.468	.017
12	.502	.598	.096	.429	.422	−.007
13	.421	.547	.126	.507	.505	−.002
Averages	.448	.555	.107	.452	.454	.002

*This listing does not mean to imply that these teachers are matched in any way.

consistently moved to higher I/D ratios, while control group teacher remained
relatively unchanged.

Table 4-2 shows what changes occurred in terms of the usage of individual
Flanders categories. Teachers in the control group showed significant increases in

Table 4-2 Summary of Changes in OD Group and Control Group Verbal Behavior (Chi-Square Analysis)

Flanders's Category	Before*	After*	Change	x^2 (df = 1)	Significance
OD Group:					
1	7	11	4	2.29	NS
2	275	413	138	69.25	.001
3	1139	1419	280	68.83	.001
4	3017	3257	240	19.09	.001
5	2475	2472	−3	——	NS
6	1693	1279	−414	101.24	.001
7	797	602	−195	47.71	.001
8	3168	3347	179	10.11	.01
9	1566	1754	188	22.57	.001
10	2173	2098	−75	2.59	NS
Control Group:					
1	11	6	−5	2.27	NS
2	265	287	22	1.83	NS
3	1153	1149	−4	——	NS
4	2957	3127	170	10.12	.01
5	2403	2387	−16	0.10	NS
6	1642	1723	81	3.99	.05
7	761	824	63	5.22	.05
8	3046	3265	219	15.75	.001
9	1475	1545	70	3.32	NS
10	2001	2147	146	10.65	.01

*Adjusted totals (total tallies minus any steady state tallies).

categories 4 (asking questions), 6 (giving directions), and 7 (criticizing or
justifying authority). Categories 8 (student response) and 10 (silence or
confusion) also increased significantly. Control group teachers, then, increased
their use of dominative contacts. Giving directions and criticizing students'
behavior or justifying teachers' authority both increased. Asking questions,
normally considered integrative behavior, also increased. However, the increase
in students' responses and in silence or confusion indicated that these were short
questions and that the interaction was being closely controlled by the teacher.

The teachers who had OD training significantly decreased their reliance on giving directions and criticizing students' behavior or justifying authority. They also increased their use of praise and encouragement (2), using students' ideas (5), and asking questions (4). Students' involvement increased significantly in terms of both their responses to the teacher and their self-initiated comments. Silence or confusion decreased but not significantly. OD teachers increased their use of integrative statements while decreasing dominative statements. The interactions became livelier, more free, and more student-centered. Students were more involved in the interaction and initiating more comments. Category 10 (silence and confusion) also increased. Coders indicated this was a result of increased pauses between questions and answers.

This evidence clearly shows changes in teachers' verbal behavior. The direction of the change indicates that teachers transferred the values and skills of OD to their classroom behavior. By being more integrative in their behavior they were giving the students more freedom to act and to interact. The OD students were becoming more active participants in the classroom. Such activity is an important aspect of classroom climate.

Results from the "Classroom Life" Instrument

The second instrument used in the research, the student perception survey, was initiated to determine the effect of the changes in teachers' classroom behavior on the attitudes of students. This instrument is made up of nine items: four that indicate students' perception of the teachers, three about the students' relations with other students in the class; and two questions about the students' perception of the class in general. The Classroom Life questionnaire was administered to the control and OD group teachers' classes at the same time that the Flanders data were being collected.

The changes found in data elicited by the Classroom Life questionnaire (see Tables 4-3, 4-4, and 4-5) indicated that students' attitudes toward each other

Table 4-3 Perception of the Teacher, Change in Classroom Life Questionnaire Responses from Pre-test to Post-test (Chi-Square Analysis)

		Change in Response*	Level of Significance
The teacher of this class knows most of the students.	Control	–	.05
	OD	–	.01
If we help each other the teacher of this class likes it.	Control	+	.05
	OD	+	.05
Pupils in this class do what the teacher wants them to.	Control	–	.01
	OD	–	.01
The teacher of this class cares how hard I work.	Control	+	.01
	OD	0	–

* + indicates movement toward more positive attitudes.

  – indicates movement toward more negative attitudes.

  0 indicates no change.

Table 4-4 Perceptions of the Class in General, Change in Classroom Life Questionnaire Responses from Pre-test to Post-test (Chi-Square Analysis)

		Change in Response*	Level of Significance
Life in this class is . . .	Control	+	.01
	OD	+	.05
How hard are you working in this class?	Control	0	—
	OD	0	—

*+ indicates positive attitude change.

0 indicates no change.

Table 4-5 Students' Perceptions of Other Students in the Classroom, Changes in Classroom Life Questionnaire Responses from Pre-test to Post-test (Chi-Square Analysis)

		Change in Response*	Level of Significance
Pupils in this class help each other.	Control	–	.01
	OD	0	—
Pupils in this class act friendly toward each other.	Control	–	.01
	OD	+	.01
Pupils in this class hang around together outside of school.	Control	0	—
	OD	+	.05

*+ indicates positive attitude change.

– indicates negative attitude change.

0 indicates no change.

improved in the OD school classrooms. Students' attitudes in the OD school toward the teacher and the class in general did not change in comparison to changes in attitudes reported by the control group students. These results may be due in part to the short time lapse (two weeks) allowed between the termination of the OD project and the final collection of data. It is possible that insufficient time was allowed for students' attitudes to reflect the changes observed in teacher verbal behavior.

Bailey (1967) explored the hypothesis that human relations training would cause changes in teaching performance, and that this performance change would be perceived by the students. His study involved two high schools: one in California and one in Michigan. Students completed the Western Michigan University Student Opinion Questionnaire on a before-after schedule. The experimental school's faculty participated in a three day and evening human relations laboratory. Bailey's results indicated that there were changes in the perceptions of the students in both schools, but no significant differences between the two schools were obtained. Bailey concluded that if teacher behavior does change, students' attitudes may not immediately reflect that change.

Students' attitudes have been shown to regress as the school year progresses (Flanders, Morrison, and Leland, 1968; Gage, Runkel, and Chatterjee, 1963). For this reason the results of this study may take on significant meaning. Not only were OD students' attitudes toward classmates improved over those of the control group students; they did not regress.

The change in students' attitudes toward their classmates may be in the vanguard of changes to come in attitudes toward the teacher and the class in general. This would follow from studies done by Flanders (1960) indicating that there is a close relationship between high teacher I/D ratios and improved classroom climate.

A study by Flanders, Morrison, and Leland (1968) indicated that the observed regression of student attitudes during the school year is related to the "externality" or "internality" of the pupils and to the teachers' verbal classroom behavior. Greater losses in students' attitudes occurred among pupils whose teachers exhibited a lower incidence of praise and encouragement than among those whose teachers exhibited a higher incidence of such behaviors. The ıcrease observed in the use of praise and encouragement may be responsible for the improvement in student-classmate attitudes observed in the OD school.

Summary of Results

The evidence from Flanders's Interaction Analysis and from the Classroom Life instrument show that OD teachers did move to more integrative contacts with their students. Their verbal behavior indicated that they had transferred their learnings from the OD project to the classroom. Results from the Classroom Life questionnaire indicated that this change in teachers' behavior was beginning to be felt in the classroom. The normal demise of classroom climate had been lessened, and students' peer group relations had improved.

Further Analysis of Data

No significant relationship was found between teachers' ages, levels of academic preparation, and years of teaching experience when compared to changes in teachers' verbal behavior. It is apparent that these variables did not contribute to the variance in change of verbal behavior among the teachers. This indicates that other variables besides these should be considered if further research is initiated.

Eisenstadt (1967) was able to account for a considerable amount of the variance observed in changes in participants' behavior by a determination of the participants' "readiness" to enter into group process training. Readiness was established by an analysis of the participants' application for training, interviews of participants, and the results of the Krout Personal Preference Inventory. This may be a fruitful path to follow in the future. Eisenstadt also found high relationships to (1) power on the job, (2) perception of relevance of the laboratory training, and (3) cognitive sophistication. Unfortunately, none of these variables was considered in this study.

Eisenstadt reports that participants' behavior during the training gave little indication of the participants' learning. This is in agreement with the results of this study. However, Miles (1964) found a high relationship when comparing trainer ratings and changes in participants' on-the-job behavior. These differences may be present because of the situations participants found themselves in when returning to their work.

Situational variables, such as the work to which a participant returns, may be more important than his level of activity during training. This may be particularly important in the case of change in a teacher's behavior, because of the isolated conditions in which teachers work. A supervisor in industry is constantly confronted with pressures from peers and superiors that tend to maintain prior behavior. A teacher, working alone in a classroom, is not faced with the same constraints. He has more freedom to experiment with newly learned or discovered behaviors. If power on the job is an important variable, as the study of Eisenstadt indicates, this could relate to the changes observed in teacher behavior, as teachers do hold considerable power in their classrooms.

During the OD project, teachers invariably mentioned the applicability of verbal communication skills to the classroom even though the trainers never deliberately mentioned the connection. Teachers' perceptions of the relevance of verbal communication skills and the concepts of OD to the classroom may have accounted for much of the transfer observed. Unfortunately, data that would shed light on this point were not obtained in this study.

Implications for Schools Undergoing Organization Development

Results from the study reported in Chapter 3 indicated that teachers adopted several small-group techniques from the organization development project for use in their classroom. The results of the research in Chapter 4 showed that teachers changed their verbal behavior toward a more integrative, student-centered style. These two findings, when combined, indicate that organization development, beyond the effects it may have in improving the problem-solving ability of the staff of a school, can change teacher verbal behavior and a teacher's skills in working with small groups of students. Adoption of either or both of these techniques, I feel, can lead to a clear improvement in classroom activity.

References

Anderson, H. 1939. Domination and social integration in the behavior of kindergarten children in an experimental play situation. *Journal of Experimental Education* 8:123-31.

_____, and Brewer, H. M. 1945. Studies of teachers' classroom personalities, I. *Applied Psychological Monographs* No. 6.

_____, and Brewer, J. E. 1946. Studies of teachers' classroom personalities, II. *Applied Psychological Monographs* No. 8.

_____; Brewer, J. E.; Brewer, H. M.; and Reed, M. F. 1946. *Studies of teachers' classroom personalities, III. Follow-up of the effects of dominative and integrative contacts on children's behavior.* Stanford: Stanford University Press.

Bailey, W. J. 1967. Student perceived behavioral changes occurring in a secondary school faculty as a result of human relations in-service workshop. Unpublished Ed.D. dissertation, Michigan State University.

Cogan, M. L. 1958. The relation of the behavior of teachers to the productive behavior of their pupils. *Journal of Experimental Education* 89-124.

Eisenstadt, Jeane W. 1967. An investigation of factors which influence response to laboratory training. *Journal of Applied Behavioral Science* 3:575-78.

Flanders, N. A. 1960. Teacher influence, pupil attitude, and achievement. Mimeograph, University of Michigan.

——; Morrison, B. A., and Leland, B. E. 1968. Changes in pupil attitudes during the school year. *Journal of Educational Psychology* 59:334-38.

Gage, N. L.; Runkel, P. J., and Chatterjee, B. B. 1963. Changing teacher behavior through feedback from pupils: an application of equilibrium theory. In *Readings in the social psychology of education.* Ed. W. W. Charters, Jr., and N. L. Gage. Boston: Allyn and Bacon.

Miles, Matthew B. 1964. The T-group and the classroom. In *T-Group theory and laboratory method.* Eds., L. P. Bradford, J. R. Gibb, and K. D. Benne. New York: Wiley.

Schmuck, R. 1963. Some relationships of peer liking patterns in the classroom to pupil attitudes and achievement. *School Review* 71:337-59.

——. 1968. Helping teachers improve classroom group processes. *Journal of Applied Behavioral Science* 4:401-35.

——, and Schmuck, P. 1971. *Group processes in the classroom.* Dubuque, Iowa: Wm. C. Brown.

——, and Van Egmond, E. E. 1965. Sex difference in the relationship of interpersonal perceptions to academic performance. *Psychology in the Schools* 3:59-65.

Walberg, H. J., and Anderson, G. J. 1968. Classroom climate and individual learning. *Journal of Educational Psychology* 59:414-19.

5

STARTING UP A NEW
SENIOR HIGH SCHOOL*

Fred Fosmire, Carolin Keutzer, and Richard Diller

In general, critics of American education have not pursued issues related to organization development. They have tended to explain inadequacies in schools by describing the quality of academic resources in contrast to the interpersonal processes through which the resources are actualized. They have pointed to inferior teachers, administrators, consultants, buildings, and curriculum materials, but not often to inadequate communication, poorly defined roles, and ambiguous procedures for decision-making. How the resources are combined and coordinated organizationally has received only cursory attention.

Shortsightedness about organizational processes in schools—even among advocates of more humanistic schools—can be carried to ludicrous extremes. Imagine the members of a football team playing a game without the benefit of practicing as a unit. Many new schools unfortunately do commence operation exactly this way—without any practice or rehearsals. After all, it is argued, so long as the teachers are capable, the administrators skilled, and the curriculum materials up to date, why spend energy on developing communication skills, group agreements, and team morale? Would not those develop naturally when a school has top-flight, highly-motivated personnel?

The answer is No. Educators, like football players, need to practice together to execute the organizational plan successfully. A school is more than simply the sum total of its individual members and curriculum materials. The staff as a staff has different characteristics from those of its individual members; and if it is effectively trained—as in this intervention—it can be more productive than would be expected from a simple summing up of individual resources.

This project shows that newly organized high school faculties can benefit significantly from OD training during their first year of operation. With so many schools commencing operation every year, OD start-up interventions as effective as this one should be done over and over again.

* John E. Wood, formerly of the Beaverton, Oregon, School District, contributed immensely to this research. The study simply could not have been done without his continued collaboration and support. Additional critical aid was provided by Dr. Al Thede and Mrs. Dorothy Bumala of Barlow High School, Troutdale, Oregon. The cooperation of the faculties and students in completing the questionnaires was indispensable to the study and is much appreciated. Special recognition for assistance should go to Mary Dell Smith, who was centrally involved in the project. Others who assisted either in data-gathering or in some aspect of training were Barbara Jones, Neil White, and Kent Davis.

Starting up a new school can be exciting, especially if an optimal degree of teamwork and cooperation can be engendered on the staff. Often, unfortunately, too little attention is given to preparing new staffs to work together effectively. We believe that the proper unit to train is the interdependent work group—the staff itself as a whole—not the individual faculty members separated from one another. We do not mean merely that every faculty member should undergo some training in group processes. We mean that the staff itself should be taught to carry out a new pattern of organizational behavior as a team.*

We had the opportunity to test the effectiveness of OD training with a new high school several years ago. A two-week "laboratory learning" experience was held for a group of thirty-five strangers who would make up the entire staff of the new school. The general objective of the training was to promote an effective social system characterized by a high degree of proficiency in basic instrumental skills (communication, decision-making, problem-solving, and conflict-management) and by an atmosphere of interpersonal openness, trust, and freedom for innovation and experimentation. The first week was primarily oriented toward developing skills, while the second week was directed more toward organization development.

Purpose of the Study

Our primary purpose for assessing the effects of the organizational training was to see if the heavy expenditures (in terms of time, money, energy and convenience) could be recovered with interest. As the consultants in the intervention, we were seeking reassurance that experientially gratifying procedures and theoretically sound principles of learning could yield a pay-off in improvement of overt behavior, social climate, and system effectiveness. Toward that end, we used a number of different "internal" and "external" criteria (following the distinction of Campbell and Dunnette, 1968) to see if we had, in fact, "made a difference."

Mindful of the legitimate complaint of Campbell and Dunnette (1968, p. 94) that most "descriptions of training programs are so incomplete as to preclude any careful assessment of the role played by these other methods," we have provided detailed accounts of the procedures used during both the summer intervention and the continuing consultation sessions during the school year (Keutzer, Fosmire, Diller, and Smith, 1969). In this chapter we will emphasize results more than training processes.

Nature of the Schools Studied

The experimental high school (EHS) opened for the first time in September 1968. EHS is in a school district in the suburbs of Portland, Oregon, which serves a population of above-average affluence. Its students are predominantly

* The interested reader may want to compare starting up a high school with starting up an engineering coporation. (See Dayal and Thomas, 1968.)

from white middle-class homes. Schmuck and Runkel (1970) provide a more complete description of the district. The school had a total certified staff of thirty-five, composed of one principal, two vice-principals, and thirty-two classroom teachers. During the first year of operation there were 600 students in grades 10 and 11 (sophomores and juniors) and no seniors. The prevailing orientation and philosophy of EHS's administrators will be described below as part of the history of the intervention.

The control high school (CHS) also opened its doors for the first time in September 1968. Like EHS, it is located in a Portland suburb and serves white middle-class students predominantly. During the first year of classes, there were thirty-three certified members on the staff, including a principal and two vice-principals. There were 560 students in grades 9, 10, and 11. Like EHS, there was no grade 12 the first year.

The general philosophy of CHS was described by one of the vice-principals as reflecting the temper of the community. A tone of conservatism prescribed somewhat stricter rules of dress and deportment than some students would have preferred; and the term "discipline" was commonly heard when the administrators discussed their roles. As the vice-principal summarized the situation; "Students were given as much freedom as they could handle; those who could not handle it were restricted."

Entry into the Experimental School

A year before this intervention, two of the writers had been trainers in a sensitivity lab for selected teachers in this school district. At a meeting with the total administrative staff of the district, the objectives and apparent outcomes of that lab were reviewed. Three weeks later, the senior author received a call from one of the administrators present during that meeting—the principal-elect of the experimental school—asking about training activities for the staff of the new school.

Consultation with the Principal

Over the course of several meetings, the principal described the physical characteristics of the new school, his criteria for selecting his staff, his general objectives for the training program, and his personal goals for the new school. The principal's philosophy of administration emphasized participative decision-making, internal control from within the system (feedback), and a permissive, open style in relating to staff members.

The principal's objectives for the workshop were as follows: to establish norms for open communication; to build productive and rewarding interpersonal relationships; to develop satisfying procedures of problem-solving and decision-making which would yield high-quality decisions and solutions; to establish a high degree of role-clarity; to encourage the staff to value students as individuals and to assume responsibility for "guiding" as well as "teaching" them; and to involve the total staff in curriculum development and appraisal.

Further mutual inquiry between the principal and consultant yielded the decision that all of the professional staff (excluding civil service employees but including administrative persons) would be required (as stipulated in their job offers) to participate, with financial compensation, in a two-week summer workshop to be held on a nine-to-five basis in the local area. To effect a continuing consultation relationship, the consultant agreed to take responsibility for the two days set aside (by contract between the district and the teachers) for in-service training.

Pre-Workshop Meeting of Participants

In the spring preceding the workshop, the senior consultant spent an evening with all of the new EHS staff members who had been recruited at the time (approximately twenty people). While discussing some of his values, concerns, and tentative plans, he invited the prospective participants to share their own fears and apprehensions, expectations, and learning-objectives for the workshop.

The Summer Laboratory Experience

First Week: Focus on Skill-Building

The lab was designed to teach some communication skills and a common language regarding interpersonal openness and trust *before* providing large blocks of unstructured time. Many of the materials and exercises used in the first week were developed by Wallen (1966a, 1966b, 1967a, 1967b). The overall orientation of the lab was substantially derived from traditional T-group methods and values, as exemplified by the ground rules which the trainers suggested. A brief rationale was presented for each rule.

1. That anything which occurred within the group session could be a legitimate object for observation and analysis.

2. That the participants focus attention on the shared, direct, immediate experiences of the group.

3. That the group adopt an experimental attitude toward behavior change.

4. That the members endeavor to provide and be receptive to interpersonal feedback.

Team-Building. The objectives of the first week were to help participants learn more about (1) the value of joint inquiry (to promote cooperative inquiry and to minimize competitive arguments), (2) ways in which to be helpful in interpersonal relations, (3) group problem-solving methods, (4) ways in which to give and receive constructive feedback, (5) group processes in general, and (6) the participants themselves in interaction with others. More generally, the objective was to build *interpersonal trust.* A variety of techniques were employed, including unstructured inquiry groups, "fishbowl" arrangements with observers providing feedback to participants, various systematic data-gathering procedures and feedback of results, mixed fishbowls across I-groups, and work in dyads. The participants received approximately ten brief lectures covering cognitive material such as Wallen's treatment of the "interpersonal gap" and his concept of openness (1966b, 1967a, 1967b), and the "Johari Window" (Luft and Ingham, 1955; see also Luft, 1969).

Inquiry Groups. Much of the work of the first week occurred in two inquiry groups (I-groups), each of which had representatives from all departments of the school. Each group, which met from four to six hours a day, began as an agenda-free group of strangers whose ordinary role statuses were irrelevant to this "here-and-now" experience. The only norms which had been given legitimacy explicitly were those suggested by the ground rules.

Allowing for considerable variation between groups, it could be said that both I-groups followed, roughly, the developmental sequence outlined by Tuckman (1965) of "forming" (characterized by orientation, testing, and dependence), "storming" (conflict and polarization around interpersonal issues), and "norming" (wherein resistance is somewhat overcome and "in-group" feeling and cohesiveness develop, new standards evolve, and new roles are adopted). Tuckman's fourth stage, "performing," was not reached in this first week.

To provide a better idea of the activities of the first week, we will describe a portion of the first day. Each I-group was begun in essentially the same manner. After introducing the "name game" (in which each member systematically states his own name and the names of all those in the circle who have previously introduced themselves, until the last person to speak has introduced himself and recited the names of all the other members) and suggesting that the group might want to adopt some agreements (e.g., confidentiality, directness), the trainer explicitly defaulted as "group leader." Since each I-group had its own history, it would be impossible, after that point, to detail any specific process which would simultaneously and validly describe both groups.

The Group Expectation Survey (Wallen, 1966a) is typical of the way in which questionnaire data were used in training. The instrument provides easily understood data about the communications norms of a group. The survey asks each member to indicate anonymously (1) what proportion of the group is interested in knowing his reactions in six situations (reported below), (2) what proportion of the group will report candidly their reactions to his behavior in the same six situations, (3) to what proportion of the group will he report his own reactions, and (4) from what proportion of the group is he interested in knowing personal reactions. The six situations are:

When he (you) does not understand something you (he) said.

When he (you) likes something you (he) said or did.

When he (you) disagrees with something you (he) said.

When he (you) thinks you (he) have changed the subject or become irrelevant.

When he (you) feels impatient or irritated with something you (he) said or did.

When he (you) feels hurt—rejected, embarrassed, or put down—by something you (he) said or did.

The survey, handed out after an I-group meeting on the second day, took only three or four minutes to complete. The results were presented graphically at the beginning of the following session. Consistent with protocols collected over a wide range of groups (Fosmire and Keutzer, 1968), the results showed that each member was saying (1) that he was receptive to interpersonal feedback but that he perceived the others as unwilling to give it, and (2) that though he would report his feelings candidly, he doubted that others would do the same. Since all members were saying this to one another it became obvious to all that attempts at greater openness might be safer than formerly believed.

Second Week: Focus on Organization Development

During the second week the transformation of the lab participants into a "work group" in a "natural setting" was begun. The focus of the intervention was shifted from assessment and training in basic interpersonal skills to a focus on the "real life" problems of a newly formed work group: e.g., decision-making, agenda-setting, and conflict management.

The overall strategy of the week called for (1) more shifting and recomposing of groups, (2) more work in groups which were working on organizational problems, and (3) the trainers acting more as process consultants (Schein, 1969) while participants worked on real-life problems. Some of the techniques employed are well known in training circles (e.g., a variety of nonverbal trust-building and warmup exercises), while others are more novel. To give some of the flavor of the meetings held during the second week, we will describe in detail the activities of the morning of the third day of this week.

The interventions of day eight of the lab were based on some shared perceptions of the training staff gathered from the previous two days of the lab. These perceptions were that (1) the participants were beginning to relate to one another in terms of their statuses now that they were working on concrete school-related problems, and the exchanges and process in general were less productive and satisfying than they had been in the first week; (2) the participants had not identified "hidden agenda" based on differences in educational philosophy and past experiences in school districts (in a few cases there was a hidden "personal" agenda emerging from prior relationships between specific individuals); and (3) there was a markedly skewed distribution of participation whenever the group worked on specific institutional problems, and once one of the high participators got the floor, he tended to give a speech. The self- and other-perceived "expertise" of the individuals seemed to be determining who spoke and for how long.

On the basis of these observations, the staff began the eighth day with an "unfreezing" activity. Specifically, each member was asked to pair via eye-contact with someone with whom he felt he had a "trust problem." Then, after pairing off, one member was to assume the role of a blind person and the other the role of "assister" and they were to spend thirty minutes exploring the environment, alternating their roles. After a brief sharing of feelings and observations about the "blind man technique," the individuals were asked to form their I-groups in the large room and spend fifteen minutes "brainstorming" for hidden agenda, or those things which any individual felt could not be talked about in the group. The participants were cautioned not to evaluate any contribution, only to note it. Then the two groups shared their lists, again without evaluation.

The final two hours of the morning session were spent in the I-groups, again with the task of creating a specific proposal for the decision-making process to be adopted by the staff. At this time most staff members wanted to reach important decisions by consensus. They understood that consensus decision-making required that every member of the staff have a chance to communicate his views and that the minority would, after discussion, be willing to go along with the majority. Such a process required that all staff members would at times participate actively in discussions. During the training session the training staff introduced a technique designed to highlight and manipulate the problems of unequal participation and speech-making noted above. Each member of an I-group was given five poker chips, each worth twenty seconds of "air time." If a person wanted to speak he was required to toss one of his poker chips onto the floor in the center of the group. This gave him the floor. At the end of the twenty seconds, signaled by a toy clicker manipulated by one of the training staff, the person had to either stop speaking or throw in another chip. The chips were not redistributed until all members had spent their chips, a procedure which forced those members who used up their chips immediately to sit silently while members who had not spoken used up their chips. Before redistributing the chips, the groups discussed the experience. The chips were reallocated four times in this two-hour work session.

Continuing Consultation

The activities of the consultants during the first school year at EHS can be seen as an extension of the summer lab experience—as "followup treatment." The following is a chronological report of the major interactions between EHS and the training staff during the school year.

Although we had planned, for reasons of research design, to have no contact with students beyond administering, periodically, a questionnaire to them—the Environmental Description Questionnaire (EDQ)—we were requested to help members of the student government work together more effectively in their task of framing a constitution for the school. Three trainers spent most of an October day with the student leaders.

Before the regular monthly meeting with the staff in November, we sent all staff members a restatement of the objectives of the summer lab experience and a summary of how they changed in their responses to the SPQ from the pre- to the post-lab administrations. (This information can be retrieved from Figure 5-1.) The focus of that staff meeting, however, was on the results of the EDQ administered to the students at the beginning of the school year. Reports of results were distributed to the teachers and they were invited to help decide on an effective way of getting the summarized results back to the students. After discussion, the teachers agreed to distribute copies of the report in the "REP rooms" (i.e., rooms in which groups of from twenty to twenty-five students formed to discuss school issues and send representatives to the lower house of student government). Some time was spent insuring that every teacher understood the entire report.

The remainder of that November staff meeting was spent in a regular business meeting. At its conclusion the consultants were invited to describe what they had observed about the functioning of the total staff. The consultants' report stimulated considerable discussion of the principal's mode of leadership in staff

Table 5-1 SPQ Item Clusters

The Situation Prediction Questionnaire was a paper-and-pencil instrument designed to assess the probability that the test-taker would respond in any of several alternative ways in a given situation. He was asked to indicate this probability by a check mark at the appropriate place on a linear scale like the following:

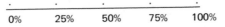

0%	25%	50%	75%	100%

The items (alternative behaviors) are reproduced below and are preceded in every case by the hypothetical situation to which they pertain. The order of presentation has been changed to provide for grouping of items within common rational clusters. The direction (+ or −) of the item's contribution to the cluster score is also indicated.

CANDOR (six component items)

In every school building there are invariable annoyances and difficulties between people who work together. The person who is dissatisfied with something another is doing (a) might keep it to himself, perhaps waiting for the problem to take care of itself; (b) might talk about it with someone other than the "offending" person; or (c) might discuss it with the person with whom he is dissatisfied. Estimate the probability that *you* would *tell the person involved* about your dissatisfaction IF:

That person is a superior (e.g., the principal) (+)

The person is a subordinate (e.g., a teaching aide or janitor) (+)

That person is a teaching colleague (+)

Suppose, in the course of your work, you feel hurt and "put down" by something another teacher has said to you. Estimate the probability that you would:

Avoid the other teacher for a while (−)

Tell the other teacher that you felt hurt and put down (+)

Tell your friends that the other teacher is hard to get along with (−)

RECEPTIVITY (five component items)

One of the main risks in confronting a person with something you don't like about the way he is behaving is that he will feel hurt, "put down," or angry. Estimate the probability that you yourself would feel this way IF:

The person confronting you were a teaching colleague (−)

The person confronting you were a superior (e.g., the principal) (−)

The person were a subordinate (e.g., a teaching aide or janitor) (−)

Suppose you are in the middle of a carefully planned classroom program in which you have invested much time, thought, and effort. A student expresses dissatisfaction with the way things are going and suggests a modification or change in the procedure. Estimate the probability that you would:

Ignore the suggestion or defer it for later consideration (−)

Check out the feelings and opinions of the other students in the class (+)

INITIATIVE/RISK (three component items)

Innovation in teaching is always accompanied by risk of failure. Suppose you have an exciting idea for a new way of teaching that could really enhance the degree of learning of students, but suppose also that there is a possibility that the new approach might not go over at all. Estimate the probability that you would try out the new method anyway IF:

There were a high risk that the new method would fail (+)

Suppose you develop a particularly useful and effective method for teaching something. Estimate the probability that you would:

Describe it briefly at a faculty meeting and offer to meet with others who wanted to hear more about it (+)

Say nothing about it unless somebody asked you (−)

CONFLICT ACCEPTANCE (seven component items)

Suppose you are present when two other teachers get into a heated argument about how the school should be run. Estimate the probability that you would:

Listen to both parties in the argument and then side with the one you think is right (+)

Try to get the two to quiet down and stop arguing (−)

Help each one in the argument to understand the viewpoint of the other (+)

Avoid getting involved in the interaction at all (−)

Suppose you strongly disagree with a procedure that the principal has outlined for all to follow. Estimate the probability that you would:

Go and talk with the principal about this disagreement (+)

Say nothing but ignore the principal's directive (−)

Say nothing but comply grudgingly with the principal's directive (−)

SECURITY (four component items)

Suppose you wanted to improve your classroom effectiveness in some area. What is the probability that you would:

Ask another teacher to observe your teaching and then have a conference with you afterwards (+)

Ask another teacher to let you observe how he teaches the material in order to get an idea how to improve your own methods (+)

Use a questionnaire to find out how your students feel about your teaching in this area (+)

Hold a free and open discussion with your students about your teaching of this subject matter (+)

meetings. The next interaction with the total staff occurred in February when a special meeting was held at the request of the principal to work on ways of increasing the amount of student involvement in the REP rooms and to increase students' desires and ability to handle their freedom more responsibly.

Having learned the technique of "force-field analysis" in the summer lab, the faculty was able to break up into six-person work groups to identify the forces which facilitate and those which impede the desired behavior. The senior consultant gave a short lecture on diffusion of innovation, and then the participants "brainstormed" the problem of reducing the forces which impede wider acceptance of the new culture by students. Each work group brought to the total group a number of suggestions for action steps to be taken immediately. Another brief lecture was given on methods of obtaining and using sociometric data in the classroom. The day ended with the staff developing plans for continuing to work on the problems of student involvement and responsibility.

The in-service training day in April was begun by introducing an exercise developed by Brissey (1968). Five-person groups generated lists of "surprises" (i.e., events which were discrepant with their expectations at the beginning of the school year), then consensually rated each item ("event") in terms of its pleasantness/unpleasantness and its importance for them. The lists were posted for review. Stimulated by the "surprise" data, interest groups were formed to discuss particular problems and to develop recommendations regarding procedures to bring about improvements. Their respective recommendations were presented orally to the total group by a representative of each work group.

Just before these oral presentations, each staff member had written the names of three persons with whom he had "unfinished business" (unresolved conflicts, ambiguous role relationships, etc.). On the basis of these data two large groups were formed and the last two hours of the day were spent working over those issues. In fishbowl style the persons on the outside observed the inner circle as they gave interpersonal feedback to one another. At intervals the observers would criticize the feedback as to the degree of its constructiveness. Then the outer and inner circles exchanged places and the procedure was continued.

At the close of the day the consultants presented (in both a written report and oral summary) the results of the November administration of the EDQ to the students. Though the consultants were pleased with the absolute scores and the apparent marked contrasts with CHS on most items, the teachers were not cheered. They were more concerned with the results of the *latest* administration of the EDQ, for they feared that there had been a downturn in student optimism, enthusiasm, and positive reactions to the school. Unfortunately, those results were not yet available and the day seemed to end on a note of guarded optimism.

Although the various members of the consultation team visited the school four times during the school year to administer EDQs to samples of the student body, and although the principal and the senior consultant talked via telephone at least once a month, these contacts were devoted almost entirely to testing, working out agreements regarding scheduling, and planning for subsequent organization development activities. Such contacts, therefore, have not been described in detail in the Procedures part of this chapter, though their influence (albeit partially counterbalanced by parallel contacts at CHS) is recognized.

Results

Situation Prediction Questionnaire

It should never be assumed that a set of laboratory experiences, however subjectively satisfying or pleasing to one's clinical judgment, will have a systematic effect on even the verbal behavior of participants. Thus we sought a tangible index of what may be termed "attitude" (insofar as predicted performance of an act indicates approval for that act) toward certain behavior. For example, if the laboratory were successful in approaching goals for which it was designed, index scores would indicate that participants had a higher level of commitment to these behaviors following the two-week experience than they had before the lab.

Items for the Situation Prediction Questionnaire (SPQ) were generated to allow predictions on the part of the faculty members with regard to their own behavior in the realms of (1) dealing with co-workers in a direct and candid manner (candor); (2) receiving direct and candid reactions from others (receptivity); (3) attempting and promoting innovation in teaching methods (initiation/risk); (4) encouraging open, direct expression and management of conflict (conflict acceptance); and (5) taking the initiative to increase critical comment on one's own work (security). A cluster of items for each domain calls for the general response on several hypothetical situations.

For ease in viewing the results, we have reduced the SPQ data by combining scores of items which, on a theoretical basis, seemed to belong together. The actual constituent items of each cluster are presented in Table 5-1.

The method of planned comparisons (Hays, 1963) was used to assess the differences, both between schools and within schools over a period of time, in the SPQ clusters. The faculties of both the experimental and control schools responded to the SPQ twice, at approximately a two-week interval, in late summer or early fall of 1968, making four responses in all. The laboratory learning experience took place between administrations for EHS: a period of normal functioning as a faculty intervened between administrations at CHS.

The first set of contrasts (whose defining weights are presented in Table 5-2) detects divergence/convergence of the two groups as a result of the experimental intervention; i.e., they test for changes in differences between the schools before and after the intervention.

The second set of weights detects changes in responses (in both groups) on the second testing which can be attributed to nothing more than a prior exposure to the instrument (the "retest" effect); the sensitizing or persuasive

Table 5-2 Weights Defining the Planned Comparisons of Means on SPQ Clusters

Comparison	EHS pre-lab	EHS post-lab	EHS May	CHS Sept.	CHS Oct.	CHS May
I. Experimental effect	−1	+1	0	+1	−1	0
II. Measurement effect	−1	+1	0	−1	+1	0
III. Divergent trends	−1	−1	+2	+1	+1	−2

Table 5-3 Results of Planned Comparison Tests on SPQ Clusters

Cluster	Contrast	SS	F	Probability Level*
Candor	I. Experimental	2.5411	7.39	p < .0039**
	II. Measurement	6.7150	19.53	p < .0039**
	III. Divergence	0.0009	0.00	p > .50
Receptivity	I. Experimental	1.1894	3.46	p < .10
	II. Measurement	1.1635	3.38	p < .10
	III. Divergence	0.1632	0.47	p > .50
Initiation/Risk	I. Experimental	0.8026	2.33	p < .25
	II. Measurement	0.0091	0.03	p > .50
	III. Divergence	0.0386	0.11	p > .50
Conflict Acceptance	I. Experimental	2.5099	7.30	p < .0039**
	II. Measurement	0.4027	1.17	p < .50
	III. Divergence	0.7479	2.18	p < .25
Security	I. Experimental	1.7820	5.18	p < .05
	II. Measurement	0.9941	2.89	p < .10
	III. Divergence	1.6851	4.90	p < .05

* The probability that apparent effects this large could occur by chance alone

** Significant finding, maintaining alpha < .05 for entire set of 15 comparisons

effect of asking the SPQ questions is "error" as far as assessment of the effects of the laboratory is concerned.

Weights for Comparison III serve to contrast the changes over the course of the 1968-69 academic year ("year-trend") on the part of the faculties of the two schools. Divergence of scores over time could be interpreted as a "multiplier effect" of continued exposure to the subculture created in the laboratory experience; convergence of prediction-probabilities could indicate that the change effected by the training was transitory. Both possibilities seemed plausible enough to merit testing.*

Table 5-3 presents the results of the planned comparison tests. The act of raising the issue of candor in the first testing seems to have had the effect of inducing greater self-reported candor in the second testing; the retest in both populations revealed higher predictions of candid behavior than did the original testing. However, the increase in predicted candor at EHS following the lab was

* A technical word about the way the data was treated should be injected here. As is frequently the case when subjects construe a question as requiring relative frequencies or proportions as answers, the data concerning likelihood of events presented a marked heterogeneity of variance. Thus the arcsin transformation of estimates provided a better estimate of mean responses than did the raw data (Meyers, 1966). The above-described analyses of SPQ responses were, therefore, performed on transformed values.

Figure 5-1 SPQ Rational-Cluster Index Scores

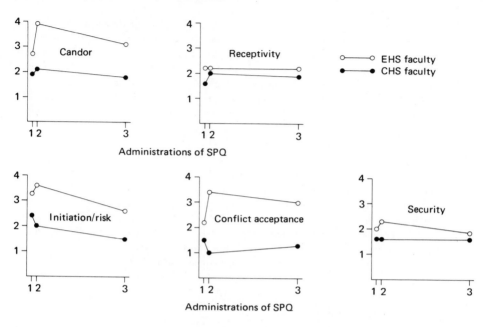

significantly greater than the increase at CHS at retest. This difference between faculties was maintained throughout the school year; no reliable differences in "year-trend" (as seen by Comparison III) were observed.

Similarly EHS showed significantly greater increase in predicted acceptance of overt conflict ("conflict acceptance" cluster) on the first retest than did CHS. Again, this difference was maintained throughout the school year and no reliable difference in year-trend was observed. The fact that no reliable measurement effect (Comparison II) was observed might suggest that tolerance-for-overt-conflict lacked the motivating aura of social desirability that seems to surround the issue of candor.

No other effect was significant at the p .0039 level to which these analyses were held. (Any less rigorous level of significance would necessitate assuming a greater than 5 percent risk of "alpha error"—that is, a risk of accepting one or more chance fluctuations in the data as reliable effects.) On the other hand, we saw no reason to ignore entirely trends which were not sufficiently strong to be demonstrated by the limited number of observations in this study but which might nevertheless suggest important effects.

A perusal of Figure 5-1, which displays the comparative changes over time of CHS and EHS, is helpful in exploring some of the suggestive if statistically nonsignificant trends reported in Table 5-3. Curiously, the trends toward a negative experimental effect (Comparison I) and a measurement effect (Comparison II) in receptivity reflected virtually no change on the part of the experimental population; rather there was a marked change on the part of the control group from first to second testing, causing them to approach closely the stable position maintained by the experimental group. With respect to the receptivity cluster, then, the laboratory was apparently no more powerful than the ordinary persuasive pressures of testing in inducing predictions of socially desirable behaviors.

While the trends with regard to the initiation of experimental-teaching methods (initiation cluster) were too weak to warrant even speculative discussion, the security cluster (the tendency to invite critical candid comment from others) aroused our interest. The weak trends toward experimental (Comparison I) and measurement (II) effects were both due solely to greater predicted activity on the part of EHS and might, thus, reflect an effect of the laboratory experience; if so, however, the effect was transitory, for an equally strong year-trend denoted a convergence of EHS and CHS.

Despite strenuous and rather successful efforts to match the two schools (EHS and CHS) on demographic variables, the matching was, of course, imperfect. No two faculties, systematically and actively recruited by different administrators with values differing to an undefined degree, could be expected to reflect the same level of commitment to the same norms. Indeed, a casual inspection of Figure 5-1 will disclose that the SPQ questionnaires were sensitive to differences in attitude even before the laboratory increased their differences in experience. The effects of the experimental procedure, it is important to note, in every instance served to *increase* these attitudinal differences between faculties.

Environmental Description Questionnaire

The SPQ data attempted answers to two questions: (1) Would the laboratory experience have an immediate impact on the participants? and (2) Would those effects endure? However, self-perceived behavior tendencies are not necessarily translated into observable behavior. As Campbell and Dunnette (1968) have emphasized, observable changes in job behavior have seldom been shown to accompany changes in internal criteria.

In an effort to look more closely at this relationship, we asked students in both schools to observe and describe the teaching environment for us. If the differences between faculties, reflected by teachers' self-reports on the SPQ, were indeed translated into differences in behavior, observations by students at the two schools would differ also.

The Environmental Description Questionnaire (EDQ) was constructed to assess the expectations and preferences of students regarding various aspects of school life. The questions did not focus exclusively on the behavior of teachers but tapped a variety of characteristics of school life so as to indicate the direction of faculty leadership in the school.

The EDQ was administered twice at CHS—to all students at the beginning of the year (September) and to a representative sample of students at the end of the year (May). At EHS, in an attempt to test each student twice, the EDQ was administered to all students in September and to representative samples of students again in November, January, March, and May. By testing at intervals we hoped to discern how quickly the students changed their expectations after gaining experience in the EHS environment. Since both schools were opening their doors for the first time, the initial responses of students were considered as expectations based on previous school experience.

Table 5-4 presents the defining weights of the three sets of comparisons planned for the analysis of these data. The first set of contrasts detects

Table 5-4 Weights Defining the Planned Comparisons of Means on EDQ Items

Comparison	EHS Sept. N = 489	EHS Nov. N = 130	EHS Jan. N = 110	EHS March N = 112	EHS May N = 78	CHS Oct. N = 441	CHS May N = 81
I. Experimental effect (comparative net growth)	−1				+1	+1	−1
II. Entropy (movement over time)	+1				−1	+1	−1
III. Initial growth (and subsequent decay)	−2	+1	+2	+1	−2		

divergence in reported frequency of events covered by the EDQ. Differences in this comparison reflect either (1) greater change at EHS or (2) opposite trends over the year at the two schools.

The second set of weights detects any general tendencies in both schools to increase or decrease over the year. The third set of weights detects deviation from a linear growth trend over the year at EHS. If both Tests I and II were significant for a given item, one could conclude that the greatest change in a characteristic which came to differentiate the two schools occurred early and remained fairly constant. If Test III alone were significant, one could conclude that the change was paralleled at CHS.

Since three contrasts were applied to each of forty items (shown in Table 5-5), it was necessary to demand that each test be conducted at the $p < .00015$ significance level in order to maintain an acceptable $p < .05$ level for the entire set. We can be more than 95 percent certain that each of the indicated critical differences is indeed a reliable difference. Since the number of respondents was fairly large, nonsignificant differences were of modest size and do not warrant even tentative interpretation.

Figure 5-2 presents graphically the means (probability estimations) for each EDQ item at specified times over the school year. These line graphs reveal that the means of student expectations at EHS did not, as a rule, progress smoothly (monotonically) from September to May; rather, many items were characterized by periods of apparent retrogression. Figure 5-2 points up, however, the rather large number of items on which EHS students described their school as clearly changing and changing in a direction different from that at CHS.

Although the satisfaction of students with their school may not be the most important criterion in evaluating school atmosphere, it may relate to absenteeism, dropout rate, and enthusiasm for learning. The EDQ sought two answers to every item: (1) the probability of the described event occurring (data reported in Table 5-5 and Figure 5-2) and (2) the frequency with which the event *should* occur (i.e., more often, less often, "same frequency as now," or "does not matter"). Comparing the two sets of answers for each school on both the September and May administrations allowed us to see whether the schools changed in the preferred direction on each item.

Table 5-5 Results of F-Tests of Planned Comparisons for EDQ Items

Comparison*

I	II	III	Item as Presented
	c	e	1. Teachers regularly check up on the students to make sure that assignments are being carried out on time.
			2. Students help one another understand the material presented in class.
b		e	3. Teachers go out of their way to make sure that students treat them with respect.
b	c	e	4. When a student expresses anger with one teacher, the other teachers soon know about it.
b	c	e	5. Teachers make students feel like children.
a			6. If a student thinks out a report carefully, teachers will give him a good grade, even if they don't agree with him.
a			7. If assignments are not clear the teachers don't mind answering all the questions that students want to ask.
a	d	f	8. Students are encouraged to help decide how the class will be taught.
b	c		9. Students say nothing in class unless called upon.
			10. Teachers treat questions in class as if the students were criticizing them personally.
a			11. If students do their work well they get a good grade, whether or not the teachers like them.
		f	12. Students feel responsibility for making class worthwhile and interesting.
	d	f	13. Students are encouraged to help decide what will be covered in a class.
			14. Teachers restate and ask questions until they are sure they understand what students are saying.
			15. When a student presents an idea no one responds.

*   [a]Indicates EHS was significantly *higher* on that reported event than CHS, with the difference being significant at the .00015 level (in keeping with a .05 level of significance over the entire set of tests).

[b]Indicates EHS was significantly *lower* on that reported event than CHS, with the difference being significant at the .00015 level.

[c]Indicates a significant tendency for this item to *increase* over time and across schools $(p < .00015)$.

[d]Indicates a significant tendency for this item to *decrease* over time and across schools $(p < .00015)$.

[e]Indicates initial *growth* and subsequent decay or leveling off $(p < .00015)$.

[f]Indicates initial *decrement* and subsequent recovery or leveling off $(p < .00015)$.

Table 5-5 (continued)

Comparison

I	II	III	Item as Presented
			16. If a student expresses dissatisfaction with the way a class is going, a teacher would:
b	c	e	a. Ignore the suggestion or wait until later to consider it.
a	d		b. Check out the reactions of others in the class.
a		f	c. Change the way he was running the class if the other students were dissatisfied.
			17. In order to find out how things were going in the classroom, a teacher would:
			a. Use a questionnaire.
a		e	b. Hold a free and open discussion with the students.
			18. In a class, students would take responsibility for changing things that seem to make some students feel insecure, "put down," or useless.
			19. Suppose a rule were broken by a student in the cafeteria, halls, or parking lot. What is the chance another student would:
		f	a. Say something to this student?
			b. Tell a teacher?
a	d		c. Bring it up to student government?
b			d. Ignore it, and let a teacher catch him?
a			20. If a student were teased to a point of anger or tears, he would get help from some other student.
		e	21. Estimate the chance that if a group of students want to organize an extra-curricular sport, such as rugby, they would get support from the physical education department.
			22. Estimate the chance that in an activity group, the goals and projects of the group are set by:
a		e	a. The students alone.
b		f	b. The sponsor(s) alone.
a			c. The students and sponsor(s) together.
			23. Estimate the chance that in unsupervised areas (cafeteria, halls, parking lots) the rules for student behavior are set by:
	d	e	a. The student government alone.
b	c	e	b. The faculty alone.
a	d		c. The student government and faculty together.

Table 5-5 (continued)

Comparison

I	II	III	Item as Presented
			24. Estimate the chance that an activity group will be formed or abolished by:
a			a. A group of interested students.
b	c		b. The faculty sponsor(s).
a			c. A group of interested students and the sponsor(s).
a			25. Estimate the chance that if a member of an activity group is unhappy with a project or the way the project is being done, he would feel free to share these feelings with the group.
			26. Estimate the chance that after a project has been decided upon in an activity group:
	c		a. The sponsor sees that it gets done.
a			b. The entire group sees that it gets done.
			c. A subgroup sees that it gets done.

According to the perceptions of EHS students, for all those twenty-six events which 51 percent or more had agreed should occur more frequently, the frequency of its reported occurrence did in fact increase from September to May. Similarly, EHS students reported a lower relative frequency of occurrence in May than in September for all ten items on which a majority preferred a lower frequency of occurrence. Thus for each of that thirty-six items on which there was a majority consensus in September, there was by May an indication of the desired change. The probability of obtaining this degree of agreement between preference and observation by chance is infinitesimally small ($p < 1/10^8$ exact test).

We calculated these concordance rates for CHS also. In contrast to EHS, there was a slight tendency for observed changes between September and May to be in directions *opposite* to preferences. Of the twenty items for which there was consensus (at least 51 percent of the students agreeing on preferred direction of change), only five changed in the desired direction. (The probability of chance disagreement this large between preference and observation is less than .25 by exact test.) The smaller number of items on which a majority of CHS students indicated a preferred change (twenty, compared to thirty-six such items at EHS) was due, in part, to a larger number of "do not care" responses at CHS.

To see how representative of Oregon high schools these two schools (EHS and CHS) were, we administered the EDQ to 100-student samples from four additional schools. Though from quite widely dispersed geographic areas, the four schools were comparable in size to CHS and EHS. According to the EDQ data, we inferred that CHS resembled EHS more closely than it resembled any of the four additional schools. More generally, the data suggested that *both* EHS and CHS were somewhat deviant in the direction of greater interpersonal openness among both staff and students.

Figure 5-2 Students' Responses to Environmental Description Questionnaire at Intervals from Beginning to End of School Year

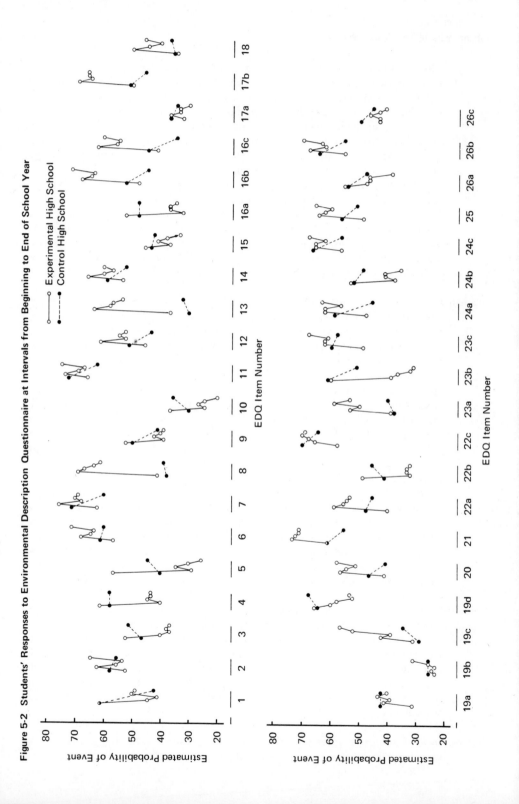

Observational and Anecdotal Data

The consultation staff had the opportunity to observe task-centered staff interactions during two staff meetings and during the day of in-service training in April. The staff behaved in a manner consistent with their self-descriptions on the SPQ. They seemed to be open and direct with one another and were skillful in their use of the language of observation and the language of introspection and empathy. Further they were earnestly trying to arrive at decisions of high quality without sacrificing commitment to carry out the decision; i.e., they attempted to find competent solutions to problems external to the staff as a social system while maintaining intra-system integrity. Conflict did not typically produce "flight" behavior, but was used instead to generate additional information; i.e., they attempted to use conflict constructively. Relations between teaching staff and administrators never appeared to be guarded or defensive. With rare exceptions, the principal modeled the skills (e.g., open communication and conjoint problem-solving) which had been emphasized in the summer laboratory experience.

Student-Faculty Relationships. Possibly most striking of all were the interactions between the staff and students; the faculty lounge was our center for observing these interactions. In line with what seemed to be a perpetual "open door policy," students would come in singly or in twos and threes (with no apparent feelings of uneasiness) to talk with individual members of the staff. In this lounge, where staff members took their coffee breaks, ate lunch, and held both formal and spontaneous discussions of school business, it was not unusual to see a teacher simultaneously eating lunch and tutoring a student. Next to that dyad might be two other teachers discussing a specific school problem while another teacher and a group of students planned a forthcoming event. Though many unrelated conversations were typically occurring at once, the noise level was not excessively high and there seemed to be an atmosphere of both seriousness and relaxation.

We were able to observe the student-faculty interactions in one other context. In our several administrations of the EDQ (each of which involved a departure from the daily academic schedule), we saw no confirmation of the widespread fear that the teacher who relates to students more on a person-to-person basis (as opposed to stylized role performance in keeping with given statuses) "loses control" of students. We observed very few instances of students responding to staff in ways which connoted disrespect or insensitivity.

Student-Student Relationships. A visitor to EHS could not help noticing a number of characteristics of student life which set this school off from the typical high school. Regardless of the hour or day that we visited, we were always impressed by the level of activity. Students were in motion—talking, arguing, laughing, meeting with teachers, etc. There was not, however, much horseplay; rather the atmosphere seemed more one of "creative chaos." Whether the students were more or less creative than in other schools, they appeared to be more involved in the school experience.

Staff-School Relationships. In spite of the selection procedures and training program, not every staff member was fully committed to the emerging organizational pattern.

In the spring, one teacher decided—conjointly with the principal—not to continue in the school during the coming year. He reported that he found the orientation to be stressful to him, that it exacerbated some of his basic fears about the morality of students in an unsupervised and unregulated situation. A second teacher decided to terminate also, although that decision was related more to a lack of personal commitment to any specific life goals than to a disagreement with the goals of EHS.

This school district has a regular practice of allowing teachers to request transfers between schools within the district if they wish. The fact that, in the spring, there were twenty-four requests for transfer *to* the experimental school and no requests for transfer *from* the school seemed to indicate considerable satisfaction with (or at least challenge by) the school among the teaching staff.

Caveat. Lest we give the impression that all hopes were realized during the first year of operation of EHS, we will reiterate some of the continuing problems which were recognized by both school personnel and consultation staff. In no particular order, the major concerns were the following:

1. The students seemed not to have the skills to take full advantage of the opportunities for self-government in academic affairs. This was especially true at the beginning of the school year, although in April there were still large differences between REP rooms (units of self-government) in terms of degree of involvement in student government.

2. A number of students did not have sufficient self-discipline to manage intelligently the amount of freedom they were given. Their "irresponsibility" most often took the form of wandering away from school during regular school hours (a particularly seductive Dairy Queen establishment was located nearby) and of failing to make normal progress in their academic learning.

3. Though the in-service training in April seemed at least partially to restore feelings of confidence and of competence, the faculty suffered a serious diminution of morale in late March and April. This "low phase" was attributed by many teachers to the recognition of the above two concerns.

Discussion and Conclusions

In this chapter we have briefly described a ten-day training program and continuing consultation provided for the staff of a newly formed high school. The impact of that learning experience on both the staff and students of the school has been the major focus. Although large amounts of data have been systematically collected and summarized in this effort, we believe that our results must depend upon external corroborating evidence for final confirmation, interpretation, and validation.

Both in practice and in principle, evaluation studies in a field setting lack the epistomological efficiency of laboratory research. As Campbell and Stanley (1963, p. 1) point out, not all important questions can be pursued "in the Fischer (1925, 1935) tradition in which an experimenter, having complete mastery, can schedule treatments and measurements for optimal efficiency, with [the details] of design emerging only from that goal of efficiency."

When it is not feasible to assign randomly a large number of cases (in the present study, the school faculty is, of course, the basic unit) to conditions which are under rigorous control for the duration of the experimental period, many variables which might influence the results remain uncontrolled; and the task of obtaining clear answers to theoretical and practical questions becomes much more difficult. Procedures by which one might approach the complex task of applied research are outlined by Campbell and Stanley's excellent article (1963).

It is clear, however, that what is lost in experimental power is counter-balanced, often very heavily, by the ecological or external validity of the results. We can be certain that the treatments in question do have a measurable effect within the environment with which we are concerned. Shaky extrapolation from a peculiar and simplified laboratory environment to a vastly more complex, interactive environment is not required to permit application of our knowledge.

Granting the problems of conducting rigorous field research on organization change, we could have increased the meaningfulness of these results had we had a somewhat more complicated design. For example, an ideal study would have had another comparison school whose faculty and students completed the questionnaires in September, received feedback regarding their responses, and completed the questionnaires again in May. Such an additional control group would have allowed some partialling out of effects deriving from data feedback alone (without training). The advantage of the additional control school not-withstanding, the extra cost in time and effort in data collection would have been prohibitive, had such a school been available.

For similar reasons of cost, we did not pay attention to a number of outcome measures and intervening variables (e.g., changes in *behavior* of teachers and students, amount of outside study, and achievement-test scores). Harrison reports significant improvement in achievement scores of students following an organization development intervention in the South Brunswick, N. J., school system (1970). That project, apparently much more extensive than the one reported in this paper, included some work with principals at labs sponsored by the National Training Laboratories before the training efforts on site with students and staff. According to Harrison, the students achieved high average scores on all four subjects (mathematics, science, reading, and social studies) of the Sequential Test of Education Progress (1970, p. 68). Efforts at assessing change in other kinds of organizations (e.g., Seashore and Bowers, 1970) yield results showing changes in what Likert calls "intervening variables" as well as changes in outcome variables (Likert and Bowers, 1969). Though it cannot be assumed that we would have obtained results comparable to the above-reported data, their consistency supports our hunch that our observed changes were probably paralleled by similar changes in intervening and outcome variables.

Without minimizing the limitations imposed by the design of this study, we would add that it is unlikely that any field study, however well-designed, can ever be sufficiently rigorous to provide the ultimate answers to critical ex-perimental questions. Converging evidence from sets of observations will almost surely be required. It is therefore most fortunate that the present results are paralleled by those of Schmuck, Runkel, and Langmeyer in Chapter 3 of this volume. This convergence of observations strengthens our confidence (1) that an interaction of subject selection and the treatment is not of primary importance in accounting for the results, and (2) that some (albeit unidentified) feature or interaction of features of the intervention *can* account for the results. For the methodological reasons discussed above, it is obvious that our observations, in isolation, cannot be assumed to generalize beyond a sample having the peculiarities of the EHS faculty. The fact that Schmuck's research yielded similar results in a sample with somewhat different characteristics gives us an indication that our results can be generalized to a less constricted population of faculties.

Further evidence for generalization of effects from our program of planned organizational change comes from the large number of EDQ items which show a net gain in positive expectations between September and May at EHS. Flanders (1968) and Neidt and Hedlund (1967) have found that students' attitudes toward school typically reflect increasing disenchantment from the beginning to the end of the school year. In comparison with students at CHS, EHS students usually manifested less loss of positive attitudes on those EDQ items which reflected net loss from September to May and often showed a gain in favorable attitudes, while CHS students reported a net loss. The EDQ results contrast sharply with other studies which also show a steady decay in enthusiasm regarding courses of study (Osborn, 1965) or methods of instruction (Devine, 1968). The EDQ results suggest that the organization development activities did produce a climate of openness and responsibility to which the students responded both in the classroom and in unsupervised areas.

Central to the interpretation of the present study is a consideration of the ways in which the procedures of our intervention and those of Schmuck and his associates are different and the ways in which they are similar and thus replicative. Though a point-by-point comparison of training procedures would reveal many differences, the aims of the two projects were nearly identical. The explicit objectives of both interventions were those of organization development; and even though personal growth and skill-building were among the subsidiary objectives of our program, the intervention had as its prime target the enhancement of system functioning.

Readers familiar with T-group or sensitivity training will recognize numerous points of similarity between the training procedures conducted for the client school and many sensitivity-training labs; however, some important differences need to be explicated. T-groups traditionally are focused on the personal growth of the individual participants, with the principal goal of increasing the awareness of self as a social object. Effort is made to facilitate the learning of concepts and skills in order to lead to "constructive openness." T-groups typically are comprised of persons who are initially strangers to one another; as a group, they have no history and no future.

In contrast, an organization development intervention focuses on organizational effectiveness (Argyris, 1962; Beckhard, 1969; Bennis, 1969; French, 1969; and Miles et al., 1967). Following systems theorists (e.g., Buckley, 1967), we assumed that the system which is most "open" is most adaptive to change and most effective. (In this context, "openness" refers to receptivity to inputs from the system environment—e.g., in the case of EHS this might include the district administration, parents, and townspeople.) Obviously, then, an OD intervention might incorporate some of the goals of T-group methods in the service of organizational objectives. Indeed Argyris (1962) argues that organizational effectiveness rests on a foundation of interpersonal *competence*. (The attribute to which he refers here is the same competence that traditional T-groups have sought to enhance.) In our view of an OD intervention, the interpersonal insights and skills become tools for evolving and clarifying *work-related* norms, customs, procedures, and policies which facilitate achievement of the organizational mission.

A slight digression to consider the meaning of the term "norm" might clarify how we view OD effects in general and OD effects at EHS. By "norm" we mean the expectations shared by members of a social system regarding the way in which the occupant of a particular role position should behave. If norms are prescribed by authority figures and enforced by management via a system of rewards and punishments, we might speak of "external" control. This approach to organizational control has been criticized by those who favor a "human relations" emphasis in management or administration (e.g., Argyris, 1962; McGregor, 1960). The "human relations" proponents contend that members of an organization are capable of evolving norms to which they feel committed and which enhance organizational effectiveness. Organizational norms developed in this manner are commonly thought to be self- and peer-enforced, yielding what might thereby be called "internal" control. And the development of "internal" control is a critical part of what we are calling OD intervention.

As previously stated, we shared with the Schmuck group a conception and commitment to organization development as the focus of the interventions; and, in spite of the differences in small details of design and the personalities of the training teams, there was great similarity in general philosophy. Common sets of concepts and skills were presented. Parallel results in the two studies suggest, therefore, that it was the broader similarities rather than the narrow details which were the effective features of both experimental designs.

A flaw in our study was a departure from experimental design. We began the study with three basic questions: (1) Will a ten-day laboratory learning experience have measurable immediate impact upon the participants? (2) To what extent will the impact endure? and (3) Will the changes in faculty produce changes in student behavior both in the classroom and in unsupervised areas? It was important, therefore, for the consulting staff to interact with students as little as possible, administering the EDQ and nothing beyond that. Yet, as we pointed out earlier, we spent one day working with members of the student government.

Probably no other departure from the research design muddies our conclusions as much as this one. Naturally, it was important that we refrain from engaging in training activities with students if we wanted to regard EDQ data (changes in students' perceptions) as a major class of dependent variables. Three of us spent most of one school day with members of student government; and, although the time was not great, these students seemed to learn a great deal. What is most important for our conclusions is that these students probably were among the most influential in the entire student body, so that one could argue that our one-day effort with them accounted for much of the change in EDQ results over the year.

As a summary of the findings of the present research, we advance the following: an organization development intervention in a new senior high school had an effect upon both faculty and students in that (1) teachers exhibited greater interpersonal openness, and (2) students saw the faculty as more receptive to student ideas, opinions, and attitudes, and as a result they became more co-active with the staff in making decisions affecting their learning, they developed stronger feelings of responsibility toward fellow students and faculty, and they developed stronger student-enforced "internal" norms bearing on behavior in unsupervised areas as well as in the classroom.

Several important questions remain. Further studies will be required to determine the extent to which organization development interventions depend on a favorable psychological setting: if not a climate of enthusiasm, at least a willingness on the part of participants to experiment with new ways of functioning. Similarly, additional investigations are needed to determine the forces which influence the rate of "fade-out" of obtained effects.

References

Argyris, C. 1962. *Interpersonal competence and organizational effectiveness.* Homewood, Illinois: Irwin.

Beckhard, R. 1969. *Organization development: strategies and models.* Reading, Massachusetts: Addison-Wesley.

Bennis, W. G. 1969. *Organization development: its nature, origin, and prospects.* Reading, Massachusetts: Addison-Wesley.

Brissey, F. L. 1968. *Personal communication.* Vancouver: University of British Columbia, School of Education.

Buckley, W. 1967. *Sociology and modern systems theory.* Englewood Cliffs, N. J.: Prentice-Hall.

Campbell, D. T., and Stanley, J. C. 1963. *Experimental and quasi-experimental designs for research.* Chicago: Rand McNally.

Campbell, J. P., and Dunnette, M. D. 1968. Effectiveness of T-group experiences in managerial training and development. *Psychological Bulletin* 70:73-104.

Dayal, I., and Thomas, J. M. 1968. Operation KPE: developing a new organization. *Journal of Applied Behavioral Science* 4:473-506.

Devine, D. F. 1968. Student attitudes and achievement: a comparison between the effects of programmed instruction and classroom approach to teaching algebra. *Mathematics Teacher* 61:296-301.

Etzioni, A. 1964. *Modern organizations.* Englewood Cliffs, N. J.: Prentice-Hall.

Fisher, R. A. 1925. *Statistical methods for research workers.* London: Oliver and Boyd.

____. 1935. *The design of experiments.* London: Oliver and Boyd.

Flanders, N. 1964. *Interaction analysis in the classroom: a manual for observers.* Ann Arbor: University of Michigan.

____. 1968. Changes in pupil attitudes during the school year. *Journal of Educational Psychology* 59:334-38.

Fosmire, F. R., and Keutzer, C. 1968. Task-directed learning: a systems-analysis approach to marital therapy. Paper presented at OPA-WSPA meeting, May 1968 at Crystal Mountain, Washington. Eugene, Oregon: University of Oregon. Mimeographed.

French, W. 1969. Organization development: objectives, assumptions, and strategies. *California Management Review* 12:23-34.

Hall, J.; O'Leary, V.; and Williams, M. 1963. The decision-making grid: an analysis of individual behavior in the decision-making group. Austin, Texas: University of Texas. Mimeographed.

____. 1964. The decision-making grid: a model of decision-making styles. *California Management Review,* Winter, pp. 43-54.

Harrison, C. H. 1970. Schools put a town on the map. *Saturday Review,* February 21.

Hays, W. *Statistics for psychologists.* 1963. New York: Holt, Rinehart, and Winston.

Keutzer, C., and Fosmire, F. R. 1968. *Situation prediction questionnaire.* Eugene, Oregon: University of Oregon.

____; Fosmire, F. R.; Diller, R.; and Smith, M. D. 1969. Laboratory training in a new social system: evaluation of a two-week program for high school personnel. Eugene, Oregon: University of Oregon. Mimeographed.

Likert, R., and Bowers, D. G. 1969. Organizational theory and human resources accounting. *American Psychologist,* 24:585-92.

Luft, J. 1969. *Of human interaction.* Palo Alto, California: National Press Books.

_____ , and Ingham, H. 1955. *The Johari window, a graphic model for interpersonal relations.* Los Angeles: University of California at Los Angeles Extension Office, Western Training Laboratory in Group Development.

McGregor, D. 1960. *The human side of enterprise.* New York: McGraw-Hill.

Meyers, J. L. 1966. *Fundamentals of experimental design.* Boston: Allyn and Bacon.

Miles, M. B., et al. 1967. The clinical-experimental approach to assessing organizational change efforts. *Journal of Applied Behavioral Science* 3:347-80.

Neidt, C. O., and Hedlund, D. E. 1967. Relationship between change in attitude toward a course and final achievement. *Journal of Educational Research* 61:56-58.

Osborn, K. H. 1965. A longitudinal study of achievement in and attitude toward mathematics of selected students using School Mathematics Study Group materials. *Dissertation Abstracts* 26121, p. 7119.

Schein, E. H. 1969. *Process consultation: its role in organization development.* Reading, Massachusetts: Addison-Wesley.

Schmuck, R. A., and Runkel, P. J. 1970. *Organizational training for a school faculty.* Eugene, Oregon: University of Oregon, CASEA.

_____ ; and Runkel, P. J.; and Langmeyer, D. 1969. Improving organization problem-solving in a school faculty. *Journal of Applied Behavioral Science* 5:455-82. (Revised slightly as Chapter 3 of this volume.)

Seashore, S. E., and Bowers, D. G. 1970. Durability of organizational change. *American Psychologist* 25:227-33.

Tuckman, B. W. 1965. Developmental sequence in small groups. *Psychological Bulletin* 63:384-99.

Wallen, J. L. 1966a. *Group expectations survey: form Q.* Portland, Oregon. Mimeographed.

_____ . 1966b. *Openness in human relations: Group task.* Portland, Oregon. Mimeographed.

_____ . 1967a. Skills in helping others understand you as a person (and supplemental exercises, "Communication of feelings F-1, F-2, and F-3"). Portland, Oregon. Mimeographed.

_____ . 1967b. *The interpersonal gap.* Portland, Oregon: Northwest Regional Education Laboratory.

6

USING SURVEY FEEDBACK
AND CONSULTATION*

Charles T. McElvaney and Matthew B. Miles

The public face presented by many educators expresses interest in educational research. Most administrators and teachers have participated—if not in a committed way, at least willingly—in a research project. But the public face often belies hidden reticence and cynicism about the research process and the usefulness of the results.

Data collected from questionnaires generally have not been useful to school people. The results often are not fed back, and even if they are, they are difficult to understand and use. The data are arranged in elaborate tables printed in obscure journals, and at best serve to help someone earn a doctorate. Although research is credited with importance, it does not seem to have had much payoff for the practical educator.

Data that are collected for the purpose of an OD intervention can be quite different in effect, however, as this chapter indicates. When survey data deal with matters of strong relevance and concern to the people in an intact working group, analyzing and interpreting them involves strong feelings and can lead to active problem-solving and change.

One of the useful contributions of this article is the explicitly-worked-out model showing just how and why survey feedback has its effects as an intervention mode. The reader may wish to apply the model to the account in Chapter 8, where data feedback failed to be useful in the work of the change agent teams.

In this study, data feedback was the main intervention mode, leading on into active problem-solving and coaching help for the top administrative team. It should be pointed out that data feedback could also be accompanied by "teaching" interventions (such as the communication skills and group process exercises described in Chapters 3, 4, and 5), to aid active problem-solving in the course of organization improvement.

Survey feedback is a procedure in which outside consultants and members of a system collaboratively gather, analyze, and interpret data that deal with various aspects of the system's functioning, and its members' professional lives. Using

* This chapter was adapted from Charles T. McElvaney and Matthew B. Miles, "The School Psychologist as a Change Agent: Improving a School System Through Survey Feedback Methods," in G. B. Gottsegen and M. G. Gottsegen, *Professional School Psychology*, III, (New York: Grune and Stratton, Inc., 1969), by permission of the publisher.

such data as a base, the participants, with consultative help, begin problem-solving efforts to improve the organizational processes and the working relationships among members.

Background

This project began with the assumption that it is essential to help school districts become *fundamentally* healthier rather than to help them solve only short-term problems. It was an attempt to go deeper, to improve the basic capacity of the school organization to survive and cope more adequately.

This assumption came from experience in two lines of work. First, there was the area of educational innovation: it had become more and more apparent that school district innovativeness really depends on "organization health," rather than on the efforts of isolated "hero innovators" as such. Intelligent innovation and its adoption are much more dependent on systems than on persons (Miles, 1965). The second influence on the project came from work in the industrial organization improvement area. Much recent work there has stressed technologies for planned change aimed at increasing the accuracy of internal communication, aiding the ability of subordinates to influence upward, and improving the procedures of problem-solving by administrative teams—approaches which try, in effect, to introduce more openness, trust, and collaborative activity into the culture of an organization. (See Bennis, 1963.) This project was devoted to adapting the tactics of organizational change used in industrial settings to the special case of schools (Bidwell, 1965; and Miles, 1967), trying them out, and assessing the consequences.

Organization Health

Some Prime Assumptions

We assumed that an organizationally healthy system could not only cope with short-term problems, but would survive—would continue to cope adequately over time—and would also continuously develop and extend its own coping activities. In short, a healthy organization was felt to be a self-renewing one (Miles, 1965).

Two particularly crucial organizational health variables examined in this survey feedback project were *communication adequacy* (how easily information travels in the organization, without distortion) and *power equalization* (a collaborative stance toward work, as contrasted with the exercise of arbitrary authority based on position). Both these variables are related to the area of *problem-solving* as a kind of master dimension of effective organization.

Some Underlying Assumptions

The approaches to industrial organization change which we now planned to use in the field of education share certain basic assumptions.

Self-Study Emphasis. The first assumption is that change efforts should involve members of a district themselves in examining the way their own organization, with its groups, roles and relationships, actually works. The data used in this study were a kind of mirror into which the members of the school district could look as a basis for self-corrective action. This approach stands in sharp contrast to approaches which depend on expert consultants recommending specific organizational changes.

Problem-Solving Focus. Motivation to change, as we will see, is sharpened by looking at survey feedback data, and by efforts to improve such skills as problem identification, problem diagnosis, and solution invention. Problem-solving is a kind of master skill, and is especially crucial at the managerial level. The criterion for management success is often the degree to which problems are solved systematically and productively as they come up.

At the process level, a problem-solving approach requires high openness of mind, and cooperation. If good solutions are to be obtained, full data must be available. Secondly, good problem-solving techniques require relatively equalized power, so that decisions can be made more on the basis of accurate information and competence than because someone in a position of formal authority says so. Thus, shared decision-making becomes more central in these improvement approaches and ideally has two effects: the decisions are of higher quality because they are made on the basis of more accurate information, and people are more committed to carrying them out. Hence, the importance of organizational norms which support openness, trust, collaboration, and willingness to change.

Off-the-Job Meetings. These approaches also involve off-site meetings of an intensive sort—usually lasting from two to ten days. Off-the-job meetings not only reduce work pressure but also enable organization members to take a self-corrective view. By analogy, it is impossible to repair a bicycle while you are riding it. Just as one must get off a bicycle while it is being examined for repairs, one has to get out of the organization, temporarily, to take a careful look at how the system is working. Such off-site meetings also offer a chance to change norms—to build a climate with more openness and more support for efforts to change.

How Survey Feedback Works

Survey feedback is an example of the planned-change processes we have been discussing above. From the start, the "client system" is usually actively involved, as Mann (1961) and Neff (1965) have pointed out. Optimally, participants themselves define the kinds of data needed and plan for the data collection. Characteristically, the instruments deal with "soft" data: employee satisfaction, concern about problems, perceived influence of self and superiors in decision-making, perception of norms and goals, and the like. It is very desirable to get "hard" data as well—that is, information on goal achievement, turnover, and cost—which let the members of the system see how well they are doing. Ordinarily, the data are fed back to an intact work "family"—people who report to a common superior, and whose jobs are interlocked in a meaningful way. The group members and their superior then begin examining and interpreting the data, start problem-solving in relation to the diagnoses they make from the data, and begin to bring about changes in both their own relationships and the home organization. Characteristically, this process then trickles further down through the organization, so that the people who were subordinates in the first meeting then lead meetings with *their* subordinates around the same set of data, and the process continues.

Figure 6-1 reviews our conceptualization of the reasons why survey feedback works. Why should it be that this process of feeding back survey data to the members of an organization and engaging them in problem-solving brings about healthy change in an organization?

Components of Feedback

Starting at the left, the process is seen as having three major components: data, meetings, and process analysis.

Data. When people start looking at the data, the information usually both corroborates their feelings and disconfirms them. Disconfirmation is usually a powerful pressure for change. Participants begin to raise questions about the data: "How could people have answered that way? They could not have answered that way. Well, they did. What does that really say about our school district?" Such questions themselves increase attention to the data and concern about the problems which they indicate. Participants stop denying the validity of the data and begin to acknowledge, for instance, that "these data on morale are really disastrous. We have to *do* something about this problem." Focused change goals (at the right of Figure 6-1) tend to emerge.

Meetings. The second component, at the left of Figure 6-1, is the meetings run by relevant work groups in the organization. Ideally, of course, they are successful. If they are not successful at first, that tends to intensify the motivation to work hard. In any event, radically increased interaction is taking place: people who ordinarily have little to say to each other talk very much, very intensively. The more one interacts with others in a valued setting, the more favorable are the attitudes both toward the task and toward the colleagues engaged in this mutual effort. Pressure to clarify one's own position during the problem-solving grows, and various pressures toward conformity occur. For example, there tends to be pressure for people to acknowledge rather than to run away from the data, and to agree that a certain goal has high priority. Conformity pressures can become strong enough, of course, to enfeeble problem-solving; people "go along" and avoid unpopular ideas and issues.

Process Analysis. The major way out of this problem of conformity, as we and others have found, is the process analysis approach—the third component at the left in Figure 6-1. This in some respects is the most fundamental component. During the course of data study, outside consultants occasionally help the people concerned to study realistically and in detail their processes, what is happening here and now in the group. For example, in the project we describe below, the data showed very clearly that the supervising principal and his associate were far apart on many issues. More and more as the meetings progressed, it became clear

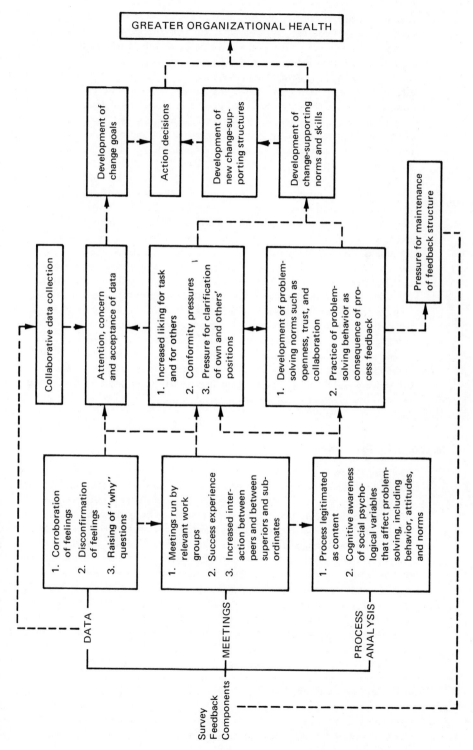

Figure 6-1 Reasons for Success of Survey Feedback

that they were in conflict with each other. Rather than avoid the problem, the authors, as outside consultants, tried to help the group examine the conflict between the two top men and the ways in which it was made evident (interruptions, failure to listen, etc.). We also helped the group to examine and discuss other issues: how trusting they were, their methods of making decisions, the effectiveness of their problem-solving, and the fact that the principals were talking much less than central office people as work proceeded.

The essence of process analysis, then, is that from time to time the group examines the procedures by which problems are being solved and discusses them. Behavior and feelings are recognized as legitimate content, rather than being discussed outside the meeting or afterwards.

Process analysis is fairly fundamental to the success of survey feedback. Through it, people become more aware of the human factors which bear on problem-solving efforts in organizations. Process analysis also tends to develop new norms supporting problem-solving: the more participants analyze the process, the more open they become. Behavior, after all, cannot be hidden. Process analysis helps participants to realize the actual effects of behavior. As participants become more open and trustful, their relationships become more collaborative. If, for example, the boss is doing something arbitrary and ineffective and a subordinate comments on it, the comment itself tends to rob the boss of the power to do such things in the future. Process analysis, by providing immediate feedback, also helps people to become more skillful at problem-solving and to display more collaborative behavior.

Such norms and behaviors also tend to operate as a pressure to keep the survey feedback structure *itself* going; superiors tend to feel that the data should be actively discussed by their subordinates, and the survey feedback model may be used recurrently through the subsequent months and years of the organization's life.

Effects on the Organization

The right side of Figure 6-1 displays large-scale organization change effects which are likely to occur. Continual re-examination of the data, as suggested earlier, tends to create new change goals, such as the improvement of communication between teachers and principals. The group also begins to make action decisions regarding the real life of the organization (for example, devoting more budget money to in-service workshops.) Ideally, such decisions are supported both by the norms and skills which support change and by new change-supporting structures. For example, the group may decide on more frequent off-site meetings, or an advisory council, or a research and development group, or a new troubleshooting consulting role to work on innovation diffusion problems. In short, the group tends to build new structures which are specifically devoted to the support of further change in the organization.

The Use of Survey Feedback in Schools

Some of the questions most frequently raised about the nature of survey feedback in school districts are as follows:

1. Q. What kind of data is usually collected?

A. Typically, attitude and opinion data about such matters as communication, decision-making, whether one's job is experienced as a "good fit," and the effectiveness of one's superior. If possible, hard data about organizational achievement should also be collected. In the case of schools, this can include achievement test results, mental health records, or other indicators of school district effectiveness.

2. Q. How are data collection instruments designed?

A. In a spirit of collaboration. It is desirable to sit down together with the participants and ask, "What questions do we want to know about?" and then build the questionnaires together with those who are to answer them. The more the "client system" can be involved, the better. As the arrow at the top of Figure 6-1 indicates, collaboration in the design of data collection procedures makes it more likely that the data will be "bought" by the participants later on.

3. Q. In what form are data fed back?

A. Characteristically, data are fed back in an anonymous way, either by role group (e.g., all principals), or by subunits (departments or buildings). Even when groups are small (e.g., the three administrators in the project described below) it is still important to present the data anonymously so as to avoid unproductive anxiety.

4. Q. How far down in the organization should data be collected?

A. Data are richer if they include the reactions of participants at lower status levels, because that is where the "real work gets done"—where the actual production procedures take place. Ideally, therefore, one ought to go as far down in the organizational structure as is possible.

5. Q. How about collecting data from students?

A. This is highly desirable. Though we limited the project discussed below to adults, adding student data would undoubtedly have enriched it. Gage, Runkel, and Chatterjee (1963) did a study of student feedback to teachers in which they showed that such feedback—even if conducted by mail—could affect teaching behavior favorably.

Survey Feedback Sessions with Green Meadows Personnel

Our first contacts with the experimental district, which we labeled "Green Meadows," occurred in late 1964. Table 6-1 gives an idea of the time sequence. Through the assistance of Dr. McElvaney, the Green Meadows School District volunteered to participate initially as a "control" district—filling out questionnaires on the understanding that professional personnel would receive a general report of the results. As table 6-1 shows, the first three measures (0_1, 0_2, and 0_3) were collected at the same time as parallel measurements made in another school district, South Stanton, which was then undergoing organization development training (See Benedict, Calder, Callahan, Hornstein, and Miles, 1967).

Table 6-1 Research and Intervention Design

Season	Year	Event	Sample Size
Early fall	1964	0_1	33%[a]
Midwinter	1964-5	0_2	33%[a]
Late spring	1965	0_3	100%
June	1965	X[b] Phase I	
Fall	1965	X[c] Phase II	
Midwinter	1965-6	0_4	100%
January	1967	X[d] Phase III	
Late winter	1967	0_5	100%[e]
Late spring	1967	0_6	100%[e]

[a]This included a random sample of teachers, and all administrators and principals.

[b]The initial data feedback meetings (four days) took place at this time. All central office administrators and principals participated; a selection of the 0_3 data was used.

[c]The data were fed back by principals to building faculty meetings as a basis for problem-solving; cross-building committee work began.

[d]A follow-up team training and problem-solving meeting took place at this time. Open-end questionnaire data were collected from administrators, principals, and supervisors and fed back to a three-day meeting of these persons, both prior to and during the meeting.

[e]A considerably reduced research package was used.

Green Meadows is on the edge of a large industrial city. The community is largely lower middle class and upper lower class; many of the men work in a single large manufacturing plant. There is a fairly large group of Italian descent, and a Negro community provides about 8 percent of the school population. Green Meadows was formed three years ago from four previously separate districts. The present supervising principal of the district was formerly the head of one of the districts. The plant includes a senior high school, two junior high schools, and eight elementary buildings. The staff includes only four elementary principals, however, since three of them are in charge of more than one building. There are about 250 professional personnel, and about 4,400 students.

Though it had not originally been planned that way, we began to get more and more interested in the possibility of carrying out a survey feedback design with Green Meadows. We proposed, "Rather than have a report on paper, how would you like it if we brought the data down to a meeting of the administrators and principals? We'll interpret them together, see what sense they make, and then the same process can be repeated at the building level with teachers. We think that would be a lot more meaningful." They agreed, and it was jointly decided to carry out the initial survey feedback design in June of 1965. Measurement took place about six months afterwards to assess follow-up effects, and 0_5 and 0_6 took place 18 and 22 months afterwards, respectively. An additional follow-up training meeting was held in January of 1967, prior to measurements 0_5 and 0_6.

We agreed that participants would go to a motel near the district for a four-day meeting. There were eleven participants from the district, including the supervising principal, his associate, the business manager, three secondary principals, and four elementary principals. In addition, there were four psychologists (including Dr. McElvaney) from the county office, two outside trainers (Matthew Miles and Bernard Bass), a data manager (Paula Calder), and two research observers (Steven Schiavo and Barbara Benedict)—a total of twenty people. Exhibit 1, which was given to participants, shows the range of data available to them; large amount that it was, it included only about half the data that we had collected. Some data were withheld to leave them "uncontaminated" by the discussion of particular items. The school district participants also brought along hard data on personnel turnover, schooltime accidents, and finances.

Exhibit 1   Data Available to Participants in the Four-Day Meeting

As you will recall, a wide variety of information was collected, using a total of ten different instruments.

To catalog all of the data which are available for use during the four days would be unnecessarily specific (and exhausting). It may be helpful, however, to make a listing of the types of data which can be called on as needed. The staff will help with suggestions when the group is planning which data to look at next.

The following general types of information are available:

A. Problems seen by people (for example, "poor relations with parents").

B. How satisfied people are with their contacts with various other roles.

C. How well people feel they fit their jobs.

D. How innovative people feel the district is.

E. The importance people attach to different aspects of their jobs, and how rewarded they feel in fulfilling them.

F. The general climate of the school district, as it shows up in informal codes of behavior—"do's and don'ts."

G. Various aspects of the administrative climate in each building, with focus on the behavior of the principal and the teachers.

H. The way in which decisions are actually made, and the way in which they "should" be made.

I. Principal-teacher relationships in each building.

J. Teachers' perceptions of how well the principal carries out various aspects of his job.

K. Relationships between principals and their immediate superior.

L. Goals of the school district and how they are seen by various roles.

M. Morale.

N. How the school district relates to the surrounding community.

O. How clear the communication is between various roles.

P. Student interest in school, as seen by teachers.

For most of the above topics, we have information for the district as a whole, information broken down by different roles (principal, teacher, administrator, etc.) and information broken down by building groups.

In some cases, we have been able to show how two items relate to each other. For example, it is possible to see whether teachers who participate a great deal in decision-making turn out to have students who show high interest. Again, it would not be helpful to detail all the available data. Generally, we have been able to plot the relationship between selected pairs of the items in this list:

a. Teacher morale.

b. Principal-teacher relationships.

c. Student interest in school, as seen by teachers.

d. Various problems as seen by different roles (for example, "poor relations with parents").

e. Principal's behavior as seen by teachers.

f. Participation in decision-making.

As the conference goes on, if other aspects of the data look promising, it may be possible with computer or hand tabulation to look at them as well.

Exhibit 2 Participation in Decision-Making as Seen by Teachers

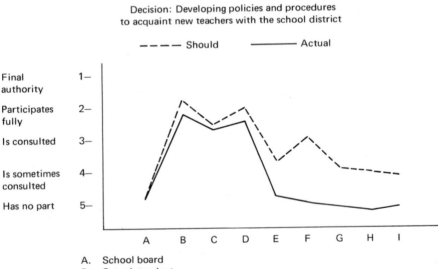

Decision: Developing policies and procedures to acquaint new teachers with the school district

‑ ‑ ‑ ‑ Should   ———— Actual

Final authority   1—
Participates fully   2—
Is consulted   3—
Is sometimes consulted   4—
Has no part   5—

A B C D E F G H I

A. School board
B. Superintendent
C. Administrators as a group
D. Principal of local school
E. Teacher faculties in the local school or department
F. Supervisors
G. Representative committee of teachers
H. Local teacher's professional organization
I. Individual teachers

Directions for "should": Generally when a decision has to be made in a school district, people have some idea about who *should* have a part in making the decision. There is the idea that particular individuals or groups *ideally ought* to be consulted, even though in fact, sometimes they may not be.

(As you think about the following decisions, please remember to think about what should, ideally, happen, rather than what official policy may hold, or what may occur in reality.)

Directions for "actual": In this section, we would like you to forget all about your answers in the last section, and think about the way things *actually* happen in this school district. Please bring to mind decisions that have been made in reality, and which persons or groups participated in making them.

Exhibit 2 is a sample data display, which shows, for example, that teachers believe that they should have considerably more to say about the particular decision noted there than they do in fact. On the other hand, teachers think that the superintendent (or "supervising principal" as the role is called in Green Meadows), the board, and the administrators as a group have about the right amount of power. It should be noted, by the way, that the superintendent, and not the board, is seen by teachers as having the most power.

Exhibit 3 is another display, focusing on goals. At the top one can see how the seven principals ranked the importance of ten different educational goals. Below is shown how teachers thought the principals *would* rank them. In effect, this is a measure of how accurately teachers really understood what the principals' educational priorities were. There was a total of about forty displays, some showing the relationship of two variables as well.

Exhibit 3 Principals' Goals

(Seven principals' ranking of goals in first table; principals' goals as 113 teachers think the principals would rank them in the second table)

Principals' Ranking of Goals	Importance Ranking				
	1	2	3	4	5
Dropout rate	0	0	1	0	6
Basic skills	0	0	1	1	5
Physical health and safety	1	0	1	0	5
Motivation and desire to learn	1	3	1	1	1
Disadvantaged children	0	1	2	1	3
College attendance	0	0	0	0	7
Discipline	0	0	1	0	6
Academic achievement	5	1	0	0	1
Moral, ethical, and patriotic concerns	0	2	0	3	2
Gifted or talented children	0	0	0	1	6

Teachers View of How Principals Would Rank Goals	Importance Ranking				
	1	2	3	4	5
Dropout rate	5	4	4	3	97
Basic skills	17	5	4	5	82
Physical health and safety	3	4	12	9	85
Motivation and desire to learn	33	28	15	10	27
Disadvantaged children	7	7	20	10	69
College attendance	1	3	2	3	104
Discipline	5	13	10	18	67
Academic achievement	28	28	16	11	30
Moral, ethical, and patriotic concerns	4	11	18	20	59
Gifted or talented children	6	3	7	19	78

The Initial Feedback Meetings

At these meetings themselves, participants had several types of experience over the four days.

Data Discussion. This involved simply looking at data, interpreting it, discussing it, arguing about it, trying to understand its causes. At first the group examined the data piece by piece, then they asked for and looked at the entire record of data for recurring themes. On request, we went to a nearby computer center and broke some of the data out by building, so that principals could see how their buildings compared with others.

Problem Identification Groups. Small groups met to identify perceived basic problems in Green Meadows, and then focused on particular data displays that could help in diagnosing the problems. Examples of problems which they identified were the school district's philosophy, inadequate communication in the district, vague role definition, deterioration of staff meeting quality since the previous year, and inadequate involvement of teachers and principals in decision-making.

Theory Sessions. The outside consultants sometimes gave short lectures on topics such as trust, decision-making, and the operation of groups in the context of organizations. In all cases, the attempt was made to link such concepts closely with what was actually happening. For example, on the first day, the participants seemed in initial discussion to be very "closed," non-trusting, and rigid. They were asked to break into small groups and generate examples of non-trusting behavior they had noticed. They came back with an enormous array of specific non-trusting behaviors (such as not talking about the names of specific teachers about whom they were concerned); this was followed by a brief lecture on the importance of trust and trust-building in organizational functioning.

Process Analysis. From time to time the group, with the trainers' help, discussed their own problem-solving processes, their feelings about the progress of the sessions, and their relationships with each other. This was occasionally helped by "mini-feedback," or brief summaries of data from reaction sheets filled out by participants during the sessions.

Task Forces. Small *ad hoc* groups were formed to discuss particular problems, such as involvement of principals in decision-making. These groups then made recommendations for improvement.

Planning for Next Steps. The group spent much time in making plans for their own future meetings, including methods for feeding data back to teachers in building meetings. They also discussed ways in which county office staff could serve as consultants. In general, the group took more and more responsibility for their own fate over the four days.

Immediate Effects on the School District

The initial purpose of the four-day meeting was to help the administrative staff interpret and analyze data from the survey instruments. However, during this period, the administrative staff became increasingly concerned with problems of organizational health as highlighted by the data and agreed that they should make plans to deal with them. It was during this phase that Dr. McElvaney's role as an inside change agent emerged. It became apparent to the staff that in order to solve their problems it was first necessary for them to improve their functioning as an administrative group. The feedback data brought them into confrontation with rather serious problems arising out of inadequate decision-making procedures, poor and distorted communications, ill-defined roles, and personal rivalries.

Action Decisions Made at Survey Feedback Sessions

In considering how they might organize and learn to work together more effectively, the administrators made three major decisions at the four-day conference.

Staff Meetings. After considerable discussion, the administrators decided that they would have periodic staff meetings to discuss crucial problems and, it was hoped, reach agreement on what to do about them. The staff, however, expressed considerable doubt as to whether staff meetings should be revived, since they had initiated such meetings the previous year but had discontinued them because they were unproductive. They pointed out an example of unproductive behavior: at one staff meeting the previous year they had spent practically all of one morning in trying to decide where to install an electrical outlet in a classroom.

Feedback to Teachers. The administrators decided that each building principal would hold periodic meetings with his staff to discuss the survey results. They had agreed that the principals would attempt to involve teachers in discussion and encourage an expression of their feelings and ideas. They generally agreed that this would be in marked contrast to their usual principal-teacher staff meetings, where discussion was minimal. The research team agreed to summarize the data in booklet form for the teachers.

Use of Consultant. The third decision made by administrators was to request the psychologist, Dr. McElvaney, to act as consultant for the administrative staff meetings and also to consult with the principals about their teacher meetings.

For the participating school psychologist, this was the most important decision made at the four-day meeting, since the administrative staff was asking him to perform in a new role. Several factors were probably important in influencing this decision. Certainly the four-day conference itself was an important factor; discussion had been focused on district organizational problems and attention had also been given to considering the way in which a psychologist might be helpful in dealing with such problems. However, this alone was not sufficient reason for the administrators to request a psychologist to help them cope with real problems on a more intimate level. Judging by the informal comments of the administrative staff, they tended to perceive the psychologist as being helpful (or at least as interested in helping), rather supportive, and concerned about their *organizational* problems. This view probably helped legitimize his new role as consultant or change agent by the end of the four-day conference.

Consultation Activities at Green Meadows

At the beginning of the 1965-66 school year, then, the psychologist became a consultant to the administrative staff. He was asked to attend the staff meetings of the administrators and principals to help make them more productive. He was also asked to consult with the principals on their teacher meetings. At the beginning, he was uncertain—even a bit apprehensive—as to how the staff would perceive his attempts to fulfill these new functions. He also questioned his ability to help the staff improve its ability to work together. The fact that he had no previous experience in working in this way with an administrative group added to his concern.

The First Green Meadows Staff Meeting

The following rather detailed report of the first staff meeting, held September 9, 1965 (also the first in which the psychologist participated), is presented in order to convey some understanding of the kinds of problems presented and the way in which they were discussed.

Present at the first meeting were the supervising principal (the administrative head of the school district), the business manager, and all the principals. The associate or assistant supervising principal for the district was absent because of illness.

The first forty-five minutes of the meeting were taken up by the business manager, who explained routine matters. The supervising principal later apologized for including this on the agenda and indicated that in the future he would instead attempt to disseminate routine information by written announcements whenever possible. (This policy was generally followed in subsequent meetings.) There followed some discussion of a teacher evaluation form that the supervising principal, with the help of the principals, had devised. The supervising principal made provision for self-rating by the teachers, followed by the principal's evaluation. The principals agreed to revise the form. Although the point was raised, the supervising principal did not ask that teachers make suggestions for revising the form.

The staff then discussed the series of principal-teacher feedback meetings which they had agreed to hold. At these meetings, the principals were to lead discussions on the survey data. They were to encourage teachers to express their ideas, attitudes, and feelings as openly as possible. After considerable discussion, decisions were made on length and frequency of meetings. It was agreed that meetings would be held once each week. (Later, however, the decision was made to give teachers released time and to hold longer meetings—about two hours in length—once a month.) The principals' primary concerns were their role in conducting the meetings and the consultative help which they might receive.

At the four-day meeting in June, the staff had requested that the principals consult with the psychologist *on an individual basis* prior to their teacher meetings. At the staff meeting, though, the principals decided that they would prefer to meet *as a group* with the psychologist both before their teacher meetings for planning and after the meetings for a post-mortem.

It was apparent that most of the principals were quite anxious about the prospect of having meetings in which teachers would be encouraged to express their feelings and ideas regarding the survey data. The principals were accustomed to conducting their teaching staff meetings in a more formal and traditional manner. Staff meetings had been held primarily for the purpose of giving teachers information; communication was primarily one-way—from the principal to the teachers. Now the principals were to encourage two-way communication. Not only would their teachers express their own ideas about the content of the data but the principals would also attempt to establish a climate and a norm supporting teachers' expression of *feelings*. Several principals expressed concern that the meetings might get out of hand and that they would not be able to cope with the situation. The principals remained anxious, even though we discussed together how they might handle their first meeting. However, the level of anxiety decreased remarkably after their first teacher meeting, when the principals found that the meetings did not "blow up" (an expression used by one principal to describe how his first meeting might end).

Following the discussion on principal-teacher meetings, the supervising principal introduced the question of the psychologist's role in the staff meetings. The group seemed quite vague in its view of what this role might be. Expressions such as "keep us on the ball" and "help bail us out when we get in trouble" were not very explicit. One principal did suggest that the psychologist act as a resource person for specific information. The psychologist suggested that it might be helpful if he played the part of a "participant-observer"; he would feel free to enter discussions in regard to content, but would also pay some attention to how the group was functioning. For example, when he felt the group was side-tracked on an unimportant detail or issue, he would call it to their attention. He also said he felt that one of the main purposes of the staff meetings would be to improve communication and cooperative planning among the administrative staff. In order to help achieve these goals, he would be interested in seeing that everyone expressed his feelings and ideas. He also pointed out that the supervising principal's role was that of the leader of the group, and that his own role as consultant should not be confused with the supervising principal's role. No one objected to these comments, and it seemed that the staff supported such views on the way in which the psychologist might participate in staff meetings.

Following this discussion, there were some rather heated comments regarding decision-making conflicts between the principals and the department supervisors. One principal pointed out that his art supervisor had turned in a large budget for art supplies. As principal he felt that he and not the art supervisor should have made the decision regarding the amount of money to be spent for art in his building. The supervising principal agreed, and the art supervisor's decision-making role on this question was not further considered at this time.

Another principal asked for clarification of areas of responsibility of the principals and cafeteria workers in matters pertaining to the serving of food in the cafeterias. The supervising principal pointed out that this problem had been clarified by the cafeteria supervisor in a letter, passed out the previous year, to all of the principals. However, two of the elementary principals indicated that they were not familiar with the letter. It was agreed that they would receive copies. The silence which followed suggested that the principals were not entirely happy with this rather arbitrary manner of "clarifying" the problem for them.

In general, the participants agreed that they were quite satisfied with the way this meeting had gone. The supervising principal, in particular, pointed out that previously he had felt that they never could have discussed matters as frankly as they had at this meeting. He attributed this to the increased openness and air of acceptance which had developed at the four-day spring meeting.

The psychologist had the impression that most staff members participated fairly actively in this first staff meeting. Although there was some expression of feeling, it seemed to him that several participants did not express themselves very freely. There was some decision-making by consensus. However, there were several instances in which people vitally affected by certain decisions were not consulted or involved in the decision-making. For example, teachers were not consulted in making or revising the teacher evaluation form; there was no decision to involve supervisors and principals on budgets involving both; and a letter written by the cafeteria supervisor *alone* was intended to clarify responsibilities of cafeteria workers and principals.

Most of the topics of the first staff meeting came up for further discussion in subsequent meetings. Action was taken on some and not on others; most continued to remain largely unresolved problems.

Other Staff Meetings

Administrative staff meetings during the school year of 1965-66 were held monthly from September through February. Meetings were not scheduled from February through April. In May, meetings were resumed and the next four were scheduled weekly meetings. The last two of these four were all-day meetings. Participation in the last four meetings was expanded to include the supervisors of physical education, art, music, and nursing.

Initially, the staff meetings were largely concerned with problems that had been highlighted by the feedback data. However, the focus of attention soon shifted from the feedback data *per se* to basic problems that were usually related only indirectly to the feedback data. For example, the supervising principal and his assistant increasingly advocated a "child-centered" approach in the school district. Much staff meeting time was devoted to discussing ways of implementing this approach. More directly related to the survey data was the growing attempt to increase teacher participation in decision-making and to broaden communication at all levels.

Feedback Meetings with Teachers

Near the beginning of the school year, soon after the staff meetings were started, the principals began meeting with their teaching staffs to discuss the feedback data. Five meetings were held (one afternoon a month) from the beginning of the school year through January. Previous to each meeting with their teachers, the principals and the psychologist met together in a group to make plans for their coming meetings. They also met following their teacher meetings to evaluate and discuss how the meetings might be improved.

The principals were generally well pleased with the way their meetings went, despite a great deal of initial anxiety. Reaction sheets (similar to ones that had been used in the initial feedback meetings in June) completed by the teachers themselves after each meeting indicated that they too were generally satisfied with the meetings. In particular, teachers made many comments indicating that they welcomed the opportunity to discuss problems on an equal basis with their principals; they had never experienced this previously. However, as the meetings proceeded, the teachers began to indicate dissatisfaction with merely discussing problems and became quite vocal in expressing a desire for action.

Task Forces

As a result of the discussion in the teacher meetings, teachers identified several areas that they felt needed attention. At the initiation of the administrative group, committees or task forces involving all school staffs and cutting across all grade levels in all school buildings were formed in eight areas: supervision, grouping, grading, reading, teacher load, teacher assignment, library, and curriculum. This led to a one-and-a-half day meeting in February for all professional school personnel, at which time the task forces discussed the eight areas and later made preliminary written reports. These reports were later discussed in several lengthy administrative staff meetings during May and June.

Results

Results as Seen by the Research Team

The research team collected data about the effects of this survey feedback project. The following section is a review of it—both quantitatively and qualitatively—as seen from outside the district. The discussion later focuses on the effects of the program as viewed from inside the district.

Correspondence Between Theory and Events. In general, it appeared that the events of the survey feedback program corresponded reasonably well to the model proposed in Figure 6-1. For example, in a specific aspect—success experiences—the rated satisfaction that people had with problem-solving increased significantly (.05 level) from the first to the last day of the June four-day meeting. Optimism regarding the effects of the meeting also increased, although not significantly (.10 level). Interaction rates accelerated a great deal. (It was initially thought that the June meeting might have equalled six months' worth of interaction on the job; the psychologist's final estimate was nearer six years.) Some new change goals were developed, as well as a few action decisions—but not many. Some new change-supporting structures emerged—e.g., the teacher task forces. Judging from the psychologist's further work with the administrative group, norms supporting change did evolve, and the group did learn some skills needed for doing things collaboratively. In general, particularly with regard to the first two columns of Figure 6-1, there appeared to be a reasonably good correspondence between theory and events, judged on the basis of observer data and participant ratings.

Quantitative Data. As Table 6-2 indicates, data were collected at three different points in time prior to the program, and the fourth data collection took place about six months following the first feedback of data. The instrument package took about two hours of the respondent's time to complete. With some encouragement through mail reminders and occasional phone calls, we obtained 90 percent, 65 percent, 80 percent, and 80 percent returns at the four times of testing. Other

Table 6-2 Ratings of Building-Level Meetings

Mean ratings of the building-level meetings given by teachers
of principals who had high and low satisfaction with the
survey feedback program.

Scale	High Group		Low Group **	
	Time 1 Oct. '65	Time 4 Jan. '66	Time 1 Oct. '65	Time 4 Jan. '66
Inactive-active (self)	4.95	4.81	4.02	4.54*
Closed-open (self)	5.60	5.13*	4.63	4.90
Ideas unused-used (self)	4.88	4.60	3.67	4.20*
Poorly-well (group performance)	5.88	5.98	4.91	5.24*
Pessimistic-optimistic (decision follow-through)	5.46	5.24	4.53	5.06*

*The change from October to January shown by the group is significant at less than the .05 level.

**The low group mean ratings are all significantly lower than the high group ratings for the October meeting. At the January meeting, the low group teachers felt less well about how the group worked together than the high group teachers (p < .05). The other January meeting ratings of the two groups did not differ significantly.

data included observer notes made at the meetings, participant ratings of the meetings, ratings of the building-level meetings, and interviews with the administrators both individually and as a group at time O_4 and six months later (O_5).

The immediate quantitative findings are disappointing. Within the administrative group thirty-six different indicators (such as questionnaire items, sociometric scores, indices, etc.) were examined. Of those thirty-six, looking at changes from Time 3 to Time 4 (six months before the feedback began and six months afterward), three came out as predicted (.05 level), one came out as predicted at the .10 level, and two came out reversed (.05 level). Of the remaining thirty, fifteen "changed" as predicted nonsignificantly, twelve were opposite, and three showed no change. Within the large group of teachers, the research team examined forty-three indicators. No changes were found in approximately thirty-four. Five indicators changed as predicted, and four changed in the opposite direction. In short, what the team had for short-term results at the quantitative level was not significantly different from chance fluctuation. That, of course, was disappointing—and naturally led to additional data analyses.

Instrument Sensitivity. To the question, "Did the instruments really measure anything?" the answer must be Yes. This conclusion is supported by other data. The principals of the buildings were classified as having either high or low satisfaction with the survey feedback program. Four principals were seen as enthusiastic (as judged from interviews and open-end questionnaires); four principals were less actively interested and/or were seen by us more as threatened or anxious as a result of the program.

When the team compared the instruments filled out by teachers of the highly satisfied and less satisfied principals, large differences were found. Teachers in the buildings run by principals satisfied with the feedback program showed higher morale and more positive feelings toward the district. They also saw their school buildings as having a more favorable climate. Thus it was clear that a number of the instruments *were* sensitive to differences within the district.

However, were the instruments sensitive measures of *change?* They were sensitive, but not sensitive enough. Some rating scale data (Table 6-2) show real differences in building meetings run by highly satisfied principals and those run by the dissatisfied. All five scales show significant high-low differences after the October meeting. Ratings filled out in January show that the high group changed on only one scale and stayed high on the others. On four of the five scales, however, the mean ratings of the low group improved. The teachers in the high group had little room for positive change, since they were so high in the first place. In effect, the work on process which began during the four-day meeting did seem to be continued at the building level with good effect for those principals who in effect needed it the most—those whose teachers had the greatest morale problems to begin with. Yet these immediate changes did not show up in our other quantitative instruments.

Interviews. Other data suggest that change was taking place—those from interviews in January and June of 1966. Communication did seem to show an improvement: six of eight principals said that communication was better. Of them, two said, "We're more open." The supervising principal said that more work on group and interpersonal processes had been done, and the assistant supervising principal said that the principals were talking more in meetings. Five of the eight principals made comments like, "We are more active. I really say what I think—I don't hold back." Three principals said in effect, "Well, I haven't changed much."

In other data on communication three principals said there was a need for more frequent and better-run administrator meetings (they had lapsed partially during the spring). Several principals spoke quite heatedly about the poor timing and ineffectiveness of meetings, which indicates that this issue was probably a source of communication difficulty. That is, the survey feedback work got the principals committed to the idea of being more open, and to having more effective meetings. When the meetings did not improve there was a violation of expectations, with resulting anger.

Perceived changes in power distribution also occurred, though not in the expected direction. Nine of the ten other administrators said that they saw the supervising principal's role as being more powerful this year than last. They said, "He set the pace, he gave leadership, he really cared, and he really chaired the meetings." The assistant supervising principal, who formerly had a strongly competitive, blocking relationship with his superior, praised him openly and meant it. The initial survey feedback work seemed to have repaired the relationship between these men in a very striking way.

The supervising principal, on his part, said he felt much more legitimate as a leader and more trusted by his assistant. This change, however, didn't increase the power of the principals. In September and October of 1965, the eight principals did hold several meetings, separately from the superintendent and assistant, to work on problems about which they were concerned. For example, they felt that when a supervisor visited the building, he should always consult with the principal before going about his business in the building. Recommendations from these meetings may have appeared threatening to the three top men. In any event, one of the administrators said, "The three of us discussed the principals' gripes and said they were wrong, and no more principal meetings were held." One of the principals said, "Our wings were clipped." In this case, a power-equalizing effort on the part of the principals was blocked by the top group.

The outstanding event in the power equalization area was the formation of the eight district-wide committees which made recommendations for changes. By June of 1966, however, the administrative group still had not responded to the recommendations. There was a growing sense of uncertainty, skepticism, and pessimism on the part of the teachers—"Will there really be changes, or not?" This raising and blocking of expectations may help to account for the lack of change in the quantitative data up through Time 4 (late winter, 1966).

Perceived Accomplishments. The dominant theme in response to questioning of administrators about program accomplishments involved improvement in interpersonal processes and working relationships. For example, the assistant supervising principal and the high school principal had entered the survey feedback meeting literally not speaking to each other, because of conflict over the assistant supervising principal's having approved of a teacher's requests for change without consulting the principal, with many resultant disruptive effects in both school and community. At the end of the survey feedback meetings, the two men were talking to each other again in reasonable terms.

All the administrators said that process improvement had occurred as a result of the group's increased ability to work together openly. Only three, however, felt that content improvement had occurred (in the sense that better decisions were now being made about the educational program). Nine persons either made no comment about content achievement, or said that the district was on the threshold of achievement, or were dubious about content work.

Perceptions of the Inside Change Agent. It is of interest to know what the administrative staff thought about the psychologist's role. In January of 1966, they made such comments as: "He's observant; he steps in and quizzes us on what we mean. He gets things straight. He's a catalyst between the administrators and the principals. Without him we would have been misguided. Without him the group wouldn't be the same. He's probably been the most important factor in keeping us going."

By June of 1966, they made these comments: "He has made his presence necessary for progress' sake. He's done a fine job of directing and redirecting the group's thinking towards specific goals. He's a big help to me in keeping my own confidence raised in regard to both content and process." The only negative comment was made by the psychologist himself (see below for further discussion). Clearly he was seen by his clients as an effective catalyst and aid to the group's processes.

In summary, the interview data do show a clear improvement in communication, at least among the top administrative group. Power equalization did not take place; if anything, the supervising principal was exerting more decisive leadership at the end of the year. The most *optimistic* conclusion from the data would be that organizational change did begin at the top of the district, then showed some regression following the initial active involvement of lower-echelon people, with the net effect that no durable quantitative changes were found. Such an effect may be accounted for by the relative lack of action decisions and the absence of new change-supporting structures to implement the work of the teacher committees. The most *pessimistic* conclusion from the quantitative point of view at this point in the study would be that the program was a momentary perturbation in the functioning of a stable system and that no really fundamental shifts occurred in information flow or power handling.

It should be noted that these views are taken from a position outside the district. It may be useful to supplement them with commentary by the psychologist who served as the inside change agent.

Results as Seen by the Inside Change Agent

General Observations. The administrative staff generally agreed that the chief task facing them was one of learning to function as a cooperative team. Participant observation of the staff meetings indicated that the two administrators and principals made progress in operating effectively and making decisions together. They also made numerous comments to this effect. On other levels, the admission of negative feelings was a step in the direction of greater openness. For example, the supervising principal and his assistant on one hand and the building principals on the other admitted to having had feelings of suspicion and distrust toward one another before the present series of staff meetings. Each felt that there had not always been mutual support. Principals cited examples in which their decisions (involving the teaching staff) had been reversed by one of the administrators—at times on the basis of a direct complaint to an administrator by a teacher. The principals also accused the administrators of giving conflicting answers to a problem. In turn, the administrators complained that the principals had not always supported *their* decisions. The very fact that both subgroups could admit to such feelings was itself a major change in the direction of more openness, as mentioned. As one principal said about expressing such feelings, "It helped clear the air." The staff came to agree that one of the first priorities was the necessity to support one another even when agreement was incomplete.

A great deal of time was taken up in staff meetings discussing and attempting to reach common understanding on policies, philosophies, and practices in the district. This was particularly true after the task force reports were completed. These reports put the burden on the administrative staff to make decisions on a number of specific issues. However, on many controversial or difficult issues, the administrators agreed only to further study. The supervising principal, in fact, did not complete his responses to the task force reports.

Despite some evidence to the contrary, improved communication among the administrative staff did seem to be a major accomplishment. Initially the principals complained about the absence or ambiguity of many administrative policies. As staff meetings proceeded, however, the principals often expressed satisfaction with the increased opportunity to express their opinions to administrators on policy matters. In addition, they felt that the increased clarification of many policies made it easier for them to function with

confidence and self-assurance. However, there was still some difficulty in understanding the child-centered approach inaugurated by the supervising principal
and his assistant.

In contrast to their previous experience with staff meetings, the administrators saw the past year's experience as very worthwhile. The discussions
were mostly concerned with basic and relevant issues, and judging by their comments, the participants appeared much more involved and interested in the
meetings. They also became more aware of the way in which their group
functioned. Some analysis of the group process was introduced; this, they felt,
gave them a better understanding of what helped and what hindered them from
operating effectively together.

The Role of the School Psychologist as a Change Agent. For the psychologist, one of the
most satisfying aspects of the year's experience was his acceptance by the Green
Meadows staff in a different role. The following year an informal survey of the
ten administrators and principals was made on his work. They were asked to
rank the psychologist's three primary activities (consultation with the administrative staff, work with children, and mental health consultation) in terms
of their "helpfulness." On a three-point scale with 1 indicating "most helpful,"
the roles of "consultant to staff" and "work with children" were tied with a rank
of 1.7, compared to a rank of 2.6 for "mental health consultation." The
supervising principal and his assistant both ranked "consultant to staff" as most
helpful.

However, his role as change agent was not without its frustrations and
problems. Often a problem would be examined in considerable detail in staff
meetings, but no decision would be taken on it. In effect, the problem would be
left hanging, only to be brought up again at a later meeting, where the process
would be repeated. It seemed that one of the chief weaknesses of the
administrative group was its failure to confront a problem, decide upon a
suitable method of dealing with it, and then act upon its decision. Its failure to
respond to the task force reports was a primary example. Action was taken, of
course, on a number of other problems, but it was difficult for the psychologist
to avoid impatience when it seemed that the group could be moving faster. The
fact that the psychologist was unable to help much in improving their problem-
solving skill contributed to his frustration in working with them. He himself felt
the need for greater skill in helping a group work together.

Earlier, we noted that other administrators perceived the supervising principal
as having assumed a more forceful leadership role. When an already authoritarian
administrator gains power, organizational effectiveness usually suffers. However,
such was not the case at Green Meadows. The supervising principal had tended
to vacillate and be indecisive; thus it was with relief that his subordinates saw
him become more decisive. It seemed that his feelings and ideas "jelled" and that
he communicated his attitudes and feelings more clearly. After his keynote
speech to the teaching staff at the February 1966 meeting, his assistant
congratulated him, saying, "It's too bad you didn't make that speech two years
ago." The supervising principal replied, "I don't think I believed that stuff
myself two years ago."

Although for the district results were difficult to demonstrate and relatively
little was accomplished in the way of specific action during the first year of the
project, it was the school psychologist's impression that an important *process*

had been initiated in Green Meadows. The year's efforts appeared to lay the foundation for more effective functioning in the future. As the supervising principal observed, the research instruments had probably not measured the "setting of the stage" adequately.

The value of the survey feedback data in initiating change efforts on the part of the administrative staff at Green Meadows was certainly substantial. However, it is difficult to convey the importance of another factor: the continued support, interest, and help of the outside change agent group. This was invaluable in encouraging the administrators and the inside change agent to continue their efforts. The importance of a human factor such as this is probably impossible to measure but, at least in this instance, it was probably crucial in both starting and continuing the change process.

Much remained to be done in the Green Meadow School district, but it seemed clear that the administrative staff was now in a much better position to deal with the many serious problems confronting it.

Continuation of Change Efforts During 1966-67

Conclusions from the account given thus far, whether drawn by researchers or change agents, will probably vary according to personal interests and views. Those impressed by the equilibrium-seeking aspects of social systems will find much confirmation for their views in the findings. On the other hand, those with interest in the problem of how to encourage change and development in a school district may be stimulated, like the authors, to further speculation and investigation.

Feedback and Consultation

Disconfirmation of expectations usually leads to heightened tension and increased exploratory behavior. The authors did continue with additional research and consultation in Green Meadows. The school psychologist continued working with the administrative group during the academic year of 1966-67, and an additional Phase III program (see Table 6-1) was carried out with the administrative group during January of 1967. The research team collected open-end data from the administrative staff on such matters as perceived changes in the district, barriers to further change, and problems on which the administrative group wanted to work most intensively. These data were fed back during a three-day meeting. The meeting was primarily devoted to active problem-solving work on topics such as the pending reorganization of the district, the role of the supervisors (who had been invited to come to the three-day meeting as well), and the use of in-service time for teachers. Interspersed with the problem-solving was a considerable amount of process analysis, both of the problem-solving quality and the interpersonal relations in the group. Short-run rating data showed much administrator enthusiasm and optimism following this intervention.

Data collected from teachers at this time and again in May of 1967 are once more not indicative of substantial change in the district. Most of the indicators studied showed little net shift from earlier levels. However, teachers did perceive that: (1) the Green Meadows district had become more innovative; (2) the climate in the district was more open; and (3) teachers and teacher groups had slightly more influence than formerly on district-wide decisions (as based on the instrument shown in Exhibit 2). From the outside view, at any rate, there is a basis for cautious optimism: survey feedback, with follow-up consulting help from *both* outsiders and a skilled insider can help move a school district toward greater organizational health.

Inside Contact

During the 1966-67 school year, the inside change agent continued working with the administrative staff in their regular staff meetings, as well as in the three-day meeting held with the research team.

Staff meetings were continued throughout the year with some modification. The administrators continued to enunciate and clarify a "child-centered" approach, and steps were taken to involve teachers more in decision-making and innovative activities consistent with the child-centered approach.

Staff meeting time was significantly increased. Meetings were held weekly and were at least a half day in length; several continued for a whole day. More participants were included in staff meetings; the supervisors in art, music, physical education, and nursing participated in meetings throughout the year, and the cafeteria supervisor was included as a regular participant late in the school year.

Some changes were introduced into the method by which staff meetings were planned and conducted. A planning session was held prior to each staff meeting: the supervising principal, his assistant, and the psychologist met to plan the agenda, incorporating suggestions from the participants. Staff meetings often broke down into subgroup meetings, either across position lines or according to position (i.e., principals, supervisors, administrators). Participants were often able to express ideas or feelings in a subgroup which they might not feel free to express in the total group, and participants also had more "air time," meeting with fewer people. Subgroups typically met for about half an hour and then reconvened and reported back to the total group. More process analysis was introduced into staff meetings; for example, a reaction sheeet was completed by each participant at the end of each meeting and discussed at the following meeting. Most questions on the reaction sheet related to how the group had functioned: "Were you satisfied with the way decisions were made?"; "Was discussion dominated by a few?"; "What hindered us from doing better than we did?"

Two in-service days for teachers were held during the year. The most popular element of the in-service days was small group discussions. (Groups consisted of about ten, meeting by subject or grade or cutting across both.) Many teachers expressed interest in having more such meetings. As a result, pupils were dismissed early and all principals held four building-level meetings in April and May similar to the principal-teacher meetings held the previous year. Decisions on topics for discussion were left up to each principal and his group of teachers. These meetings were so well received that the administration and school board decided to dismiss pupils one half hour earlier two times a week during the 1967-68 school year in order to give teachers more time for meetings and planning. At the present time, meetings continue to be scheduled in each building at least weekly— a real departure from the past.

In looking back over the 1966-67 school year, we felt that, although there had probably been improvement over the previous year, the administrative staff as a group was still slow in making decisions and in taking action. The supervising principal had still not responded to the reports of the task forces, and now that his response had been delayed for so long it was unlikely that he would respond in the future.

Another important factor that has undoubtedly contributed to the uncertainty and anxiety felt by all the staff has been the new child-centered approach advocated by the supervising principal and his assistant. Much time was spent in discussing the implications of this approach in staff meetings. However, when it came to specifics, even the supervising principal and his assistant often seemed vague as to what action would be consistent with it. It was obvious that other staff members were not always in agreement with one another in interpreting the implications of this approach. This lack of clarity and differing interpretations were transmitted to teachers, resulting in some confusion and uncertainty.

From a positive point of view, however, increased staff meeting time, the introduction of supervisors into staff meetings, and more teacher meetings on school time all indicated greater commitment to improving communication and involving more people in decision-making.

In working with the Green Meadows school district in the role of a change agent for more than two years, the school psychologist has been impressed with the difficulty of the job. The combination of survey feedback data, occasional "outside" intervention, and the continuing availability of "at-the-elbow" consultation with an insider all seem to have contributed to the improvement which has been made. Although constructive change has often seemed to be painfully slow, the authors feel it highly probable that basic methods of functioning have changed for the better and that the health of the district will continue to improve.

References

Benedict, B. A.; Calder, P. M.; Callahan, D. M.; Hornstein, H. A.; and Miles, M. B. 1967. The clinical-experimental approach to assessing organizational change efforts. *Journal of Applied Behavioral Science* 3:347-80.

Bennis, W. G. 1963. A new role for the behavioral sciences: effecting organizational change. *Administrative Science Quarterly* 8:125-65.

Bidwell, C. E. 1965. The school as a formal organization. In *Handbook of organizations,* ed. J. G. March. Chicago: Rand McNally. Pp. 972-1022.

Gage, N. L.; Runkel, P. J.; and Chatterjee, B. B. 1963. Changing teacher behavior through feedback from pupils: an application of equilibrium theory. In *Readings in the social psychology of education,* eds. W. W. Charters, Jr., and N. L. Gage. Boston: Allyn and Bacon. Pp. 173-181.

Leavitt, H. A. 1965. Applied organizational change in industry: structural, technological, and humanistic approaches. In *Handbook of organizations,* ed. J. G. March. Chicago: Rand McNally. Pp. 1144-1170.

Mann, F. C. 1961. Studying and creating change. In *The planning of change,* eds. W. G. Bennis, K. D. Benne, and R. Chin. New York: Holt, Rinehart, and Winston. Pp. 605-615.

Miles, M. B. 1964. On temporary systems. In *Innovation in Education,* ed. M. B. Miles. New York: Teachers College Press. Pp. 437-490.

_____. 1965. Planned change and organizational health. In *Change processes in the public schools,* eds. R. O. Carlson et al. Eugene, Oregon: Center for the Advanced Study of Educational Administration. Pp. 11-36. .

_____. 1967. Some properties of schools as social systems. In *Change in school systems,* ed. G. Watson. Washington, D.C.: National Training Laboratories. Pp. 1-29.

_____; Calder, P. H.; Hornstein, H. A.; Callahan, D. M.; and Schiavo, R. S. 1966. Data feedback and organizational change in a school system. Paper read at American Sociological Association, August 29, 1966.

Neff, F. W. 1965. Survey research: a tool for problem diagnosis and improvement in organizations. In *Applied Sociology,* ed. A. W. Gouldner and S. M. Miller. New York: Free Press. Pp. 23-38.

7

ENTERING AND INTERVENING IN SCHOOLS

Dale G. Lake and Daniel M. Callahan

Beginnings tend to foreshadow much of what follows; things begun carry their own momentum. At least, this is what biology tells us. Is it true for social systems? Lake and Callahan suggest that it is so, and draw our attention to the very first things that happen when a client group and consultant meet and begin to plan their work together.

Their article is interesting because it draws attention to aspects of school OD programs which tend to be overlooked or taken for granted when the planners focus their attention on organization problems, the interventions needed, and their hoped-for outcomes. It differs from most of the other studies we present in describing cases of OD failure, which are always instructive, and in focusing on a concept, illustrated by many examples and descriptions, rather than on a single situation.

The authors' emphasis on the importance of conceptual underpinnings for organization development programs is well taken. If the reader will examine the three studies of successful "comprehensive strategies" in Chapter 1 (pp. 12-13), as well as those studies described in Chapters 2 to 6, he will note that all of them had a very well-worked-out conceptual rationale. Coherence makes a difference. (In passing, for one of the best analyses of entry processes available, see Greiner's description of the Sigma case (Journal of Applied Behavioral Science, 1967, 3:51-86), one of the three successful programs discussed in Chapter 1.)

Lake and Callahan do not point out explicitly that one of the major aspects of entry situations is the feelings they generate. Issues of trust and suspicion, well-being and dissatisfaction, investment and cautiousness, and openness and "closedness" are very near the surface. It may well be that direct acknowledgment of such prominent feelings is a prime requisite for making a good contract. Relationships of any sort cannot be forged on the basis of task agreements alone. The reader may want to look at the cases presented and his own experience with this concern in mind.

Most OD programs involve at least the following phases: (1) contact between the consultant and client, (2) entry into the system and formulation of a psychological, financial, and services contract between the OD consultant and client, (3) diagnosis, (4) intervention activities, and (5) evaluation. This chapter focuses specifically on issues related to entry into school districts and on a conceptual framework for classifying the interventions that follow entry.

In the OD field, especially in schools, we believe that not enough attention has been given to the process of entering the organization. While aspects of entry such as contract formation, point of entry, etc., are mentioned, we know of no systematic attempt to deal with these issues as important parts of organizational improvement efforts. In several representative treatments of organizational change (Argyris, 1965; Bennis, 1966; Schein and Bennis, 1965; Bennis, Benne, and Chin, 1969), the issue of entry is not treated as a separate problem nor can the term be found in the subject indexes of these books. One could conclude that the topic of "entry" is not very important in OD; however, we contend that entry, as the first step in the planned organizational change effort, is very important and deserves systematic treatment.

For one thing, the style and focus of entry often determine whether the OD program will survive or collapse, as we shall show in case studies. More than this, barriers to OD in schools are not minor, as Blumberg and Schmuck (in press) have pointed out; unskilled or naive entry efforts may simply never succeed.

In addition, it is during the contract-making phase of entry that system members and outside consultants envision the sorts of interventions which may lie ahead. Unless a consultant has a clear conceptual framework for the sorts of work he will be doing with the system and can explain this framework to the client, the likelihood of a productive, eventually self-renewing OD program is small.

We begin with a conclusion. At this point in the history of OD, it is *not* possible to determine precisely, through the use of well documented case studies or other respectable data sources, the particular entry strategies that are most likely to lead to long-term successful outcomes. In lieu of such data, this chapter reviews some entry strategies which have been tried, sets forth some recommendations as to what adequate entry strategies may entail, and presents a general conceptual framework for thinking about interventions, with some specific examples.

Case Studies of Entry

Entry into a Large Urban School District

A study showing a direct connection between entry and the failure of an OD effort in a large school district was conducted by Derr (1970) and his associates from Harvard and MIT. Briefly, this team of OD consultants undertook to help the urban district analyze the problems of fourteen departments and to suggest ways to reorganize for greater effectiveness. Data were collected via interviews with twenty-four persons from a diagonal cross-section (known as special services) of the fourteen departments. Following analysis of the data, the results were fed back to department heads and other representatives. These feedback sessions were successful in that the diagnoses were confirmed, and the participants were generally enthusiastic about the laboratory training method employed.

However, following the feedback meetings, things appeared to go awry. Top administrators were given a written report of the diagnosis; however, they refused to work collaboratively with the OD team in order to take the next steps in solving the district's problems. Instead of trying to resolve the problems uncovered by the diagnosis, the top administration was satisfied to receive the "final report" and let it drop there. After a year, follow-up interviews of the participants in the feedback meetings revealed that none of them had seen the report and that the same organizational problems still existed.

After review of this study it seems clear, as it did to the study's author, that entry was poorly accomplished. Several weaknesses are apparent. (1) There was no agreement about collaboration at the top administrative level. In fact, the associate superintendents were suspicious of the OD team's efforts. (2) The data collection began even though the OD team was not convinced that the school authorities understood or approved the methods to be used or were willing to abide by the results. (3) There was no sharing of expectations. Top administrators simply wanted a report to support a political power play, while the OD team wanted to practice OD methods in the district.

The fact is that the contract between the OD consultants and the district was extremely vague—so vague that there was in effect no contract at all. This allowed top administrators to demand, and get, a report even though submittal was contrary to the intentions of the OD team. This vagueness also allowed the administration to refuse to comply with demands of the OD team. They refused to collaborate in the problem-solving process, and they refused to share the report with others (especially with those from whom the data were collected). Thus it is clear that the OD consultants did not enter the district at the top of the power structure. They entered lower down, and although they got cooperation there, they were successfully resisted by top administrators. It was as if they were in competition with the administration. (Not surprisingly, one of the major problems revealed in the diagnosis was the prevalence of dysfunctional power struggles in the district.)

It became clear later that the OD report was being used to support the administration's request for additional staffing. It also became clear through follow-up interviews that the fourteen departments (supposedly the *client*) were not helped. Thus, uncertainty at entry resulted in a lack of clarity about the contract, a lack of clarity about the point of entry, a lack of clarity about who the client was, and the use of interventions which provided short-run satisfaction and no long-term help. Further, this uncertainty resulted in the involvement of the OD consultants in a power struggle with the client, a situation which was symptomatic of the client's major problems.

Entry into "Old City"

Our second case is drawn from the work of COPED (Cooperative Project for Educational Development), a large-scale enterprise involving collaboration between school districts and university-based OD consultants.*

"Old City" was a community with a population of about 150,000, retaining few of the families which once gave it historical distinction. About 70 percent of the children in its elementary schools were non-white. Middle and upper class citizens had moved out to the more comfortable suburbs.

---

* See COPED (1970, Vol. 2) for the complete case. The interested reader is encouraged to examine the nine other cases presented there as well; they are well-documented and instructive. Also see Chapter 1 of this volume for more information on COPED.

Chronology. The following is a simple chronology of events related to the OD entry process:

1965	Dec.	Invitational conference with representatives from nineteen other districts
1966	Feb.	Exploration of consultants with Old City cabinet
	Mar.	First off-site meeting
	Apr.	Beginning of task force meetings
	May	Completion of task force meetings with reports
	June	Beginning of meetings with cabinet
1967	Oct.	Completion of evaluation of meetings and closing of project

For the purpose of discussing entry we intend to look at only those events which occurred between December 1965 and June 1966. The first event, a one-day invitational conference, included many districts in addition to Old City. Participants were invited by the university-based COPED staff through a letter to superintendents. In order to attend they had to agree to bring a team from their district including members of the board and central office, a principal, and a member of the teaching staff. They were told to expect that the conference would describe a new federally supported change project and that they would have a chance to actually begin diagnosing their own district's difficulties.

What the members of the teams attending the invitational conference actually learned about the intentions of the university change team sponsoring the conference is difficult to assess. Data collected at the conference show that the participants believed it to be "successful," and that they thought they understood better some of the problems of planning for change. But there is no evidence to show that the participants had an understanding of what would be expected of them if they were to collaborate with the university change team, nor who from within the district would be involved, nor how a contract with a clear budget agreeable to all parties could be formed.

The second contact with Old City, in the February exploration meeting, helped to clear up some additional matters for negotiation. For instance, dollar costs of becoming involved were determined; it was indicated that the change strategy called for intensive work with the administrative cabinet before going to other parts of the district; and it was clarified that the change effort was not just "sensitivity training."

It was also agreed that the way to begin was with a one-week summer meeting of the administrative cabinet. The superintendent of Old City was amenable to the idea of having such a central group provide leadership to the project. However, immediately after returning to the district, the superintendent called and said that he could not commit his cabinet to the summer meeting. He reported that many of his cabinet staff had already made summer plans (even though they were on a twelve-month salary) and that others did not really see the utility of a one-week meeting. About half of the cabinet did volunteer to attend such a conference, but it never materialized.

The first district-wide entry activity consisted of the off-site workshop for seventy-five persons selected from every level of the school district. The participants enrolled with cynical expectations, i.e., "Another set of meetings to go to"; "all talk and no action."

The workshop was designed by the consultants to start with diagnosis and, along with increasing the participants' problem-solving skills, to work toward collaborative solutions to problems diagnosed. The data for the workshop were collected from participants through a questionnaire.

The immediate structural outcome of this workshop for the district was the creation of five task forces which would work through the rest of the spring and submit reports for action to the superintendent at the close of the school year. The task forces did work diligently, using some released teaching time, and were ready to report in June. The presentations, given to an assemblage of some three hundred persons, were creative, using a variety of media. The superintendent closed the meeting by indicating the particular reports he intended to implement immediately and which he intended to put on the summer agenda of the cabinet.

However, the cabinet never met to work on the reports. Instead, an advisory group was set up to meet and carry through on the task force reports. The consultants described the outcomes of this advisory group as follows:

1. Little was accomplished regarding team effectiveness. Members arrived late for the opening meeting and for the opening session on the second day; they decided to end the meeting a half day earlier than planned. . . .The only decisions made resulted from a proposal outlined by the superintendent, the rest of the group contributing mainly by helping work out details for implementing it. As one member said during the meeting, the only time the group was able to work was when they were operating in their old familiar way—"all sat back and waited until the superintendent presented an idea," then later many criticized him for dominating the meeting. There was some process analysis—discussion of how the meeting was conducted and how members viewed it—but the main thing this revealed was members' discomfort in doing process analysis, and thus the training seemed to strengthen resistance to any further team-development meetings.

2. The task force recommendations were discussed, but no steps were planned to implement them. However, high concern was displayed about lack of action regarding the task force reports, and about maintaining the involvement of the many teachers who took part in the task force work. (COPED, 1970, 2:7-8)

The advisory group also devised a plan to continue OD work at the building level, over the strong objections of the outside COPED staff, who felt that such efforts would fail unless more commitment were developed at higher levels (the cabinet, the advisory group itself, and the principals). Some building-level work, aided by training for building leadership teams, did take place, but the summer cabinet meeting did not occur, and it appeared by the fall that no continuing commitment to OD was likely. External funding of the project ceased at this time.

In December of that year, a problem survey was undertaken again by interviewing a sample of seventy-five participants. Analysis of these data indicated that participants agreed that the workshop had been an excellent way to open up communication between roles, to identify problems, and to improve teamwork, but there was even more agreement that follow-up implementation of the work started at the conference had been disappointing. The disappointment was felt most keenly by principals. One indicated, "At this point, I don't see any results that are of any significance." Another said, "Too much talk, superficial change." Others said: "Aspirations were raised but poor follow-through left us worse off than before," and "When the consultants were no longer in charge, as in the workshop, things fell apart." A central office person asked of the consultant, "How come you didn't warn us ahead of time that you didn't have the resources to follow through with the task forces and see that the changes stuck?"

Comments

Certain major problems in entry are apparent in this case. The first problem that any entry process encounters is that of *expectations*—those of the consultants and the clients. In this case, some of the participants in the workshop fully expected that the consultants were going to solve the various problems listed (e.g., racial imbalance, poor public image, lack of materials). The consultants tried to shift expectations about themselves from "dispensers of solutions" to experts in developing rational ways for the *clients* themselves to carry out open, collaborative problem-solving. The consultants in Old City fully expected that once their clients had experienced improved problem-solving in the off-site setting they would then be able to carry over these skills to the "back-home" situation. This proved not to be the case.

A second set of problems which often arises in the entry process might be summarized under the question, "What is to be exchanged?" That is, what will the client receive for his money and energy investment? Technological help? Conceptual help? New methods? What, precisely, is being exchanged between client and consultant? This is, of course, a central problem of contract-making.

Again, in our example, it is painfully clear that clients and consultants did not share a common image of just how the consultant was to be helpful. In fact, definite *mis*perceptions were created. As we have seen, many of the clients in the first workshop thought the consultants were experts on the *content* of such problems as racial imbalance or junior high discipline (a misperception created by the questionnaire itself). Therefore, many came to the workshop expecting to hear lectures on these topics. It was difficult for these participants even to recognize that the teaching of problem-solving skills was, in fact, helpful. The participants expected new ideas but received new skills.

Other issues raised by the entry process in Old City can be phrased as questions. Why start with a workshop? What were the objectives for which the workshop was supposed to be an adequate solution? What other start-up methods might have been used? Where was the entry supposed to lead: i.e., what would have been an adequate step after the workshop? When could initial expectations be renegotiated?

Summary

These case studies revealed similar kinds of entry problems. In the large urban district, as in Old City, there was no sharing of expectations between client and consultant. Had expectations been fully shared, the consultants might not even have entered the district in the former case, and in the latter case might have planned different kinds of activities for district members.

In both districts the goals had not been clarified. In the urban case, the consultants were ready to provide their clients with increased skills in diagnosis and problem-solving in exchange for their active participation in the OD method. It was not too clear who the client was in this case, but if it were the top administration, they wanted a final report to use in their negotiations with the board of education. In Old City, the consultants wanted to provide the clients with skills (problem-solving, decision-making, etc.). The clients, however, expected solutions to problems they were facing.

Finally, the consultants in both cases were not very clear about their own purposes in engaging the clients in specific intervention activities. If the consultants in the large urban district had been clearer about who the client was and clearer about the client's expectations, would they have used the data feedback design? In fact, would they have done anything with the district at all? Similarly, the connection between the off-site workshop in Old City, at least as an initial district-wide entry activity, and the consultants' goals was not clear. Before taking such a step, the consultants should perhaps have been surer that the superintendent and his cabinet were willing to work collaboratively with them.

The issues and questions raised by these case examples point to the need for a thorough conceptual-empirical base with which to start entry processes in school districts and guide the interventions which follow. Below we describe such a framework.

Concepts for Entry and Intervention

It seems to us that the complexity of modern organizations in general, and of school districts in particular, requires a set of principles as comprehensive as that of general systems theory to promote understanding. School districts are continuously interacting with their environments. Their boundaries are very permeable: parents, textbook salesmen, facilities salesmen, professional associations, drug pushers, local businessmen, and others find little difficulty in gaining access to the management and influence structures of the schools. Miles (1967) has documented this permeability in his article on the vulnerability of schools. In general systems theory, this permeability of boundaries would classify the school district as an open system. In the words of Kast and Rosenzweig (1970, p. 119):

The open system is in continual interaction with its environment and achieves a "steady state" or dynamic equilibrium while still retaining the capacity for work or energy transformation.

In the case of a school district, this means that it receives *inputs* from the society in the form of people, materials, money and information; it *transforms* these into *outputs* of products, services, and rewards (to the organization members and the larger society) of sufficient quality to maintain their participation. Kast and Rosenzweig (1970, p. 119) have diagrammed this relationship as follows:

Figure 7-1 General Model of Organization as an Open System

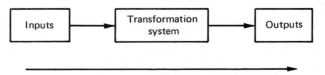

Flow of material/energy/information

Transformation Subsystems

Now let us elaborate the transformation system in order to pinpoint the area into which the organization development consultant makes his entry. Again, following Kast and Rosenzweig, we have:

Figure 7-2   Organization as a Socio-technical System

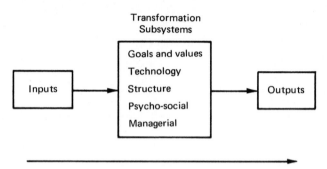

Transformation
Subsystems

Inputs → Goals and values
Technology
Structure
Psycho-social
Managerial → Outputs

Flow of material/energy/information

The essential point is that each of the subsystems in the transformation system is essential to the successful accomplishment of the organization's mission. Another implication of this scheme is that it is within the transformation system that the consultant develops expectations and formulates the contract with school district clients. That is, the OD consultant makes his entry (and intervention) directly into one or more of the subsystems of the *transformation system.* He is not initially in the business of trying to improve the nature of the inputs in a school district, as someone selling new curriculum materials might be. Nor does he initially aim to modify the output, as an evaluator might. (Of course, it is expected that continued work at improving the transformation system will ultimately modify and improve the outputs of the system and probably reduce the number and types of dysfunctional inputs. However, the transformation system is the initial basic target.)

Interventions into the Transformation Subsystems

In this section, we review some sample interventions for each of the transformation subsystems shown in Figure 7-2. Some of these may occur during or very near the entry process. Even if they are used later, consultant and client ordinarily need to be very clear that such types of intervention are in the offing. The nature of the exchange must be mutually agreed on.

The task now will be to describe how and what the OD consultant can do in each of the subsystems.

Goals and Values Subsystem. Most OD consultants try to improve the goals and values subsystem of schools by focusing upon the *way* goals are formulated. A first step is to examine the goals currently in operation and how they came to be formulated.

Entry into the goals and values subsystem is achieved when both the client and the OD consultant have agreed that this is an important area for investigation and that the development of a set of procedures for improvement is necessary.

Many procedures for work in the goals and values area have now been developed. For instance, the Educational Policy Research Centers at both Syracuse University and Stanford Research Institute have developed procedures for future prediction and focusing on long-term goals.

One such method developed for schools is a modification of the Delphi process (Hudspeth, 1970). The process requests a wide range of persons in the school district and local community to "conjecture some events which might take place during the next fifteen years that you perceive may have some impact on . . . education. In your conjectures think about things that might happen that would affect: administration of schools, industrial training programs, manpower needs, etc." (Hudspeth, 1970, p. 1, Appendix). Subsequently the respondents are asked to assign dates to their conjectures, which are then processed via computer and fed back. After this, respondents are asked (1) to examine the range of dates provided, (2) to assign a value estimate to the event, and (3) to write a very short description about the possible consequence of the event in question.

Ultimately, the purpose of this Delphi method is to help the person setting goals to assess strategy options for his goal against the beliefs, attitudes, and consequences felt and seen by various members of affected groups and to help him determine the value of achieving his goal.

In addition the OD consultant may focus on short-term goal setting. Some systems have experimented with developing work plans and with "management by objectives" (which may improve both the goal subsystem and the managerial subsystem). One such program is currently under way in a Connecticut school district, conducted by TDR Associates (Genova, 1970). Their Professional Development and Appraisals Program is designed to allow teachers, support personnel, administrators, and school board members to interact through specific goal-setting and planning in an educational program for students. More will be said about this program in the section below on the managerial subsystem.

Technology Subsystem. Kast and Rosenzweig (1970, p. 141) have defined this subsystem:

> In the most general sense, technology refers to *knowledge* about the performance of certain tasks or activities. Jacques Ellul (1964) gives a broad connotation to technology or, as he calls it, technique. Technology is far more than the machine and refers to standardized means for attaining a predetermined objective or result. Thus, technology converts spontaneous and unreflective behavior that is deliberate and rationalized. "In our technological society, *technique* is the *totality of methods rationally arrived at and having absolute efficiency* (for a given stage of development) in *every* field of human activity" (p. XXV). Technology has come to dominate every field of human activity and is geared to the achievement of maximum efficiency in all human endeavors.

While OD consultants hardly ever work with technological hardware, some have developed systematic data collection and analysis systems which can be utilized as school management information systems. For instance, Miles,

Hornstein, Callahan, Calder, and Schiavo (1969)* developed instrumentation for a survey feedback program for school districts which encourages the constant monitoring of performance. To quote from these authors:

Survey feedback is a process in which outside staff and members of the organization collaboratively gather, analyze and interpret data that deal with various aspects of the organization's functioning and its members' work lives, and using the data as a base, begin to correctively alter the organizational structure and the members' work relationships. (P. 458.)

Survey feedback meetings occur in off-site meetings in which the participants, with the active help of the outside consultants, develop a diagnosis of the organizational problems. During this process, system members are helped to acquire new skills (e.g., how to collect and use data for diagnosis and problem-solving) so that organizational change programs will be ongoing rather than single events that occur only when outside consultants are present. The OD consultant, then, not only takes a major role in initial diagnosis and problem-solving activities, but teaches relevant skills to selected members of the system so that they can continue such processes. The goal of the OD consultant is thus to make himself unnecessary to the organization—to work himself out of a job.

A related kind of technology was developed in COPED (COPED, 1970, Vol. III) to aid school districts in diagnosis and problem solving. Using data collected in a large OD project in schools, a "data bank" was constituted for use in in-service programs for teachers. A brief description of this program follows.

A unique feature is the "data bank," a set of cards containing the actual data from a set of school buildings and staffs of various types, to which the participants in the in-service action program will be referred for answers to some of the inquiry questions they develop after confrontation with some of the specific problems faced by the staffs of two specimen schools. The program is designed to involve a staff first in confronting some of the problems of professional climate through simulation—that is, by using two schools about which real data have been gathered. After the participants have had a chance to be confronted with some of the typical problems faced by these schools, examine data that may illumine problems and lead toward diagnosis, raise additional inquiry questions about these schools which may be explored through use of the data bank, and serve as consultants to these school staffs in laying strategies for improvement, the payoff question is faced: "Do these problems and diagnostic procedures have relevance for us? Do we wish to become engaged in a problem-solving effort within our own school directed toward improving the climate here?" If so, guidelines are set for a continuing problem-solving program that may involve the staff for the rest of the year (COPED, 1970, Vol. I).

Structural Subsystem. Kast and Rosenzweig (1970, p. 170) have defined the structural subsystem:

Very simply, structure may be considered as *the established pattern of relationships among the components or parts of the organization.* However, the structure of a social system is not visible in the same way as [that of] a biological or mechanical system. It cannot be seen but is inferred from the actual operations and behavior of the organization.

The distinction between *structure* and *process* in systems helps in understanding this concept. The structure of a system is the arrangement of its subsystems and components in three-dimensional space at a given moment of time. . . .Process is dynamic change in the matter-energy or information of that system over time.

Many consultants or organizations have concerned themselves with the arrangement of the organizational chart and with such questions as: Who are "staff?" What are line role requirements? What is the maximum unit for "span

*See also Chapter 6 in the present volume.

of control?" OD consultants typically examine and try to change such variables as: (1) the proportion of behavior that is controlled by specified rules and regulations of the organization; (2) the degree to which role expectations are clear to those who are interdependent in their working relationships; and (3) the degree to which the organization's form contributes to its ability to adjust to internal and external changes in a manner that promotes organizational survival and development.

Much work needs to be done in this area. At entry, school personnel may think of the OD consultant's wares as essentially training-oriented or "person-changing," and not envision structural changes as possible. Yet relatively simple structural interventions can be very useful.

One striking example of structural change which promoted innovation was tried in a Long Island, New York, district. A change management team was created to search continuously for new ideas from the teaching staff. As an idea which seemed worth trying was discovered, the teacher initiating the idea was given a budget. The "sponsor teacher" used the budget to hire substitutes so that he or she could give demonstrations, to release other teachers to visit such demonstrations, or to purchase materials with which to develop the idea. Both the change management team itself, and the tying of budgets to innovative teachers were examples of structural changes which promoted innovation.

Psycho-Social Subsystem. Kast and Rosenzweig (1970, p. 211) have defined the psycho-social subsystem:

> The psycho-social system—the individual in social relationships—can be understood in terms of motivation and behavior occurring in an environment which includes: status and role systems, group dynamics, influence systems, and leadership.

Schein, in his book *Process Consultation* (1969, p. 4), has defined the OD consultant's task in this area by stressing the need to change three major human values in the psycho-social perspective on work. They are: "(1) increasing the importance of human over task concerns, (2) shifting the emphasis from short-run to long-run effectiveness, and (3) shifting emphasis from administration by rules to open and perpetual diagnosis."

One example of a rather long-term (4 years), well-documented effort to intervene directly with the psycho-social system occurred in a school district in eastern New York with a community of about 10,000 people. The initial entry strategy involved creating an experimental sensitivity training group including the superintendent, two board members, several high school teachers, and three students. No effort was made to deal with "system" problems as such; the group experience was aimed at increasing open, direct communication among the members. Satisfaction with this first group experience led to a vigorous expansion of the strategy—informal, relatively unstructured, mixed groups (i.e., students, teachers, parents and administrators), increasingly staffed by a cadre of local teachers and parents themselves.

The format of the adult-youth (or AY) groups has been described by an outside evaluation team (Benedict, Emmett, and Singer, 1969) as follows:

> The participant in an AY group is involved in a six-week experience which includes a weekly group meeting and two intensive weekends, all held at _____ high school.
> The atmosphere at a typical group is informal but expectant. Members and trainers sit wherever they can find rug or chair space until the group has assembled. Occasionally a

trainer will "open" a group but more typically the beginning, content, and structuring of the group process is in the hands of the members. It is assumed that they will learn more from actions and explorations which they determine for themselves.

In this situation the trainers play a participant model role. We saw in the groups, and had reported on questionnaires, the importance of trainer modeling [of] openness, warmth, supportiveness, and willingness to confront others with feelings. Early in the life of the group, most trainers focus on helping members to feel and genuinely express their feelings for one another. It is acknowledged that these feelings may be confronting, that members may find some of the events either painful or pleasurable.

In order to hold such events within reasonable bounds, norms about limitations on permissible behavior are both reported by trainers; and as we saw it, practiced by the trainers. Some are: "people shouldn't be pushed to do things they don't want to do"; "don't go into personal historical data—stick to the here and now"; "limit some self-disclosures"; "don't play therapist and attribute motivation to others." In order to promote the exploration of feelings, other norms are in evidence, such as "be supportive but open"; "check how people are feeling and reacting"; "stop intellectualizing when it goes on too long"; "use yourself to confront others."

The tone of a group varies greatly from session to session and from one part of a meeting to another. Adults and youth, from what we could see, frequently do some very "straight" talking to each other which gives rise to the feeling that they can meet as persons. (P. 19.)

The outside evaluation team interviewed many of the participants, collected questionnaire data, and observed many sessions of the group meetings. Some of their evaluation comments follow (Benedict, Emmett, and Singer, 1969):

We emerge with the following impression: In some if not many cases, participation in the AY program has been very useful and meaningful to individual students and faculty, and has led them to be more creative and effective. It also appears to have increased the cohesiveness and warmth of some sub-groups within the school. . . .

The quantity of rumor and exaggeration which we have heard surround the groups makes it clear to us that this is an emotionally charged issue, which cuts to the core of many people's value orientations. . . .

The board expected these groups to increase unity and cohesiveness within the community. From our point of view it is doubtful that this will happen.

It seems likely that the present program, should it continue, would produce better understanding and interaction among individuals within the school community. However, it seems very unlikely to impart to the system the understanding, and the problem-solving and decision-making skills needed to cope with conflicts and tension between groups and in group settings. . . . Even if one works on the theory that working with individuals is the way to change a social system or facilitate creative problem solving, at the present rate, working with only some of the teachers within the school, it would take an indefinite time to reach a "critical mass."

The outside evaluators were specifically requested to search through the community to see if anyone had been harmed psychologically by the group program. The evaluation team interviewed all members of the mental health profession in that community:

Although there were repeated allusions to cases "which we all know about," only three concrete instances of moderate to severe psychological disturbance reportedly resulting from experience in the groups were brought to our attention. In only one of these cases— that of an adult—does this contention appear to have any solid basis in fact. In one of the other two cases, severe upset did occur; but the individual in question, it turned out, had not been in a group, but in some other experience. In a second case, substantial disturbance also seems to have occurred, but remotely enough in time from the group experience and with so many intervening events, that in our judgment it is difficult to assign direct causal responsibility to the group experience. (P. 24.)

Thus the intervention focused largely on opening communication and increasing the "humanness" of interaction in the district. In addition, much of the work of the OD consultant in the psycho-social subsystem deals with *norms,* those explicit/implicit expectations that we have for each other's behavior. Norms of particular interest are those of (1) authenticity: the degree to which persons are interpersonally genuine, (2) owning: the degree to which persons take responsibility for their own ideas, goals, and feelings, (3) inquiry: the degree to which persons are questioning, hypothetical, and (4) openness: the degree to which persons give feelings and seek the expression of feelings from others.

Another major emphasis within the psycho-social subsystem is that on conflict and its management. Most OD consultants begin with the assumptions that conflict is a normal condition for schools in our turbulent culture and that the productive management of conflict requires an important set of skills. The consultant can help by teaching skills, by helping district members analyze the source and nature of conflict, and by providing substantive help in the management of intergroup conflict.

Managerial Subsystem. The managerial subsystem has been defined (Kast and Rosenzweig, 1970, pp. 340-41) as follows:

> Everyone is a manager, if only of his personal affairs. Our primary concern, however, is management in organizational settings—the coordination of group effort toward an established purpose. This coordination is effected primarily (1) through people, (2) via techniques, (3) in an organization, and (4) toward objectives. Essentially, management is the process of integrating human and material resources into a total system for objective accomplishment.

This subsystem typically has been a focus of major concern to the OD consultant. It includes such critical areas as decision-making, control and influence, coordination, recruitment process, orientation process, reward process, and leadership. One such program which combines work on leadership, communication, control, and coordination simultaneously is called the Professional Development and Appraisals Program (PDAP).

Genova (1970) describes the program:

> Professional Development and Appraisals is essentially a system of planning, implementing and evaluating improvements and innovations in ways that promote and widen personal accountability. Many people set and accomplish goals anyway, but under PDAP, goals are more explicitly stated, time schedules are set, and the measurement of goal attainment is defined in observable terms. Staff members are provided with released time for goal setting and goal attainment, and administrators have roles and accountability for goal attainment with their staff members. (P. 2.)

The teacher's first experience with PDAP is a conference with his supervisor during which they agree on criteria to evaluate the teacher's classroom performance and identify the assistance that the teacher will need. After this, the supervisor makes at least three one-hour visits to the class to assess how well the teacher is measuring up. Conferences are held after each visit. Finally, the supervisor makes his recommendation concerning reappointment or not, based upon his assessment of the teacher's performance and his potential for improvement.

After one year of operation, outside evaluators were brought in to determine how effectively the PDAP was working. The PDAP participants and a sample of non-participants were asked to rate how the PDAP methods compared to traditional methods for each of twelve issues, such as "my influencing school district goals." In the largest difference found, 23 percent of PDAP participants felt that traditional teacher evaluation was an above-average or excellent method for improving classroom teaching, while almost 72 percent felt that PDAP was an above-average or excellent method. The next largest difference was for determining administrator competence and cost effectiveness, where the advantage for PDAP was 30 percentage points in both cases.

Thus, the evaluations show that the PDAP approach is seen as more successful along a number of important dimensions. In addition, the district now has excellent data on specific objectives of teachers, contained in regular progress reports coming out of the appraisal sessions.

Concluding Comments

In this chapter we have attempted to stress the importance of the "entry-process" and to provide a conceptual framework within which it can be viewed. First, two case studies of OD efforts in school districts were presented, and then notions from general systems theory were discussed.

The case studies highlighted certain difficulties which were encountered at entry and suggested how these may have related to the lack of success of the change efforts. In both cases similar entry problems were found: lack of clarity about the consultants' purposes and the particular activities clients were being asked to engage in; little or no sharing of expectations between client and consultant; vague contracts which could be (and were) easily broken. In one case, there was also lack of specification about who the client was.

We maintain that an OD consultant using the concepts of a transformation system as his conceptual base is in a good position to make a clear contract with a client. From his initial contact with the client, the consultant can specify the subsystem or subsystems with which he is willing to deal. Then the diagnosis and ultimately the intervention plans he and the client work out collaboratively will be in terms of one or more of these subsystems. This approach will help the OD consultant working with school districts to avoid giving the impression that he intends to have a direct effect on system inputs or the outputs. More important, the transformation system concepts help the consultant get his purposes straight in his own mind. As a result, he can help clients become clearer about what they are buying when they contract for OD services.

References

Argyris, C. 1965. *Organization and innovation.* Homewood, Illinois: Irwin.

Benedict, Barbara; Emmet, G.; and Singer, D. 1969. Evaluation report: The East Williston [New York] School District adult-youth program. Mimeographed.

Bennis, W. G. 1966. *Changing organizations.* New York: McGraw-Hill.

_____; Benne, K.D.; and Chin, R., eds. 1969. *The planning of change.* New York: Holt, Rinehart, & Winston.

Blumberg, A., and Schmuck, R. A. In press. Barriers to training in organizational development for schools. *Educational Technology.*

Buchanan, P. C., and Chasnoff, R. E. 1970. COPED in Old City: interventions, dilemmas and change in a school system. In *Cooperative project in educational development,* ed. Dale G. Lake. Final Report V. II, Office of Education Project No. 8-0069.

COPED. 1970. *Cooperative project in education development, final report,* Vols. I, II, and III, Office of Education Project No. 8-0069.

Derr, C. B. 1970. Organization development in one large urban school system. *Education and Urban Society.* September.

Ellul, J. 1964. *The technological society* (trans. John Wilkinson). New York: Knopf.

Genova, W. 1970. Professional development and appraisals program. Wellesley Hills, Massachusetts: TDR Associates. Mimeographed.

Hudspeth, D. 1970. *A long range planning tool for education: the focus Delphi.* New York State Education Department, Bureau of Two Year College Programs.

Kast, F.E., and Rosenzweig, J.E. 1970. *Organization and management: a systems approach.* New York: McGraw-Hill.

Miles, M. B. 1967. Some properties of schools as social systems. In *Change in school systems,* ed. Goodwin Watson. Washington, D.C.: National Training Laboratories.

_____ ; Hornstein, H. A.; Callahan, D. M.; Calder, Paula; and Schiavo, R. S. 1970. The consequence of survey feedback: Theory and evaluation. In *The planning of change,* eds. W. G. Bennis, K. D. Benne, and R. Chin. New York: Holt, Rinehart, & Winston. Pp. 457-68.

Schein, E. H. 1969. *The process consultant.* Reading, Massachusetts: Addison-Wesley.

_____ , and Bennis, W. G. 1965. *Personal and organizational change through group methods: the laboratory approach.* New York: Wiley.

Watson, G., and Lake, D. G. 1967. Self renewal in schools: Some concepts and an example. Paper read at the American Orthopsychiatric Association Meetings.

8

USING TEAMS
OF CHANGE AGENTS*

Max R. Goodson and Warren O. Hagstrom

The vogue of educational innovators during the early 60's was the change-agent team—a vertically composed cluster representing several professional roles in the district. Such groups were charged with organizing themselves cohesively around a current innovation and convincing others in the district to try out the new practice. The theory was that a representative group with whom it would be easy to identify could more easily gain widespread allegiance than a single administrator or small cluster of curriculum specialists.

With this in mind, many school districts at one time or another during the past ten years have tried to establish small teams for stimulating change. Unfortunately, most often such teams sputtered quickly and became non-functional. Reasons for failure were multiple, of course, but one could argue—as Goodson and Hagstrom do—that in order to succeed such teams must learn the skills, norms, and procedures needed to sustain a concerted effort when the going gets rough. In terms of the organizational development cube presented in Chapter 1, Goodson and Hagstrom used mostly soft modes of OD training in preparing the change-agent teams.

This study shows that even those change-agent teams that are carefully selected, trained, and supported by skilled outside consultants have difficulty in carrying out their primary purposes. Although each of the teams studied still exists, none has been able to mount an effective change program in its district. And when change projects of a promising nature were commenced, they were aborted by the succession of key administrators and also because of high teacher turnover. More basically, the top administrators never seemed to own the change-agent teams as important and legitimate parts of their districts. Perhaps, too, the OD training given to the teams and other district members did not involve enough "hard" interventions.

Whatever the answer, few studies of the effects of change-agent teams as a strategy for organization development have been done as carefully as this one.

* This chapter was adapted from Max R. Goodson, and Warren O. Hagstrom, *Changing Schools: Case Studies of Change Agent Teams in Three School Systems,* Technical Report, Center for Research and Development in Cognitive Learning (Madison: University of Wisconsin, 1970). We are greatly indebted to Mrs. Joanne Soraya and the late Leo Hilfiker for their contributions to the larger project and this report.

In the spring of 1966 some Wisconsin school districts cooperating with the Research and Development Center for Cognitive Learning were invited to participate in a two-year project in planned change. Eight districts were involved. All provided information through a questionnaire to their personnel in 1967 and again in 1969. Five districts each established a district-wide subgroup called a "change agent team." These teams were constituted of personnel from all parts of each district to represent the largest conceivable organizational unit. Three of the five districts involved their team in training designed to improve competence in interpersonal communication, problem-solving, and planned change.

The rationale for our change agent team approach has five key points: (1) it provides entry into a district by an outside consultant team as represented by our Wisconsin staff; (2) it assumes an integrated character embracing several components and avoids selecting one of the district's components for special treatment; (3) it maximizes opportunities of school district personnel to determine priorities for change and to control development of district groups in accordance with their priorities; (4) it provides greater opportunity for a school district to continue developing after the outside consultants are withdrawn; and (5) it improves relationships among district components and increases possibilities for all parts of the district to receive attention.

This approach also has at least two limitations: (1) the starting point is far removed from students for whom the district functions, and (2) there is danger of spreading efforts thinly over a large district—a condition which can lead to positive results only after considerable time, in contrast to the immediate results that may come through more concentrated efforts.

Change Agent Teams

Whether school districts know it or not, agents for change function in all of them. Various persons in diverse roles from the superintendent to the kindergarten pupil have a potential to modify themselves and to create change in others. Different people, of course, do have different degrees of power and resources to act innovatively. We assumed that change agents who were cognizant of their resources and mission and appropriately authorized by those with district-wide responsibility for making decisions would be more effective in planning and managing change than those who were not aware of their potential. The role played by expectation is also an important condition; those who are expected to be change agents are more likely to perform appropriately.

Role of the Change Agent

Historically, the change agent of a school district has been the superintendent, although recently administration theorists have sought to change this one-office-one-man authoritarian approach. Data from our eight school districts indicate the importance of the function which the superintendent plays in influencing general educational matters as well as innovative processes. To deny the superintendent the role of change agent is unreal and unwise, but to look to him as *the only* possible change agent is naive. This implies that no other staff member has the interest and capabilities necessary to contribute creatively. While it is true that the superintendent or members of his staff should be included in a change agent team because of their key position in decision-making and their broad view of the district, other personnel should also be included. Teachers, principals, and school board members should collaborate in change efforts which can utilize their ideas and abilities and their linkage roles. In the final analysis, the success of a change project will depend upon how well all key members of a district plan and manage the process by which it is accomplished. This view led the Wisconsin staff to the concept of an internal team designed for school district innovation. (See Goodson and Hammes, 1968.)

Criteria for Change Agent Teams

Criteria for change agent team design were formulated as follows:

Size. A team should be large enough to use the potential of several individuals representing a variety of roles but small enough to meet as a face-to-face group. The ideal size is from five to eight members.

High-Level Representation. The superintendent or his central office representatives should be on the change agent team. Such representation provides the team with legitimacy, broad perspective, and leverage for implementation.

Vertical Role Representation. Principals, teachers, and school board officers should be members of change teams. This more readily insures diverse thinking in problem-solving and provides necessary linkages throughout the district.

These criteria, along with a statement of team functions, were communicated to the superintendents of the three districts involved. Two main functions were projected. One was to assist colleagues in developing and maintaining a climate in which innovation might flourish as a natural state of affairs. The second was to plan and manage specific innovations which a district might need or desire.

Within these broad functions more instrumental strategies of change agent teams were described, as follows: (1) to give attention to the school district as a whole and consider needed changes, (2) to plan and coordinate strategies for initiating and maintaining change processes, (3) to consult with central office colleagues and school faculties concerning a particular innovation and to consider the prevailing climate regarding needs and efforts in improvement, including resistances to change, and (4) to act as a resource to colleagues in planning and managing change.

Structure of Change Agent Teams

Each of the three districts that received training responded in a different manner to these general conditions of team design. District A created a new team with eight members, consisting of a school board member, assistant superintendent, the elementary and junior high school principals, psychologist, and three teachers representing the elementary, junior, and senior high school levels. District B modified an already existent high school curriculum council composed of department chairmen. It was chaired by the coordinator for instruction. An elementary school principal was added, to make a group of fourteen members. District C used as its change agent team a standing Improvement Committee composed of the superintendent, two coordinators, one high school principal, and two elementary school principals. This structure was later modified to include teachers and related teams in buildings.

Interventions by the Outside Consultants

The outside consultants served two functions: (1) to observe and analyze the change process and (2) to offer human development training and interpersonal support without deliberately influencing the districts toward any particular innovations. The design involved the Wisconsin staff working as an outside change agent with the three internal teams, which in turn functioned as innovators within their respective districts. The interpersonal and problem-solving processes ("Dialogue-Inquiry-Action Model") used by the outside team served as training strategies for the internal teams, which could use them subsequently with their colleagues. Thus there was a mirroring or simulation of processes thought essential to creating changes, with continuous and reciprocal feedback between colleagues, the internal change agent team, and the Wisconsin staff.

Style of the Intervention

The intervention used by the outsiders rested upon two considerations: one involved trust and respect and the other the use of a therapeutic philosophy. A school district has an integrity that requires it to be respected ethically and factually by an outside agency. As outside consultants, we tried to be sensitive to the districts' indigenous qualities and to respect the realities and the personalities involved.

Leonard Duhl (1967) has described the therapeutic model by drawing a parallel between the patient-therapist relationship and the processes involved in planned social change. He states: "When a patient comes to a therapist reporting a current crisis, he usually asks for help in reaching a certain goal. If the therapist were a planner, he would probably . . . outline five steps for the patient to take. If, however, the therapist simply gives a patient five steps to follow, nothing will happen. He must initially teach the patient the *step-by-step process of assimilating new information, of reconceptualizing the world, of looking toward generalized goals, and of thinking about how certain immediate steps may be directed toward these generalized goals.*"

This therapeutic model emphasizes autoplastic development—growth from *within* the system. Development in which the change process originates *outside* the system and exerts influence from that position in modifying the inner workings of the system is described as alloplastic development. In relating to the change agents of the school districts, we used the therapeutic model with a decided emphasis on autoplastic development.

Human Development Laboratory Training

The University of Wisconsin consultants offered training to the school districts consistent with their concepts of trust and autoplastic development. The training program was called the Human Development Laboratory (originally named the Human Relations Workshop) and met for sixteen hours, typically eight hours per day on a Friday and Saturday. Laboratory sessions were designed to help participants develop abilities in two areas: (1) interpersonal competencies involved in relating and communicating with others as well as understanding oneself and (2) competencies necessary for activating a problem-solving process ("dialogue-inquiry-action model"), including establishing priorities, planning strategies, handling data, and using external resources.

One goal of the laboratory training was the acquisition of a sharpened diagnostic sensitivity. Another was the growth of self-awareness. The training also aimed at helping participants to experiment with and practice ways of intervening in relationships with others. Finally, an important goal of laboratory training was to afford an opportunity for participants to reassess and modify appropriately their deep-seated dispositions and stereotypes regarding role groups and certain individuals in the district.

The laboratory training design was a set of related dialogue-inquiry-action sequences that participants and trainers activated and attempted to maintain. Three elements were generally incorporated: (1) a basic group variously named "encounter group," "sensitivity training group," "T-group," or, as we called it, a "dialogue" group (D-group), (2) focused or structured exercises, and (3) information-giving sessions in which theory was succinctly presented.

The Human Development Laboratory was designed to enhance and further develop two interpersonal and problem-solving competencies. The discrete competencies (or components thereof) were always related to personal functioning and were conceptually brought together in the trilogy of dialogue-inquiry-action. A training sequence that influenced both competencies consisted of two complementary phases with an interlude between Session I and Session II of approximately six weeks. Our design emphasizing interpersonal competencies always was antecedent to the problem-solving.

The main goal of the laboratory training was a functional integration enabling participants to use interpersonal and problem-solving skills appropriately in dealing with tasks. One trainee described the effect of his laboratory training on his work at school. He said: "I can now better sense when I should speak, when I should listen, when I should state alternatives or raise questions, and when I should press for action."

The D-group is usually an intense experience for the participants. It becomes appropriate, if not a matter of felt necessity, for participants to disclose themselves through overt actions and to receive feedback from others. Feelings become very much involved, highlighting the learning process taking place for each member. The procedure for growth is the reverse of that in other methods, such as reading or listening to lectures. We believe that experience precedes conceptualization. Words and symbols become attached to events and summarize segments of experience. The use of symbols which have been enriched by meaningful experience enables members to communicate, often at an abstract level, and reflect upon experiences in the D-group. When learning is occurring, the emphasis is on the here-and-now and not something outside the present which can be described only abstractly.

Another important aspect of the training group is the trainer's behavior. As an authority (a typical assumption of his position made by the members), the trainer violates their ordinary expectations. He does not provide external structure; rather, members generate structure through attempts at interpersonal influence on the basis of the needs and concepts they bring.

A Model for Planning and Action

In planning the laboratory design, we used a dialogue-inquiry-action model. A term used interchangeably with dialogue-inquiry-action in this chapter is "problem-solving." Very few human situations can be reduced to a one-problem analysis. The actuality of problem-solving requires the merging of cooperative inquiries and dialogue among group members. Since the formulation of a problem is only one step in the larger process of changing reality, the more complete phrase, "dialogue-inquiry-action," is preferred.

The model relates the mission of a school to its realities and has mediating functions which a professional staff must perform and take responsibility for if the school is to improve. The reality of a school is multiple. Parent expectations, interpersonal norms of the professional staff, behavior and goals of students, structures of the school, teacher and administrator competence, and organizational climate and other conditions represent segments of reality that may need attention. When during training a staff focuses attention upon a particular segment, both careful description and careful evaluation are needed. Dialogue and shared inquiry among members of a staff facilitate the description and evaluation of reality.

Describing and evaluating reality lead naturally to formulating problems and identifying needs and also toward setting goals in accordance with reality which are consistent with missions of the school. The next stage involves elaborating and examining alternative plans. These activities are related to the evaluation of reality in terms of problems and needs determined by participants. It is during the planning phase that ideas from outside innovators become relevant as alternatives to be examined. The last phase involves implementing plans and is of greatest importance in ultimately determining the success of a change process.

Another important feature of the model is that it involves both figure and ground, in the Gestalt perceptual sense. Figure is represented by the dialogue-inquiry-action process itself. It is a *primary* process from which *secondary* functions emerge. Dialogue is interaction among professional colleagues, and it is from such dialogue, facilitated by the interpersonal competencies of participants, that the activities in the model are generated and given meaning. Dialogue activates inquiry. It enables group members to raise questions and to state and consider alternatives. Dialogue-inquiry terminates in a resolution—a decision or settlement which motivates change agent team members to go on the next function.

The ground may be conceptualized as the normative and motivational conditions of a school district. A previous study by a colleague (Hilfiker, 1969) demonstrated a relationship between norms of trust, openness, adaptability, and problem-solving adequacy, and the outcomes of innovativeness. The intensity of norms influences the degree to which participants take part in dialogue-inquiry-action processes. The norms, therefore, determine the dynamic characteristics of a school. Intensely positive feelings shared by participants about such norms enliven and nurture activities in the model. At the opposite extreme, "hopeless" or "don't care" attitudes among educators do not facilitate but rather depress dialogue-inquiry-action.

Elements of Laboratory Training

Initially, the University of Wisconsin consultants carried major responsibilities for designing and implementing Human Development Laboratories. Later change agent teams assumed more responsibility for setting goals, describing and diagnosing their schools, formulating problems to be solved, and identifying needs to be satisfied through training. The change agent teams used the dialogue-inquiry-action model in guiding their respective activities and in planning cooperative activities. Thus, the model provided a reciprocal mirroring between problem-solving processes of the outside consultants and those that change agents needed to institutionalize in their districts. The outsiders also needed continuous evaluation and feedback to reinforce their efforts to clarify and enhance problem-solving processes, for they also faced the task of upgrading performance.

Three elements were generally incorporated in laboratory designs. They were the D-groups, structured exercises, and information-giving sessions.

Dialogue Groups (D-Groups)

Basic to human development training was the formation of D-groups. These are generally constituted of nine to twelve members free to discuss any subject, including interpersonal problems, and to give feedback to others concerning reactions and feelings. Exercises to facilitate interpersonal inquiry and self-disclosure for learning used with D-group members are as follows:

Self-Description and Prediction. Based on first impressions among the D-group and on their own experiences in groups, participants make predictions of their own behavior by responding to the following directives:
  Select the person whom you feel will act most differently from you.
  List words or phrases describing your predictions as to how he will behave.
  List words or phrases which describe your predictions as to how you will behave.

Group Interaction Predictions. At the D-group's onset, members are asked to predict who will be high and low participators and who will have high and low influence. They are also asked who will try to create a congenial atmosphere, who will create an atmosphere of disagreement, and who will try to create an atmosphere of calm.

Membership Exercise. Participants are asked to look for behaviors during D-group discussion and to respond to the following directives:
  List members who tend to support one another.
  List members who tend to oppose one another.
  List members of the group who seem to be most "in."
  Note what member of the group seems most "out."
  List the conditions under which people come into and move out of the group.

Reaction Scale. Participants are asked to answer questions such as: To what extent are your opinions being solicited by the group? How satisfied do you feel with your participation in moving toward a decision? How much frustration do you feel as the work on the decision goes on? How good is the decision your group is making?

Positive and Negative Elements in Self-Image. All participants are given lists of 220 self-descriptive adjectives which include words such as: aggressive, caring, confident, dependable, lively, nervous, over-emotional, powerful, rationalizing, rigid, serious, strong, vulnerable, and zestful. They choose three positive traits which they have and would like to retain and three negative traits which they also possess but which they would like to do away with. After they have completed this by themselves each member selects a partner. The two exchange papers and discuss reasons for their choices. All participants are then reassembled to report on their partner's lists. In this way, an individual reveals himself to another person who then edits the findings and reports back to the group. Group members might ask questions, make comments, give suggestions, or agree or disagree with an individual's perceptions of himself.

Structured Exercises

Structured exercises were also incorporated into the laboratory. Four of these exercises are included here:

Listening Exercise. Participants are grouped in triads and given eight to ten important topics for discussion. In each triad one member acts as the mediator or evaluator and the other two discuss the topics. Roles are reversed after approximately five to seven minutes of dialogue, so that each member is given the opportunity to be a participant and a mediator. Before a member may speak he must summarize (in his own words) remarks made by the previous speaker, making it necessary for the participant to listen and comprehend.

NASA Exercise. Members are grouped in clusters of six to ten people and asked to complete by themselves a worksheet determining priorities in the selection of items for survival on the moon. After individual sheets are completed, clusters meet to determine priorities of their group. Consensus must be reached by the group to rank the items. (See Pfeiffer and Jones, 1969.)

Five Square Puzzle. Participants are divided into groups of five. Each member is given an envelope containing puzzle pieces for forming squares. The group task is to form five squares of equal size. During the exercise no member may speak. No member may ask another for a piece or in any way signal another member and ask for a piece. Participants may, however, give pieces to other members. (See Pfeiffer and Jones, 1969.)

Conflict and Collaboration Exercise. Participants are divided into two groups, which are then asked to determine solutions to a problem. The problem should be such that the groups will develop significantly different solutions. The groups then choose representatives to work out a common solution. Both groups are present when the discussion occurs but are on the opposite sides of a negotiations table. Each group can communicate with its representative by way of written messages. If representatives are unable to agree, problem-solving suggestions are made by the consultants to give practice in collaboration. (See Harrison, 1967.)

Presentation of Concepts

Cognitive inputs were used by the University of Wisconsin consultants as needed. The presentations were designed to present concepts for understanding the experiences. The basic rationale of laboratory training is to facilitate for the participant a better integration between his emotional experiences, his behavior or action, and his referential or cognitive processes. The following ideas were used frequently, either for summarizing an experience or for initiating a training experience:

Self-Disclosure and Feedback (Johari Window). A process of learning for a D-group member is self-disclosure and feedback. This is the initial aspect of the training experience. As a member discloses himself by self-references (feelings, self-concepts, etc.), he initiates a positive gain in self-awareness and effective participation. The consummation of the learning process comes through feedback from other group members (their responses to acts of self-reference and disclosure). The process may be diagrammed as in the Johari window. (See Luft, 1969.)

Criteria for Effective Feedback. During encounters, members of D-groups are likely to experience anxiety. Feedback is an important procedure in learning how to handle anxiety. It needs to be done as competently as possible. This means, among other things, that the anxiety level of the receiving person should be kept low, for anxiety contaminates and attenuates such critical processes as self-awareness, sensory acuity and discrimination, dialogue, and inquiry—the very processes that the D-group is designed to enhance. Attention, therefore, must be given to the following characteristics of constructive feedback: (1) it is specific and not general; (2) it is tentative and not dogmatic; (3) it informs and does not order; (4) it describes behavior and one's perception of behavior and does not generalize on it or categorize it as good or bad; (5) it describes one's own feelings, underscoring the "I-Thou" relationship and avoiding making the other into an object; (6) it is not name calling; (7) it does not accuse or impugn undesirable motives to the recipient.

Dialogue-Inquiry-Action (Problem-Solving Model). This model was described earlier in this chapter. Our experience indicates that the orientation to a sequential problem-solving process should be brief. The model may also be used effectively as a guide to certain junctures in the sequence: for example, when a group is moving from selecting an action plan to implementing of the plan. Its most effective use, however, is in conceptualizing the process and inviting dialogue-inquiry regarding the process itself after participants have experienced the various steps.

Other Concepts. Other cognitive inputs included different personality styles and their effect on social interaction, Erikson's (1963) eight stages of the life cycle and teacher or administrator influence, Jones's (1968) ideas regarding creative learning in contrast with anxiety, and survey data feedback. (See Chapter 6.)

Training the Change Agent Teams

After formation of the teams, a series of training sessions was held. The three teams attended jointly. The first session was held in the spring of 1967. The major goal was improving the group processes of change agent teams through human development training.

Participants came prepared for a typical in-service workshop with lectures on team functioning and oppo tunities to work on problems. When this did not occur many participants became confused and uncomfortable. Shortly afterward a member of one of the change agent teams evaluated the session as follows: "After the initial shock of being exposed to this type of training, I feel much can be accomplished." Another stated: "If I had this to do over, I would have stayed home." While a third participant responded: "It was a new experience for me to explore this technique. I was amazed at the evolving structure of the various groups, and the patterns that I observed and even the evident change in some of the personalities. I believe that I have profited from this experience and trust that I will be able to carry over what I have learned into all my future meetings."

Even two years later when members of the change agent teams were planning Human Development Laboratories for colleagues, they sometimes referred to the confusion and distrust that was felt when they first participated in these sessions.

Most of the initial Human Development Laboratories combined process and task orientations, although one or the other usually predominated. For example, one of the initial sessions began with members of all three district teams meeting separately in three D-groups. Following this, members of the teams were mixed together to form three heterogeneous D-groups. After some time they stopped to analyze what they had learned about one another and how that affected their team's work. Later each team worked together on a task while the other teams observed to see how the group functioned and made suggestions on how the team could work together more effectively. Finally there was a time when each team worked on its problem only, using a force field analysis: a problem-solving technique wherein forces, both positive and negative, affecting the task are diagrammed and weighted. In this laboratory session both the problem (the way in which the team worked together) and the task (the problem on which it worked) were discussed.

Goals of the next two laboratory sessions planned for change agent teams included: relating D-group training to the functioning of change agent teams "back home," learning and using problem-solving techniques, and providing additional information regarding district problems through survey data feedback. By the fourth session, change agent teams had accepted and become enthusiastic about the results of training.

The change agent teams were asked next to decide on an innovation which they would introduce into their respective districts. We outsiders provided guidelines for choosing an innovation as follows: (1) Has your team developed an operational definition of an innovation? (2) Has your team developed a system of priorities for innovations which you think are relevant and desirable locally? (3) Which of the innovations can be processed through your team? (4) What levels of decision-making should be used in achieving the change: teachers, administrators, school board members, or the electorate? (5) What limiting variables should be considered before the final selection of innovation?

Using these criteria, District A chose to work on the introduction of independent study, District B selected modular scheduling and independent study, and District C began the formulation of a philosophy of education.

Change Agent Team Activities

The change agent teams also met independently of the outside consultants. Each of their meetings was tape-recorded; later the tapes were analyzed by us. Through this analysis we were able to see effects of the Human Development Laboratory and to note each group's progress. Although the teams had identical laboratory experiences, participated in sessions involving human development and problem-solving areas, and were provided with similar criteria for selecting an innovation, each team had developed diverse characteristics, goals, and problems.

District A

District A, the largest of the three, employed approximately 500 professionals and had two senior high schools. The District, like the city in which it was located, was generally considered conservative and slow to change, but also had the reputation of being solid. In general, when innovations were introduced, they were carried on in a few schools as pilot projects and introduced in other schools slowly. In a recent study involving eight districts, School District A ranked sixth in innovativeness (Hilfiker, 1970). The city itself, which was a small manufacturing community, was growing but at a slower rate than many other cities in Wisconsin. Some of its major industries were moving elsewhere. The term "stable" best described both the city and the schools.

The change agent team began with six members (five administrators and one board member) selected by the Superintendent of Schools. During the first year an elementary and a senior high school teacher were added to the team. This group chose the introduction of independent study as its goal. This project aimed at helping teachers to give students opportunities to progress at their own rate and to adapt instruction to individual differences, especially in elementary schools. Approximately twenty elementary teachers and administrators from three schools were initial participants. They attended two training sessions (planned by the outside consultants and the change agent team) involving interpersonal relations, communication, problem-solving, and an introduction to independent study.

During one of the training sessions a problem concerning independent study was identified and analyzed. The procedure is summarized as follows:

Problem: How can we best organize the curriculum to achieve more independent study?

Possible solution: Employ both a director of elementary education and a director of secondary education. This would provide (1) greater involvement of teachers with internal consultants for curriculum change; (2) more positive forces (continued coordination and flexibility of classroom instruction); (3) coordination of elementary, junior, and senior high school programs; and (4) strengthened in-service training of teachers with the use of released time, para-professionals, resource persons, and consultants, and a clarification of the total program.

Participants (central office staff, principals, teachers, and the change agents) discussed this problem and solution. It was decided to ask the school board to create the two new positions. This was done: job descriptions were written and the central office staff in School District A now includes a director of elementary education and a director of secondary education.

In addition, approximately forty participants (including the entire guidance staff, several teachers and administrators, and the change agent team) attended the two Human Development Laboratories planned for guidance personnel.

Since the beginning of the planned change project, sixty-nine people have received a total of 3,536 training hours. A two-day planning session was held by the change agent team at the end of the school year to determine goals for 1969-70, to plan for Human Development Laboratory training for an additional seventy teachers interested in independent study, and to develop a budget for the project.

During this time the change agent team evaluated the project in this manner:

In accord with the objectives of the project our change agent team has undergone a series of training sessions in human development and problem-solving areas, has determined educational needs within the school district and has begun to introduce a particular innovation—independent study—into the schools. This has been done by determining where and with whom the innovation should be introduced and by re-educating personnel of the system through sensitivity training, in-service sessions, observations, and planned meetings.

Of particular value to the change agent team during the three years of involvement in the project have been: (1) consultant services of members of the Wisconsin staff; (2) the makeup, continuing membership and stability and the increased maturity of the change agent team which has made this group more effective; (3) Human Development Laboratory training, which has promoted positive change in attitudes on the part of educators involved; and (4) enthusiasm and interest shown by members of elementary schools involved in the independent study projects.

Negative aspects of the project as seen by the change agent team include: (1) limited use of feedback from data collections; (2) lack of time for the change agent team to meet and work; and (3) resistance to change by some professionals.

The change agent team believes that Human Development Laboratory training has resulted in an increasing sense of trust and respect within the district and that additional sessions should be conducted under the direction of trained leaders. It also feels that this project should be continued and the members of the Wisconsin staff should be maintained as consultants. The focus must now be on our school district, however, and the change agent team must make decisions and move out on its own.

The makeup, continuing membership, and training of the change agent team in District A proved advantageous to the project, as did the support of the Superintendent of Schools, the approval of the Board of Education, the guidance of the Wisconsin staff, and the enthusiasm of those who participated in Human Development Laboratories. The size of the district and the lack of time to plan and implement change seemed to be the major obstacles to the attainment of some goals.

District B

District B is also located in a manufacturing center. The community has a population of over 10,000 and is growing rapidly. This growth has forced the district to expand and presented the opportunity for innovation as the district constructs new schools. There are approximately 200 professional employees in the district. In 1967 this district was rated as the most innovative system of the eight in the sample; hundreds of teachers and school administrators have visited it every year to observe its innovative procedures. Partly because of rapid changes in the community, this district underwent several great changes during the time of the project. These included a change in the superintendent and the subsequent resignation of two school board members, the passing of a twice-defeated bond issue, and the planning of a new high school.

The change agent team consisted initially of thirteen members, including the district director of instruction, nine members of the high school faculty, three members of the junior high school faculty, and an elementary school principal. After approximately eight months of work, the new Superintendent of Schools felt that a new change agent team should be elected. All members of the original change agent team were re-elected with the exception of one faculty member. Several months later the superintendent again decided to reorganize the team. In the new group he included fourteen members: one from each of the departments in the high school and the director of instruction. The new change agent team included only three of the original team members.

The District B team went through two periods of training and identifying district needs. The initial team had focused on modular scheduling and independent study as innovations which they felt should be introduced. After the team's reorganization a bond issue was passed. This gave the new change agent team a goal: to help train colleagues to carry out innovations in a new high school.

In order to do this, the change agent team decided to establish a Human Development Laboratory which would include all 100 members of the high school faculty. The team and the outside consultants spent a day and a half in preparation for the laboratory. Goals for their planning meeting included: (1) to prepare a diagnosis of the school's faculty meeting, (2) to consider operational plans for the day of training and (3) to develop training exercises and instruments to be used in faculty and departmental meetings.

The change agent team identified goals and problems, and listed and assigned priorities to these. The group also developed a force-field analysis of the task of involving the entire staff of the high school in a Human Development Laboratory. The team decided to function as co-trainers with the outside consultants and assisted in the planning and preparing of the training design. (See Chapter 5 for description of another start-up laboratory.)

During the training event, the faculty's role in decision-making became a prominent topic for discussion. At one point members of the change agent team and the superintendent met in an inner circle with one empty chair to discuss recommendations concerning decision-making which had been formulated by small clusters of the new faculty. The remainder of the faculty was seated in a larger outer circle. They observed the inner group's process and could participate in the discussion by sitting in the additional chair in the inner circle.

Several recommendations on decision-making were made—among them the following: (1) we believe that decisions affecting teachers should be made cooperatively; (2) we are agreed that a definite problem exists regarding communication between staff and administration, and that change must take place concerning communication among all; (3) in any instance of contention with faculty decision, the school board or other members of this community may call a public meeting to discuss the action of the faculty and overrule it; (4) a well-defined communications system that allows for a free flow of ideas among all parties should be structured so that decisions are reached with mutual trust and confidence.

One member of the change agent team evaluated the Human Development Laboratory in this manner: "People told me this was the best in-service we've ever had. They expressed very positive personal feelings. My own were a little less positive." Another stated, "People see us trying to make progress and feel better about the change agent team." A third stated, "Frustration was high after the meeting. People felt they were cut off too soon. Some self-condemnation: people felt they had been hypocritical." Still another said, "What are the next steps? The staff is ready for more involvement."

The initial team after training was ready to begin incorporating the innovations which they had chosen, but when the group was reorganized, training of the new team, reidentification of needs and problems, and the selection of a new innovation had to be done again. Human Development Laboratory training, commitment of members of the change agent team to the project, and the support of the Wisconsin staff seemed to be factors which contributed to the success of the new group. On the other hand, the lack of change agent team stability, uncertainty about the future of the team, reorganization of the group, the need for retraining, and lack of support from the Superintendent of Schools were major obstacles encountered by this team in the attainment of its goals. The change agent team in District B decided to continue meeting during the following school year. They were committed to the project. During the two years approximately 125 professional members of the district received 2,408 hours of laboratory training.

District C

District C was the smallest in the study. It served two villages and consisted of two elementary schools (one in each village) and a high school. Approximately eighty professional workers were employed by the district. It was a new district and also highly innovative; it ranked third in innovativeness among the eight districts studied in 1967. It was somewhat restricted, however, by being located in a conservative area; a survey of parents in 1969 showed that 46 percent felt that "too many" new ideas were being tried in their schools. Another problem in this district was high staff turnover, due in part to the hiring of young teachers who were married to students at the University of Wisconsin.

The initial change agent team was made up of five administrators. During summer 1967, the district acquired a new superintendent. He became a member of the change agent team. The group was later expanded to include four teachers, bringing the total membership to nine. A unique situation occurred in this district. A member of the Wisconsin staff was also a resident of the district and a member of the school board, and had been instrumental in unifying the district and planning for the new high school. This undoubtedly encouraged involvement in and continuation of the project.

Because many of the original members of the change agent team left the district after the first year, the group was reorganized during 1968. The structure of the team was changed at this time. Three committees (one in each school) plus a coordinating committee of the three principals were formed. The superintendent was no longer a member of the change agent team after its restructuring.

The goal of the initial change agent team had been to write a philosophy of education for the district. This was a very appropriate project. Because of the high turnover in the district, a written philosophy would be valuable for new teachers and would give the new superintendent a chance to shape and influence policy.

The procedure for writing it, however, caused problems in the district. The statement of philosophy written by the change agent team, whose members were largely younger and more innovative teachers who remain in the district only a year or two. Since older teachers who had taught in the schools for many years were not involved, feelings of resentment and a division between the two groups developed at this time.

After this project was completed, the change agent team focused on the implementation of ungraded elementary schools. With the reorganization of the team, improvement of the format of high school classes and the introduction of multi-unit elementary schools became major goals of the group.

During the project's two years, approximately 65 percent of the professional staff in District C spent a total of 1,440 hours in Human Development Laboratory training sessions.

The initial group chosen by the change agent team to participate in the laboratory training was composed of the six members of the high school English department, their principal, and six upper primary teachers from one of the elementary schools. The elementary school was to initiate team teaching and ungraded classes in the fall. The members attending the session would be working as a team at that time. We hoped that this session might bring the groups into dialogue and that the elementary school faculty would be helped to implement their new procedures.

Originally the design called for D-groups made up of members of both the secondary and elementary faculties. The format was changed, however, when it became apparent that the English team had personal and philosophical differences which needed to be explored. Because of this, the English team and the elementary faculty met separately to discuss problems and procedures in preparing for the innovations.

The English team had varying reactions to the training. Two members left early and did not return. Others felt that the session has been very helpful. Some members were simply confused by what had taken place. Most seemed to agree that problems buried before had now been revealed. By the end of the semester, however, the English team disbanded. This was blamed, by some, on the laboratory training. It had a deleterious effect on the subsequent labs since it frightened potential participants and caused the superintendent to become unsure of the training. Subsequently anxiety feelings at the beginning of further sessions in District C were always higher than in any other district.

In comparison, the elementary faculty members attending this session had a very successful experience and asked to come back later with their principal, so that they could make more progress in preparing for changes. As a result, a second training session was held for this group.

After the reorganization of the change agent team, a combined training session was planned and executed for members of a standing teachers' in-service committee and the change agent team. The final laboratory training session focused on problem-solving techniques and the use of consultants for training in a specific area. Participants included the faculty of the other elementary school in the district which requested the training before initiating plans to become a multi-unit, team teaching school.

A questionnaire was sent to members of the professional staff in this district which asked them to evaluate the change agent team. Typical responses to the question, "How is the change agent team different from other school committees?" were as follows:

The change agent team deals with people working on various levels in the district. It is more of a planning and thinking committee.

It works in a larger area dealing with the whole school. Other committees deal with a specific area.

The change agent team seeks to improve the *whole school district.*

The small size of the district and the innovativeness of its faculties were the greatest assets to this change agent team. District C had only eighty professional employees. The change agent team could, therefore, see progress in a relatively short period of time. Due to normal teacher turnover, however, the composition and structure of the team changed almost entirely during the second year of the project. This, and a seeming lack of commitment to the concept of the change agent team and the Human Development Laboratory training by some of the professional staff members was probably the major obstacle to the team's success.

Research Evaluation

The Wisconsin staff collected observations on support for change agent teams and laboratory training, observations of growth in the effectiveness of persons and of change agent teams after laboratory training, evaluations of the program from anonymous questionnaires, and systematic data on changes in attitudes and behavior from questionnaires administered at the beginning and conclusion of the project.

Effects of Laboratory Training

Leaders in the experimental districts evaluated effects of laboratory training positively. After observing some outcomes, they committed substantial resources to further training. Although our Research and Development Center covered the costs of training, the districts were responsible for costs of meeting rooms, meals, overnight lodging, and salaries for substitutes to replace teachers who were participating. Given the many hours spent in these sessions, these were sizeable investments, and it is unlikely that the schools would have invested so heavily had the training not been perceived as useful.

The change agent teams that had laboratory training survived and continue to exist. In contrast, the teams established with no laboratory training or external support in two of the five control districts withered and died before they became well organized.

From observation of the teams during training sessions and from listening to tape recordings of their regular meetings, the Wisconsin staff became convinced that the human development training was being used outside of the training sessions and was increasing the teams' effectiveness. For example, one tape revealed a confrontation between two members, who were discussing the absence of one of them from the previous meeting. The member who had been present was angry and felt that this absence denoted a lack of commitment. Business was set aside until this confrontation was satisfactorily resolved and the group was ready to work again, thus showing that the group had the wherewithal to solve its own process problems. In another meeting a group member remarked, "I have often sat at this table and felt frustrated and afraid to say anything." There was a moment of silence and then a shocked, "In this group?" from another member. The first immediately exclaimed, "oh, no! I meant with other committees that meet in this room." This was followed by a relieved, "I couldn't imagine that you wouldn't feel free in this group." It seemed apparent that openness and freedom of communication had primary goals for this change agent team.

Similar observations revealed the personal growth of teachers and administrators who had experienced human development training. A specialist who had worked with personnel in several schools asked to participate in the training because, she said, "During the year I noticed that suddenly a teacher would become more easy to work with, listen more, and be willing to try out my suggestions. Then one day I discovered all the teachers who had changed had been going to the training sessions." A teacher reported that training had improved her teaching. One of her children had even told her that the class enjoyed school more, "because now you treat us more like people." Another team member found a particular structured exercise carried out at one of the laboratories very helpful to him in understanding others. Two years later when another laboratory session was being planned in the same district one of his teammates suggested that the exercise be used again. Turning to the member who had originally found the exercise valuable she remarked, "You remember that exercise—the one that changed your whole life!"

Human development training seemed to create an opportunity for people to explore change. In one district the change agent team brought together the faculties of three elementary schools to discuss introducing independent study in the classroom. During the meeting one teacher explained in strong terms to the superintendent why she opposed independent study and why it would not work in her classroom. Following this discussion, she and others who opposed independent study, along with some who were in favor of it, formed a study committee to investigate it for themselves. A few months later the Wisconsin staff received a tape recording of a meeting of the change agent team with this group of teachers. On the tape the teacher who had opposed independent study was heard to say, "I don't see why we can't go ahead with independent study right away. I'm already using it with my class. Why are you administrators always slowing things up?"

Another group of teachers used the laboratory setting to plan for an innovation that was to be introduced during the following fall. After much discussion they arrived at the conclusion that they were blocked because the aims of the principal, who was not present at the laboratory, were not clear. The group then talked with the principal and arranged for him to attend a second laboratory session in order to eliminate the ambiguity.

Responses to Questionnaires

These casual observations concerning the effectiveness of the training were corroborated by the response to questions asked of samples of more than two-thirds of the professional staff members of the three experimental systems in 1969. About 22 percent reported attending meetings arranged by the Wisconsin staff, and about 17 percent reported attending laboratory training sessions. Of the 96 attending such training sessions, the average number of sessions attended was 3.23. Those who attended were asked, "How valuable have these laboratory training sessions been to you personally?" The distribution of responses in each district was as follows:

Table 8-1 Perceived Personal Value of Training

Value for You Personally	District A	District B	District C	Total
Great value	36%	31%	21%	32%
Some value	35	34	42	36
A little value	9	19	33	16
No value	15	16	0	12
More harmful than valuable	5	0	4	3
Total Percentage	100%	100%	100%	100%
Number of Cases	66	32	24	122

About one-third of the total reported that the experiences were of great personal value to them. They were also asked, "How valuable do you think these laboratory training sessions have been to your district?"

Table 8-2 Perceived Organizational Value of Training

Value for School District	District A	District B	District C	Total
Great value	22%	22%	17%	21%
Some value	43	28	42	39
A little value	18	31	33	24
No value	7	19	8	11
More harmful than valuable	9	0	0	5
Total Percentage	100%	100%	100%	100%
Number of Cases	67	32	24	123

About 60 percent reported that the training sessions had at least some value for their districts. The responses are more positive for value to persons than to districts. This was in accord with our expectations, for we felt that the value of training for the district would become evident only after changes in individuals and small groups. The differences among the three districts shown in these data are not in accord with our personal judgments, however, for we felt that staff interventions were most effective in District A and least effective in District C.

These judgments of value correlated with morale of teachers and the support for norms of openness, trust, and innovation. An index measuring morale (i.e., satisfaction with schools and feelings of solidarity with staff members) had a product-moment correlation of 0.31 with responses to the question about personal value and of 0.29 with responses to the question about value for the district. An index of support for norms of openness, trust, and innovation had a correlation of 0.47 with responses to the question on personal value and 0.36 with responses to the question on value for the district. Our impression is that these correlations indicate that persons who developed these attitudes found the training more valuable, rather than that those who found the training valuable developed higher scores on the variables.

These data tend to support the notion that the interventions by the Wisconsin staff were effective. Other data do not. Comparison with other questionnaire responses for 1967 and 1969 provide no evidence that either individuals or districts exposed to the interventions improved significantly more than those not exposed.

Teachers and administrators were asked many of the same questions in 1967 and 1969. Included were questions about morale and support for norms of openness, trust, and innovation, as noted above, and questions about the amount of effort devoted to teaching innovations, the adequacy of staff meetings, and the quality of relations between teachers and principals. Data for 248 persons were available for these two time periods, although less than 13 percent (or 34 persons) of these 248 had attended any laboratory training sessions. No significant correlations existed between any of these change measures and frequency of exposure to training. For example, the correlation between an index of support for norms of openness, trust, and innovation and frequency of attendance at the Human Development Laboratories was 0.03 for the 1969 responses and 0.14 for the 1967 responses. These correlations would have to be much different to show that the training had a positive effect; to demonstrate such an effect there would have to be a significant positive correlation between exposure to training and the 1969 measure with the 1967 measure held constant. For the other dependent variables, correlation values were even smaller.

These results reflect either failure of the interventions to produce effects on the larger population of teachers and administrators or errors of measurement. There are several possible sources of measurement error: the samples from both the 1967 and 1969 populations may be non-representative; there may have been errors in merging data from the two points in time; or the measures may be too unreliable to detect change (measurement unreliability attenuates correlations among change scores far more than correlations from raw scores). Although some evidence indicates that the sample of persons for whom change data are available is unrepresentative, it is not believed that this error or other measurement errors account for the low correlations, because the correlations would have to be much larger than they are to attain significance. It seems more likely that the limited amount of training most persons received was not enough to produce lasting changes in the dependent variables. This is especially true for teacher innovativeness and relations between teachers and principals, which were not expected to be affected *directly* by the training. It remains likely that some teachers and administrators who received more intensive laboratory training were strongly affected by it, but the questionnaire data cannot demonstrate these effects either.

The data for changes in districts are superior in quality to the data for changes in individuals: the samples are larger, since it was not necessary to rely only on data for persons who answered questionnaires in both 1967 and 1969; and averages tend to be much more reliable than measures for individuals. Yet the average measures fail to show that the three districts with which the Wisconsin staff worked intensively improved more than the five control systems. Some of the data are shown in Figures 8-1 and 8-2. Figure 8-1 shows average responses of teachers and administrators in the eight districts studied to an

Figure 8-1 Mean Values of Support for Norms of Openness, Trust, and Innovation, Eight Wisconsin School Districts, 1967 and 1969

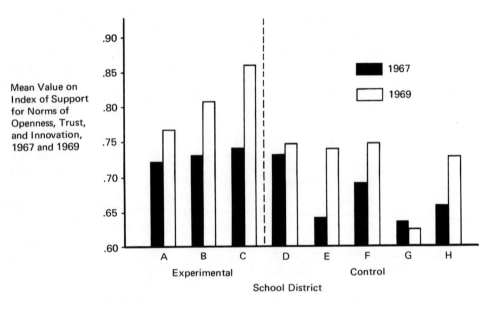

eleven-item index measuring support for norms of openness, trust, and innovation. While the three experimental districts showed the highest average support for these norms in 1969, they also did in 1967. The two districts showing the greatest improvement were in the control group.

The data in Figure 8-2 show changes in average responses to an 8-item index of morale between 1967 and 1969. The index was based on questions such as "I find my job very exciting and rewarding," "I feel involved in a lot of activities that go on in this school," and "I really don't feel satisfied with a lot of things that go on in this school." Changes in the response categories, from "always" to "almost never" in 1967 to "completely agree" to "completely disagree" in 1969, probably account for the lower average scores in 1969 than 1967, but this bias should be consistent across the eight districts. The graph shows that two of the three experimental districts had less improvement in morale than two of the five controls.

Data on teacher innovativeness, the adequacy of staff meetings, and the executive professional leadership of principals also fail to show that the experimental districts improved significantly more than the controls.

The failure to demonstrate the effectiveness of our interventions in changing basic norms and behaviors in districts may stem in part from the limited intensity and duration of the interventions; in order to make a basic change it

Figure 8-2 Relative Improvement in Mean Scores on Morale Index, Eight Wisconsin School Districts, Between 1967 and 1969

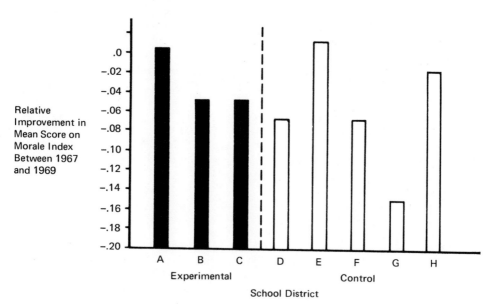

may be necessary to train more members of the staffs more intensively and for longer periods. (See Chapters 3 and 5.) In addition, other events and processes occurring in these districts, events and processes not at all under our control, were having large effects on morale, norms, and innovativeness. These events and processes include administrative succession and staff turnover.

Administrative Succession

During the project two of the three experimental districts experienced major changes in administrative personnel, while this was true of only two of the five control districts (where in any case the changes were less important). These experiences of administrative succession had great effects on personnel in the experimental districts.

District A had the same superintendent, director of instruction, and high school principals throughout the course of the study. Our staff felt that the project was most effective in this district. Part of the reason for this success was the continuing stable support for the project from the school administration.

In District B the superintendent resigned after the first collection of data (1967) and the establishment of the change agent team. His resignation was partly caused by the defeat of a bond issue in two successive elections and by disagreements with important board members. He had been known as a permissive leader in an innovative district. His successor, brought in from outside, was helped by the resignation of two board members and by the passage of the bond issue for a new high school; he may have been partly responsible for the latter success. At about the time of the second data collection, he announced his resignation. In the two year period the director of instruction and the high school principal resigned and were replaced. The new principal lasted only one year and was succeeded again. The succeeding superintendent was far more directive and dynamic than his predecessor and his contribution in terms of educational design for the new high school will be felt for a long time.

Administrative turnover was just as great in District C. Again the new superintendent took over from his predecessor after the first wave of data were collected and after the district's commitment to the project. His predecessor was the second of two superintendents of this highly innovative district. The two years saw the replacement of the superintendent's major administrative assistant (a role corresponding to the director of instruction), the high school principal, and both elementary school principals. One of the new elementary principals was in the district for a year and was replaced. In addition, during part of this period the central office had a special consultant—a dynamic woman associated with another innovative project.

In contrast, only one of the controls experienced the succession of superintendents, although the superintendent of another district became ill, which had a disorganizing effect on the district. Generally fewer changes occurred among the principals of the control districts.

In both 1967 and 1969 teachers and administrators were asked, "In general how much influence do you think the following role groups (listed below) now have in determining educational matters (e.g., curriculum, policy, etc.) in your school?" Response categories ranged from 0 for "none" to 4 for "a great deal." Respondents rated the local school board, the superintendent, the principal of their school, teachers in general, and a variety of others. The data were analyzed by summing the mean ratings for school board, superintendent, principal, and teachers in general, and then dividing each component by the sum. Thus the relative power of each role, using this index, could logically range from 0 percent, if the mean rating for the role was "none," to 100 percent, if the mean rating for the one role was greater than "none" and the mean rating for the other three roles was "none." Obviously all roles had at least some influence in each district, and the four roles do not exhaust sources of influence, so this index merely represents the *relative* influence of each.

The data indicate that in District B the superintendent's role gained greatly in perceived relative influence, mostly at the expense of the school board. In District C, the other district with a new superintendent, the role was perceived to lose influence very slightly. However, the data show that in District C teachers gained greatly in relative influence, entirely at the expense of principals. That administrative succession does not have uniform effects on authority patterns is also shown by results for two control systems in which the superintendent either resigned or became ill. In one district the superintendent lost influence almost equally to principals and teachers, and in another the superintendent was perceived to lose influence mostly to the board. The effects on influence patterns of administrative succession depend upon personal characteristics and also upon the state of the district at the time of succession.

Administrative succession has many effects upon other characteristics of districts, including the formalization of rules and norms about communication and innovation. Since our staff did not collect data systematically to study the effects of succession, we can only speculate about effects through prior research and theory (e.g., Gouldner, 1952 and 1954.)

A new official in any organization will probably be insecure, especially if he is appointed to change some policies. His superiors, not having full confidence in him, will monitor his behavior closely. Without informal relations with others, he will lack many important sources of organizational information. His subordinates are also likely to be insecure, especially if his predecessor has been permissive and democratic. They will attempt to extend their spheres of autonomy and will withhold information from him if they feel he may act against their interests. In such a situation, the new official is likely to move in two inconsistent directions: he may try to formalize rules and communication patterns and he may also engage in what Gouldner calls "pseudo-gemeinschaft" behavior with his subordinates, i.e., superficially friendly behavior designed to elicit trust and informal support that is treated with skepticism by others. In other words, the administrative successor will often increase aspects of the organization our interventions were designed to diminish: centralization, formalization of authority and communications, and reciprocal distrust. It is likely that these behaviors will be transitory; as the successor develops confidence and an informal network of work associates, distrust will diminish and the perceived importance of centralization and formalization will decline. In school districts this is likely to take at least two years, however.

We hoped that change agent teams would be able to assist in the transition process, but they did not, probably because they were not institutionalized at the time of transition. The succeeding superintendents evidently distrusted these "new" teams and the university group. One joined the change agent team as its leader, and initially its only other members were principals and other administrators. Only after about a year did he have enough confidence to include teachers, and during this period the team had been relatively ineffective in reaching its goals. The other superintendent drastically reorganized the team, although he did not join it; its leader, the director of instruction, and most of its members were newly appointed or elected. Nevertheless, this change agent team was suspicious of the superintendent. For some time they devoted much time in their regular meetings to discussing the extent to which the superintendent would permit them to influence district policies; skeptical that their effort would have any real effect, they devoted little time to important district policies and yet they failed to discuss these concerns with the superintendent openly for more than a year.

A well established change agent team should be able to aid in the transition when a new superintendent assumes office. They may serve as a channel for communicating the informal culture of the district and the hopes and fears of its members to him, and they may also serve as a sounding board for his ideas about possible district changes. The change agent teams under examination could not do this, for they were not well established, and the succession of superintendents made it difficult for them to become so.

Teacher Turnover

Turnover of teachers also has important consequences for districts, although these are not usually as dramatic or visible. More time is required for newcomers to be integrated into informal primary groups than into the formal organization; while formal rights and obligations may be quite explicit, informal procedures may be implicit and can be learned only through face-to-face interaction. Thus, when turnover rates increase, patterns of informal communication are less well developed. This means that high turnover makes it difficult for a district to transmit its distinctive culture to newcomers. Furthermore, when high turnover rates exist for a time, school staffs come to expect it to continue at a high rate. As a result, individuals will lack commitment to the school and will expect that others will also have low commitment. High turnover rates probably lead to lower levels of reciprocal trust, for there is ordinarily less reason to trust another who has no commitment to one's school.

Sometimes high turnover makes innovation easier. However, high turnover also makes it difficult to institutionalize change, also reduces levels of trust, and tends to emphasize power based upon formal position rather than upon competence. Thus, high turnover makes it more difficult to change districts in the ways attempted by the Wisconsin staff.

District C had the highest staff turnover in the sample of eight districts, although District B also had a relatively high rate of turnover. Table 8-3 indicates the range of turnover among the eight districts.

Table 8-3 Turnover in Eight Wisconsin School Districts

District	Percentage of Staff Employed for Less than Two Years	Percentage of Staff Hoping to be Employed in the Same District in 1974
Experimental:		
C	34%	46%
B	32%	52%
A	25%	60%
Control:		
E	21%	46%
G	21%	51%
D	20%	64%
H	13%	61%
F	12%	59%
All districts:	21%	58%

When, as in District C, more than one out of three teachers or administrators have served for less than two years (with more than one of six currently in their first year of service), and when fewer than half hope to be in the same district five years hence, it becomes difficult to institutionalize new norms regarding trust, cooperation, communication, and innovation. Even if satisfaction with teaching and administrative leadership is high, as it was in District C, commitment and involvement may be relatively low.

Data Feedback

One important aspect of the original intervention was the feedback of data from questionnaire surveys to change agent teams and others. Our staff felt this information would be useful in participants' efforts to diagnose problems in their schools and in their plans to solve problems. Thus, after the data from

1967 were compiled, a small portion of the results were discussed at meetings with change agent teams and others and printed memoranda containing these were distributed.

This feedback seemed to be without effect on activities of the experimental districts. For example, a discussion of low teacher morale and its correlatives received polite attention but elicited little discussion. A discussion of administrative succession and its correlatives aroused more interest; teachers in districts affected by new superintendents recognized the validity of the presentation and discussed it a little, but only in the session at which the material was presented; it appeared to have little effect on their later work. At another session the great differences in the morale of teachers and students in the two high schools of one of the districts was pointed out, but the discussion produced no further action. Somewhat later there was a student strike at the high school with low morale; while this suggests that our procedures might have some diagnostic validity, this knowledge is of little gratification, since in fact the data were not used for problem diagnosis or problem-solving.

It is evident that data, however valid, will not be used by change agent teams or school administrators unless they feel they already have a need for the data and a theory of action that will make the data relevant. (For further discussion see Chapter 6.) If data feedback is to be effective, the demands for data probably must come initially from participants: in this case the change agent teams or school administrators. We have not yet solved the problem of stimulating demand for data. Perhaps such demands will only arise if school personnel feel they have influence over school policies, if they can choose between real alternatives, and if they can see need for information about alternatives.

Alternative Futures

This chapter reports on two years of cooperative effort between a group of outside consultants and three school districts. What could have been done differently to have made the effort more productive?

A More Compelling Approach vs. the Therapeutic Model

The therapeutic model supports training in interpersonal and problem-solving competencies and emphasizes responsibilities of internal change agent teams to generate targets for change and to improve structures for facilitating change. We may have placed too much confidence in "process training," which assumes a discovery approach rather than the authority of a university expert to instruct personnel in problem-solving. The staff could have made a more aggressive thrust by directing the attention of school personnel to areas of school life requiring diagnostic effort and systematic planning for change.

A possible shortcoming of the nondirective approach is the seductiveness of sensitivity training. A lack of emphasis upon directly changing reality was recognized by a Wisconsin staff member, who described it in the following memorandum to his colleagues:

There is possible weakness in training for improvement of interpersonal relations. Such training offers only one component of a strategy for solving problems. To develop the point, consideration may be given to what is involved in improving a school. In addition to sensitivity training, problem-solving activities and their improvement as performed by school personnel are strategic. Human relations training is only one rubric of necessary activity. An accurate statement is that sensitivity training that emphasizes interpersonal relations is a necessary but not a sufficient activity in an effective strategy. The equally necessary rubric of problem-solving involves several sub-activities: describing and diagnosing reality, formulating problems, identifying needs, deliberate selecting of change targets (characteristics of the school reality that require change), planning and carrying out appropriate actions, evaluating outcomes so as to keep problem-solving in contact with reality, interpretation of data systematically collected about a school district, and similar activities . . . mounted by school personnel if improvements are to be made. Included also are activities of searching for and installing innovations that offer the prospect of changing the realities of the school.

How could our staff have been more forthright and helpful, followed through with more dispatch, and helped teams to become effective without investing more time and energy? Effective instruction involves motivation and self-direction of the learner that is facilitated by the instructor. Our staff's position is that only the educators themselves can make decisions but that the external agents may have to suggest strongly that focusing upon decision-making and specific action steps is necessary.

Improvement of Change Agent Team Structure

The status of change agent teams in Districts B and C was in doubt at times. Both groups lacked continuity of membership. The District B team did not have vertical role representation; it was composed primarily of high school representatives with an elementary principal as liaison. This was only a gesture toward the concept of a district-wide team. In District C the central change agent team enabled building teams to be formed. There was, however, a lack of coordination at the district level which was due, in part, to the fact that the central administrative staff members saw the district as being small and not needing a systematically operated structure to introduce and implement change.

Additional community involvement in change agent team activities would have been desirable. District C found that perceptions in their community indicated that the district was possibly too innovative. Helping community leaders to see goals and assist in setting expectations for public education is an important aspect of improvement.

District A had a school board member on the change agent team. This is one way to provide a link between schools and the community. Another way is to create problem-solving teams that include parents and pupils at the building level. This involvement of students and parents is calculated to open doors for more community, school, and professional dialogue, inquiry, and action.

Improvement of Human Development Laboratory Sessions

A mood of indecisiveness was projected at times by our staff, whose members were as dependent upon change agent teams as the teams were upon them. This was due in part to the group's own risk-taking efforts. The staff needed the opportunity, which the project provided, to explore techniques and to develop training designs. If a similar project were undertaken again, members of our group could act with more confidence and greater sensitivity and expertness at critical points in developing and executing training sessions.

Would additional or longer training laboratories have produced more penetrating effects? One and one-half days is not much time for a session of this kind. Districts intending to use this type of training might find ways to create a greater training density than that produced by sessions that last only one and a half days. The kind of schedule reported here did work well in the three districts. It is calculated that such is possible and compatible with the norms of many districts. When limited experience with training is seen as beneficial to a staff's improvement of group processes, perhaps the norms could be changed to allow for three to five days for the training laboratory in order to benefit the change agent team and its colleagues.

There could have been advanced laboratory training sessions for the change agent teams. During the second year of the project the teams themselves had no laboratory experiences for improving their own processes, although there were efforts by the Wisconsin staff to help the change agent team in District B work through its authority problems with the new superintendent. The members of the change agent team in District A felt the need for additional training but never implemented their own diagnosis.

Maximum learning requires experience in the full sequence of the dialogue-inquiry-action model. The teams had only limited opportunity for experiencing the full cycle. There were few instances in which changes in reality came about as a result of the problem-solving activities. The administrative additions made in District A after a training laboratory were a success for the team and its colleagues, as was the training day for the high school faculty in District B. These were probably the most obvious successes for any of the three teams. Had there been a greater number of successful experiences in carrying through the full process, the training would have been more effective.

More Meaningful Data Analysis

There could have been more focused training sequences for change agent team members involving them in collection and interpretation of data. Involvement through training and action in planning data collection would have given teams an opportunity to determine questions to which they wanted answers. Data analysis would then have likely become more relevant and useful to change agent teams.

Additional Technical Consultation

Our staff could have encouraged use of consultants in implementing of various changes selected by change agent teams: introduction of independent study, development of a PERT chart for the conversion from old high school to new high school in two years, and implementation of ungraded and unitized elementary schools. Districts A and C did use consultants on two occasions. Additional attention could have been given with profit, however, to enabling teams to define needs, state questions, and use outside resources and consultant services.

Creation of Structural Changes

Creation of three new structures within the districts was projected at outset, but these structures were never realized. The development of a structure for environmental scanning or reconnaissance and the introduction and operation of such a mechanism to find innovations in school environments (including neighboring schools, research and development centers, etc.) were projected as a functional outcome of the work of the change agent teams. Such a project might have been associated with a complementary mechanism within the Wisconsin Department of Public Instruction to provide basic information to the local district upon request. This kind of local mechanism, coordinated with a state-wide facility, is still believed to be important. Through systematic searching for innovations and gathering of information regarding their educational capabilities and applications, a district could enrich its problem-solving capabilities. Such institutionalized mechanisms are important in assuring the continuous self-renewal of a district. Competent personnel and budgetary allowances would be required for this type of structure.

Establishment of a mechanism within the district for the continuous assessment of needs and problems that suggest changes in processes, new structures, and new learning-teaching instrumentation was also projected. Such a mechanism would provide decision-makers with a rational basis for selecting and trying innovations suggested by the scanning function described above. The change agent teams functioned in a preliminary and exploratory manner as the initiating structure of such a mechanism, but no district implemented a well-designed structure during the course of the project.

Involving professional staff members and organizing an office within a school district to carry out training represents another potential structure that might have been initiated. Staff members operating as trainer-consultants could then be made available to professional and student groups needing further self-examination, greater awareness of interpersonal relations, more thought in introducing changes, and more skill in applying problem-solving approaches to various situations. (For further discussion, see Chapter 10.) One school district considered training its current staff members at the outset of the project but because no funds were allocated, the project was dropped. District A currently has this matter under advisement.

A Positive Note

Two favorable points can be made concerning this project: an observation regarding similar changes in business organizations and a limited but positive statement regarding the project itself. It is Likert's observation (1961) that neither the testing of a theory nor the alteration of an organization to allow full-scale application of the theory can be hurried. There is no substitute for ample time to enable the members of an organization to reach a level of skillful, easy, and habitual use of new practices. Likert maintains that a period of two or three years is usually required to introduce a major change in an organization with less than two hundred members and believes that in organizations with more than two or three hundred employees an additional five or more years may be required to bring about substantial changes. Consequently additional time may be needed to determine the full effects of change agent teams and it may be that the two-year cycle is not sufficient for institutionalizing new structures and processes at a level of maximum effectiveness. It may be that at least four years of cooperative effort between an outside agency such as ours and a district are required to introduce and institutionalize new structures for change. Continuous effort is required over a period of time and a greater saturation of training is needed than occurred in any of our districts.

There is further evidence regarding relationships among the innovativeness in a school district, the functioning of change agent teams, and the laboratory training of personnel. Over a period of two years District A moved two positions upward in its innovativeness within the eight school districts sampled, while its companion district decreased in innovativeness. District A developed the most ideal change agent team and made the greatest investment in training. This in itself suggests the value of the change agent team and laboratory training.

It is the conclusion of our staff that while certain activities might have been done more effectively, our approach promises long-term lasting effects that a more highly engineered approach from the outside might not offer. A result, and usually a quick result, is expected in schools by our pragmatic society. More attention is needed to developing competencies in interpersonal relations and problem-solving skills which will give more substantive and lasting results in the future. These competencies represent the capital human resources for a better future. Those persons associated with organization development in schools should resist efforts to make a show too quickly in favor of a less spectacular approach that emphasizes processes and the development of people.

The three change agent teams have continued to function after the completion of the project, thus demonstrating that members of these groups and district officials believe there is value in creation and maintenance of a structure for change within districts. We recommend, as an alternative to the preservation of a status quo of questionable value in our schools, the creation of change agent teams adapted to meet the needs of individual districts and defined by function and purpose, and the use of laboratory training as developed and applied in this project.

References

Duhl, Leonard. 1967. Planning and predicting: Or what to do when you don't know the names of the variables. *Daedalus, toward the year 2000: Work in progress* No. 3, Summer.

Erikson, Erik. 1963. *Childhood and society.* New York: Norton.

Goodson, Max R., and Hammes, Richard. 1968. *A team designed for school system changing.* Theoretical Paper No. 11. Madison, Wisconsin: Research and Development Center for Cognitive Learning, University of Wisconsin.

Gouldner, Alvin W. 1952. The problem of succession in bureaucracy. In *Reader in Bureaucracy,* eds. Robert K. Merton, Alisa P. Gray, Barbara Hockey, and Hanan C. Selvin. Glencoe, Illinois: Free Press. Pp. 339-351.

_____. 1954. *Patterns of industrial bureaucracy.* Glencoe, Illinois: Free Press.

Harrison, Roger. 1967. Training designs for intergroup collaboration. *Training News,* 11: No. 1.

Hilfiker, Leo R. 1969. *The relationship of school system innovativeness to selected dimensions of interpersonal behavior in eight school systems.* Technical Report No. 70. Madison, Wisconsin: Research and Development Center for Cognitive Learning, University of Wisconsin.

_____. 1970. *A profile of innovative school systems.* Madison, Wisconsin: Research and Development Center for Cognitive Learning, University of Wisconsin.

Jones, Richard M. 1968. *Fantasy and feeling in education.* New York: New York University Press.

Likert, Rensis. 1961. *New patterns of management.* New York: McGraw-Hill.

Luft, Joseph. 1969. *Of human interaction.* Palo Alto: National Press Books.

Pfeiffer, J. William, and Jones, John E. 1969. *A handbook of structured experiences for human relations training.* Iowa City, Iowa: University Associates Press.

9

CHANGING SCHOOLS THROUGH STUDENT ADVOCACY *

Mark A. Chesler and John E. Lohman

Many consultants, and some of their clients, have begun to argue that the OD models in widest use are overly restricted to trust-truth assumptions (see chapter 11). Most OD interventions rely too heavily, the critics argue, on open, supportive communication and the systematic exchange of valid information as keystones for organizational renewal.

This chapter provides a decisively alternate approach: that OD is centrally a matter of clarifying and strengthening expressions of the conflicting interests of diverse groups, and of radically redistributing decision-making prerogatives so that low-power groups can have more influence over an organization's fate. In particular, Chesler and Lohman focus on the students—those low-power clients who are usually somehow allotted the back seat in educational OD programs. The authors, in effect, argue not only that students ought to have more power in schools but that they are in a much better position than educational professionals to transform schools in desirable ways.

Instead of being grounded in systematic data, like most other chapters in this book, the treatment is an outline of an alternative OD model, that of power and conflict. Underlying assumptions, operating principles, and illustrative examples are presented. Some readers may view the tone of the article as too polemical; it is clearly "value-centric," to use the authors' term. We hope the article is successful in disturbing prejudices and traditional ways of thinking about OD. Perhaps, too, it may "raise consciousness," as OD practitioners come to realize how much they have collaborated to further the interests of professional educators and how little the interests of students and parents.

Power-conflict models are perhaps too new for much empirical data—other than anecdotes and descriptive accounts—to have been collected on their processes and effects. Some studies are essential and we look forward with anticipation to seeing them, from the authors' Educational Change Team, or elsewhere. Otherwise, we will not know whether the difficulties and risks of such approaches, which could be major, are commensurate with the outcomes, which may be more far-reaching than those achieved by other OD programs.

One additional point should be made. Chesler and Lohman quite rightly emphasize that redistribution of power is a central priority. Decision-making is in effect a master variable; changing its locus and improving its quality can alter

* The authors have drawn many of the ideas and examples discussed here from the thinking and work of their colleagues in the Educational Change Team of the School of Education, University of Michigan. This chapter is a product of their combined efforts.

most aspects of life in school districts. But we wish to suggest that equivalent attention should be given to the structural redesign of school districts. Even a power-equalized organization may emit unimaginative decisions which only serve to support the existing structure and practices. Public education is in need of social architects who can create designs for more effective behavior settings in schools. Some groundwork already has been laid for such roles by Perlmutter (1965), Fantini and Young (1970), and Janowitz (1969).

American high schools typically do not involve students in the legitimate exercise of influence or control over their school life; the major educational decisions are made by trained professionals. Young people are expected to obey such adult decisions and to believe that their best interests are being served thereby. In more and more schools across the country, students are expressing their alienation and anger at this situation. They are advocating their own definitions of "what's good for them," and are demanding new and more responsive forms of school governance. In this article, we review some of the problems and potentials of greatly increased student power in the conduct of school matters, and some relevant training programs and organizational renewal strategies.

Current Political Issues in Schools

Contemporary events in secondary schools reflect a breakdown in the traditional operation of professionals and professional systems. Haug and Sussman (1969) detail the generic phenomenon: "Students, the poor and the black community no longer accept uncritically the service offerings of the establishment . . . this is the revolt of the client."

Bases for Client-Professional Conflict

There are three general bases for the current conflict between professionals and clients. First, many students and parents have argued recently that educators are not automatically competent and may in fact lack the technical skill to make and implement decisions in the interest of other people's welfare.

In a second and more value-laden context, it is clear that some clients do not define their interest in the same way that professionals define the clients' interest. Since professionals and clients sometimes come from different backgrounds and cultures, they may have different perspectives and goals. For example, a secondary curriculum drawn from a certain historical context may be in conflict with many youngsters' preferences and needs. When the professional defends and implements the historical plan he may run counter to his clients' notions of their self-interest. As Bennis (1970) points out:

Questions of legitimacy arise whenever "expert power" becomes ineffective. Thus black militants, drug users, draft resisters, student protesters and liberated women all deny the legitimacy of those authorities who are not black, drug-experienced, pacifists, students or women.

Moreover, the very roles of professional and client may provide another basis for value conflict—as witnessed by student and teacher conflicts over the definitions of such things as dress, grooming, and order and discipline during class. To the extent that professionals retain the power to make decisions for others, they are vulnerable to the challenge of conflict over moral choice.

A third base of contention derives from experience with professionals' gradual accretion of privilege, which now must be defended against violation or intrusion. The economic and political self-interests of a class of professionals establish new bases for interest-group conflicts. For instance, teachers who have gained power over clients are now unwilling to relinquish that aspect of their role. The professional tradition of accountability to peers protects the educator from client evaluation and interference. This protection may or may not be in the client's best interest, but it surely adds to the comfort and power of the profession.

Consequences of Client-Professional Conflict

Clients recognize that professionals have interests that may be in conflict with their own and they naturally experience a loss of trust in the ability of professionals to act in the best interest of clients. The following statement from a student we worked with may exemplify this loss of trust.

What's very important is that you need trust. It's got to the point where nobody don't trust nobody, and that's all the student body got to look up to. If you've got a problem you're supposed to take it to the administration—if you feel that your teacher or counselor can't handle it—you go to the administration. When you can't do that because you don't trust them, what can you do with your problems?

Deterioration of trust in schools is not, in our view, to be conceived primarily as a problem in interpersonal relations. Individual predispositions and expectations surely play a part, but the erosion of trust noted here is essentially *systemic*. It is established and maintained by organizational assumptions, priorities and role structures. For example, educators insulate themselves from students both through lack of contact and elaborate control devices (passes, locked toilets, etc.). Similarly, students employ defenses of distance as a protection against the distrust they feel. But distance will not do as a solution; since school does matter to most youngsters they must somehow insure its relevance for them. Without trust in the system to meet their needs in their own terms, these clients must take the management of their interests into their own hands. In order for them to do so, power entrusted to professionals must accrue to clients.

Lack of interpersonal trust and organizational role reciprocity between students and educators, and stress upon adults' control of youthful clients, make it clear to students that they are without authority. Thus the lines of distinction between the "rulers" and the "ruled" are overt, visible, and liable to attack. A greater potential for highly escalated conflict exists where such role characteristics constantly remind students of their lower status and influence.

Kvaraceus (1965) points out that a heavy stress upon external and adult controls "tends to deepen the misunderstanding and resentment that exist between youth and adult," and notes further that when strong bureaucratic controls in the school are successful they create "a reluctant and recalcitrant conformist living close to the letter of the law." On the other hand, if unsuccessful, they create "the overt aggressive delinquent who is a member of an 'outlaw gang.' " Neither of these alternatives is an attractive educational outcome, although only the latter presents a challenge to good order and harmonious relations in school.

When large numbers of students resent and distrust the control mechanisms employed by educational professionals, the effect is to undermine the collective and legitimate authority of the school. Continued belief by clients that those in authority are abusing their prerogatives sooner or later leads to a denial of the legitimacy of that authority. And students no longer believe that school personnel will act in their immediate behalf, or even in their long-run best interest; thus they are more likely to rely on coercive influence attempts. This proposition is further explicated in Gamson (1968). For students, who have few legitimate channels for the exercise of influence or control over school life, coercion usually means the use of disruptive power. The traditional distrust and powerlessness of clients in the educational system thus sets the stage for the unmodulated and disruptive exercise of power.

When previously impotent groups finally do attain the right and opportunity to influence policy, they are often treated by prior influentials as unwelcome. They may also lack experience and skill in the judgment of issues that do require some professional expertise. Educators faced with such new definitions of the relations between professional and client, and with clients' use of power to redress past relations, often feel severely threatened and generally resist both a redefinition of the role of expert and a reallocation of power within the organization. The cultural clash between the revolutionary demands of many young people and the reformist or essentially traditional change goals of those in power makes this conflict even greater.

Rationales for Change in Power Relations

Regardless of their social, ethnic, or racial backgrounds, or their level in the status hierarchy of the school, many students are engaged in a common quest— the search for some control over their lives in school. The disparity between students' actual influence and the educational rhetoric of democracy, community, national solidarity, etc., is particularly acute when youngsters attempt to change something. One urban teen-ager we know asserted that:

... administration's always saying they wanted student participation ... it seems to me that all they wanted us to say, lookit, there's kids that are participating, there's kids that want to do something ... but they don't really want us to get what we're asking ... they just said why don't you wait until next week, and why don't you wait until next month? Talk to some more people. Pretty soon everybody [in the group] quit. Got tired out.

Some of the issues in the student search for power are evident in the following quotes from other students:

The administration invited us to this meeting, and said how they wanted us to make a new dress code and how it would be real nice ... and then they said that the only problem is that the Board of Education won't permit the different schools to have different dress codes—that's not true. There's high schools all over—two in one district—that have different dress codes. I don't know why they said that. Guess they really don't want us to have a new dress code.

The principal was supposed to bring it to the Board. He went to the Board meeting and he didn't bring it up. He just talked to them a couple seconds before the meeting. And they said, "Well don't bring it up now, we've got too much to do." And then later he told the student council advisor that students shouldn't come to the Board meeting any more because they might mess something up.

Last time all the kids went to the Board meeting for something all they did was kick 'em out of school.

These comments indicate a confusion or lack of clarity on the part of students about their appropriate participatory roles. Administrative evasion and false rhetoric serve to muddy these dangerous waters further. Students have a great deal of pluralistic ignorance about a political system in which the real mechanics are invisible to them. The power structure is more visible to teachers who do participate in some decisions, or at least are acquainted with the vagaries and nuances of school decision-making. Likewise, students who hold office and go to meetings have greater sophistication (and often cynicism) about what is happening there. But many others, uninvolved and ignorant about influence processes, are confused when asked about their influence. They are certainly not informed rebels or followers, but *non-citizens* of the most potent political organization in their lives so far.

Chesler (1969) suggests that students' desires to control their own lives and to influence the behavior of others in order to make their demands heard and implemented are at the root of many protests and school disruptions. Although these issues may be surfaced most dramatically in protests, Duggal (1968) argues that the level of student participation is low for our schools regardless of their "unrest."

On what grounds can such proposals for change be made? We believe there are three important bases for the claim that increased student power is desirable: educational, moral, and political.

The Educational Rationale

Youth are clearly justified in feeling that their power is a key variable in determining the quality of life in school. The degree to which influence is shared among the various parts or levels of institutions affects members' feelings of involvement and commitment.[1] When an organizational structure does not permit student participation in decision-making, the results may thus be political alienation, rebellion, and efforts to exert coercive influence or control.

Wittes's (1970) study of crisis-torn high schools indicates that students' perceptions of their ability to influence school policy have important implications for their desire to achieve academic success. When students feel they have

---

[1] Several theorists of organization development (Likert, 1961; McGregor, 1960; Argyris, 1964) also have postulated interdependent relationships among the formal structure of an organization, the perceptions and norms of the organization's members, and the individual's performance. Currently we know far less about the way such factors interact in schools than we would like; few studies have been carried out. Three major difficulties discourage research on such factors in schools: (1) difficulty in specifying the criterial measures; (2) long delays in school feedback loops (knowledge of results); and (3) the hesitancy of researchers and administrators to deal with "political" variables.

influence, and when they are in a peer group that has access to school power, they more often believe that they can control their own educational fate. Participation in influencing school policy, then, may be meaningful for educational outcomes and purposes in one's personal life.

In a similar vein, Polk (1968) found that students who attended a high school with modular scheduling (emphasizing the students' responsibility for their own learning progress) were more likely to score higher on Rotter's scale of internal control than were comparable students who attended traditional high schools. Coleman's (1966) nationwide survey of schools found that the feeling of being able to control one's own environment was related more highly to the academic achievement of students than all other characteristics of a student's background put together, or than all other school characteristics put together. Thus there is clear evidence that school political structures are not trivial, but are associated with student attitudes and perceptions that are important for successful academic performance.

Educationally speaking, changes in the allocation of decision-making power may also be supported on the basis of the added perspective and expertise that students may bring to organizational management and administration and to the conduct and supervision of learning experiences. Only students, of course, can truly represent their own unique interests, views, and preferences in school life. Organizations that do permit representation and utilize the skills of all their component groups are more likely to fulfill most members' needs.

The Moral Rationale

The reasons for increasing student power lie only partly in research indications that people are more likely to increase their learning in and commitment to organizations in which they are involved and for which they make important decisions. Among the other stimuli for change are more philosophic considerations of the justice and appropriateness of institutions' being governed by those people who live in and are affected by the decisions of those institutions.

More democratic forms of management and instruction may also be important models for students' personal and intellectual learning about the nature of and opportunity for democratic political influence in American society. This is not to suggest that such learning is the only issue; but the absence of democratic procedures in any of our social institutions obviously weakens the entire society.

The Political Rationale

Some very pragmatic political considerations also make reallocation of power imperative. Changes which meet the demands of protesting student groups may help cool the crisis in American secondary schools. But more importantly, they may also permit students legitimate power to alter the other things that make school life untenable. Since most school management is reactive rather than pro-active or creative in character, increased student power does provide very real promise that needed educational reforms will come about.

Meaningful student involvement may very well *not* "cool the crisis" but may increase conflict, since students—like other role groups—have unique goals and priorities which compete with others' goals and priorities. Obviously, political accommodation is in itself an insufficient rationale for student power; such accommodation only has viability when implemented for reasons or in ways that complement other more positive philosophical and educational rationales.

The Exercise of Student Power

If student power is to become real, not just a hoax or a cynical token to protesters, it will be expressed in procedures and structures that not only deviate from but even threaten current major institutional traditions and ways of life in school. It is crucial, therefore, to distinguish between programs which alter basic power arrangements and those activities which are limited to opening communication channels and encouraging informal influence or advice. The increase of communication and advice is a worthwhile activity, but it does not constitute sharing power; essentially power remains located in the same places while efforts are made to engender a psychological sense of participation.

Domains of Student Power

Some features of what we mean by the exercise of student power should help make the above distinction clear. It is our view that students should exert significant control over major portions of the formal activities and events of the school, including budgetary and fiscal policy; hiring, salary, and tenure of teachers; development and approval of curriculum and course offerings; development, approval, and enforcement of regulations governing conduct on school property; local graduation requirements; the school's role in the community; and development and implementation of procedures during crises.

Students, along with persons from other role groups in the district, must have adequate and timely access to information about the internal functioning of the school and its external transactions with the environment. If they are to have real power, students must have the opportunity and freedom to make mistakes. Along with other participants in the decision-making process, their roles must be legitimized by the school district, and their behavior made accountable to those who are affected by their decisions. The entire purpose of increased power of students is to expand the process of adult accountability to their clients. Some of these areas of decision-making deserve more comment.

Curriculum. One of the areas of school life where students can exercise power most immediately is the determination and implementation of the curriculum. The content of the curriculum, organization of classes, choice of classroom method, paths of curriculum sequencing, and criteria for success and fulfillment of a high school education all can be subject to review, guidance, and management by students. At the present time, many students who feel strongly about such matters vote individually by dropping out, sleeping in class, avoiding certain courses, and the like. Others rebel and organize protests to seek redress and change. Still other students obediently move through the system, having learned that power is not shared and, for them, is not worth arguing about. Yet they chafe at the lessons of impotence and exclusion and feel the alienation and distance between students' needs or goals and the organized content of instruction.

Finance. Students also need to play a role in the administration of school finances and in the allocation of moneys among various portions of the budget. Since innovative school activities and programs often founder on inadequate, unwise, or controversial allocations of funds, control over such areas may be required before anything else productive can happen. To shield students from making decisions on fiscal matters is to remove them from confrontation with some of the harshest realities (and most closely guarded preserves) of the school.

Personnel Matters. Student participation in decision-making also means that the qualifications of teachers as they are recruited, evaluated, considered for merit pay and promoted or transferred must be open for student review. Student voice in making decisions about the professional staff may also extend to the selection and evaluation of the high school principal. A great deal of arbitrary behavior by educators could be curtailed by using personnel procedures that reflect accountability of this sort. The development of criteria for teacher behavior, of observational or attitudinal instruments, and of methods for providing performance feedback would be helpful supports for such decision-making activities. Students' exercise of this responsibility is not merely self-serving; many teachers could benefit from knowing how their students experience the classroom and what suggestions or preferences they have. There is no reason why such a help or growth focus could not be built into student decision-making. Greater acrimony and distance between students and educators is not inevitable.

In these examples, we have gone beyond suggesting that students can be advisors to adult policy-making groups, or that the acme of student power is for students to have autonomy over their own social and athletic facilities and activities. Clearly, open channels of informal influence and autonomy in extracurricular activities are important innovations, but they represent only the beginning of strategic reform.

Of course, unilateral student control over clubs, dances, and other school-associated social or athletic events may be helpful in developing certain student skills and can lead to involvement in more sophisticated and serious efforts. For student decision-making to have the educational effects noted above, however, students must have real power, real authority, and hence *responsibility* for educational decisions and administrative governance of the school.

Suggestions that actualize these perspectives clearly threaten current legal and professional definitions of administrative power, union or association standards and agreements regarding teacher security and tenure, criteria for high school graduation, and customary notions of students' appropriate roles in school. (The professional reader who doubts this should pause at this point to envision what his role and his school would be like were student power to increase substantially—and to experience his feelings as he does so.)

A final aspect of involving students in decision-making should not be overlooked. It is best described in terms of the pluralism of interests among students on many issues. It is as overly simplistic to describe *the* student viewpoint on any educational issue as it is to assign a single viewpoint to *the* community of which the school is a part. Although there are some basic and pervasive issues on which a large proportion of students may be in agreement, adequate structures for student involvement in decision-making must acknowledge, legitimate, and be responsive to legitimate differences among students' values, goals, and life styles.

A New Model of Student Advocacy in School Change

Bold new approaches to fundamental educational change are needed. In the remainder of this chapter we shall describe one approach to educational change that is emerging out of our work with secondary schools facing severe conflict and crisis throughout the country. This approach might best be described as a *power-conflict model*.

While the foregoing analysis documents the systemic nature of educational problems, and our approach to educational change involves multiple role groups in school districts, we shall focus primarily upon the part student advocacy plays in our approach. This bias is justified, we believe, partly because it serves to highlight unique aspects of our work in schools and partly because in secondary schools today this is "where the action is." Student advocacy strategies are in use in many relatively spontaneous movements for school change. The development of a student Bill of Rights in New York City (Reeves, 1970), the Freedom Annex School in Washington, and free schools throughout the country represent such programs. The crucial question is whether professionals in organization development and training can (or will) adopt and use some of these strategies.[2]

Some Underlying Assumptions

It may be helpful at this point to clarify some of the distinctions between the power-conflict model of change proposed here and other approaches to organization development. Three premises or assumptions are present in our previous diagnosis of schools which most other OD models do not discuss explicitly. The first premise is that schools as social organizations are strain- and conflict-producing systems; that is, legitimate but competing and sometimes incompatible interests are endemic in the current structure of the school organization. Recognizing the need for legitimacy of pluralism, with the inevitable conflict that attends it, necessitates OD strategies which use conflict in an overt and constructive manner.

The second assumption in our model is that the members of a school district—students, teachers, and administrators—occupy roles and structures and operate with professional and organizational norms and procedures which keep them separate, and work against formal (and even informal) interaction and the development of cross-cutting ties of common interest, values, or feeling.

The third assumption is that all of the legitimate power, authority, and expertise in schools (and much of the informal power) presently resides entirely in the hands of boards, administrators, and some teachers in the school. A sizeable proportion of the total school district therefore has no formal access and (because of the communication and role barriers discussed previously) little informal access to power, influence, and control. The power-conflict model overtly addresses the distribution of power in the system by helping participants become aware of the nature of power inequities, and the feelings and behavior which such inequities engender in people. It focuses directly on strategies for power equalization.

---

[2]Some of the issues relevant to the difficulties of advocacy for professional educational consultants are discussed in Chesler and Arnstein (1970) and Guskin and Ross (in press).

Crucial Variables in Organizational Change

Katz and Kahn (1966) and Buchanan (1967 and 1969) review several approaches to OD and change. As they point out, few of these approaches attempt to change such major variables as the distribution of power or the priorities placed on the organization's goals. Thus they do not deal centrally with structural characteristics of the organization but focus on attitudinal and interpersonal modifications. The most frequently documented models of OD in schools focus on opening communication channels and improving communication skills, increasing skills in "consensus" decision-making, or developing sophisticated data-gathering procedures through which "problems" can be detected and remedied by supervisory and administrative elites. The power-conflict model differs from other OD strategies in the emphasis which it gives to certain organizational dimensions and variables.

Conflict. The power-conflict model explicitly recognizes and legitimizes pluralistic or multiple goals and the goal and value conflicts which follow. As Leavitt (1965) suggests, most approaches to OD do not deal explicitly with this dimension, or make naive, idealized, and questionable assumptions (e.g., that organization goals and values are widely shared). Other strategies, assuming falsely a general commonality of interests, are vague about goal-setting or use only such criteria as expertise and a general organizational perspective in dealing with the issue.

An assumption common to many OD approaches is that decision-making by consensus is possible and desirable; this often ignores the possibility of incompatible differences. Such an approach may in fact be highly coercive: it results in action taken on the assumption of consensus where none may exist and moves decisions out of the public domain because of fears of "destructive and unmanageable" conflict.

The power-conflict model, on the other hand, assumes that differences are inevitable and that processes (such as voting or coercion) which include dialogue and negotiation and which enable decisions to be made in the face of strong opposition are at times necessary. The acknowledgment of such goal differences reinforces the moral or philosophical position that all relevant parties need to be actively involved in goal-setting.

Yet this perspective on the normality (and even virtue) of conflict is rare in educational circles. Campbell (1968) points out, for instance, that literature on the government and administration of education would lead one to suspect that there is high consensus within schools and little evidence of conflict. Such a public presentation is perhaps predictable: the literature is created by, written for, and consumed by educational professionals and members of community elites. No manager wants to hear that his operation is in conflict, and few who serve managers get around to saying it openly.

Yet "harmony" of this sort is quite atypical of schools. The assertion of harmony is especially preposterous in heterogeneous communities where there is high conflict and rapid change in the social, economic, and moral character of school life.

Social theorists and researchers have suggested certain organizational conditions most likely to make positive use of conflict and to avoid crisis. Social systems (such as schools) that do not recognize the existence of internal differences in values and interests and do not respond to or organize in terms of such divergence have no buffer against highly escalated conflict.

Yet conflict need not lead to the crisis or chaos which many educators fear and experience directly. For instance, Coser (1956) argues that conflict is most likely to be functional when groups are not completely polarized but when there are some possibilities of individuals' having membership in several groups at once. Smelser's (1963) concept that system stability is dependent on multiple internal cleavages is essentially the same.

In most schools, however, sharp divisions between people of different status and race do not permit overlapping or multiple memberships. Teachers who try to "fraternize" with students are rebuffed by students and viewed askance by peers. The reverse occurs as well; studei ·s cannot gain membership in the school faculty.

Power. A second principle is that groups in conflict may be able to negotiate and adjudicate differing interests when they have relatively equal amounts of power in an organization. However, it is quite clear that such parity does not exist in schools; there is not even the appearance of legitimate power-sharing among adult educators and their students. Largely for this reason, protesters seek the use of illegitimate and highly coercive power to force the school to respond to their interests. Temporary power balances can of course be brought into being through the use of disruption, but the issue is more one of developing new legitimate power structures. Laue (1968) argues similarly in reviewing the use of direct action techniques in community desegregation efforts. He notes that through the use of their bodies, blacks "developed a new source of power" as a substitute for participation in normal political channels. Excluded as they were from normal democratic means, they invented new procedures for influencing policy.

Power, including not only formal and legitimate organizational authority, but informal influence, is a crucial concept in our model. While many OD strategies focus on developing procedures and interpersonal skills for gaining access to influencing key decision-makers in organizations, we are also concerned with more formal and permanent structural changes, including the introduction of multiple roles in legitimate authority positions and decision-making groups. We do not necessarily assume, as others apparently do, that such power will be shared benevolently by those in authority. Power may have to be taken, as well as given up, in part because those newly in positions of authority need to test the limits of their power, and in part because those already in authority, despite noble intentions, are likely to see their self-interest (and probably the interests of the organization) threatened by any new power distribution.

Trust. A key variable in many of the person-oriented OD models is trust. Such strategies focus on opening up channels of communication about feelings, and require the development of an atmosphere of openness, support, and trust. The trust that develops is essentially personal or interpersonal in form: one trusts in the benevolence and common interests of other persons.

Trust is a key variable in the power-conflict approach as well, but it may take a different form. Trust that others will behave with your best interest in mind is less prevalent. Instead, one develops trust that others will adhere to certain norms or procedures: the "rules of the game" by which all parties have agreed to abide—rules for handling conflict, making decisions, upholding bargains, and so forth. Dahl (1967) has pointed out, for example, that conflict is most likely to be productive amidst organizational agreement about the fairness of the rules and the legitimacy of different parties' interests. Thus, in our model, *procedural* trust and *functional* trust—confidence that each will perform his organizational duties and responsibilities effectively—replace *interpersonal* trust as the basis for organizational integration to bind and hold the structure together.

We must point out, however, that such procedural consensus on the morality of protesting interests and issues does not typically exist in schools. Educators often do not believe that students have real grievances or, indeed, the *right* to be aggrieved, and students often do not trust educators to deal fairly with their concerns. In high-conflict situations, whatever trust students have in administrators' sense of fair play may evaporate quickly. The schools' organizational failure to maintain trust is only partly an issue in personal or interpersonal integrity. It also stems from students' exclusion from the decision-making arena, and their suspicion about the processes that go on in it.

Communication. As indicated above, other OD strategies tend to emphasize the opening of communication channels and the removal of barriers to the honest sharing of information.

Communication may also be dealt with differently in the power-conflict model. The political nature of communication is explicitly recognized, and restricted access to certain information across status and role groups is legitimized. Such an emphasis is particularly important under conditions of unequal power, when authorities are less vulnerable than others to the abuse and misuse of such information. We are not advocating deception and chicanery, but pointing out that naive assumptions regarding common interest and collaborative decision-making do not take into consideration the constraints on communication which usually are considered management's prerogative. These restrictions on "openness" are typically encountered not only in "regular" organizational functioning but also in efforts to innovate in and change any system.

Structure. One final aspect of the power-conflict model, already alluded to, is the importance of relatively long-term structural changes in the organization of the school. Our approach recognizes the need to restructure schools to provide students and teachers with formal access to authority and decision-making procedures and with the necessary organizational support structures, such as active constituency and interest groups. At the same time, we also believe (like other OD practitioners) that it is necessary to provide training to help participants develop the necessary personal and organizational skills to operate effectively in new structures.

New Models for Organizational Governance

New organizational forms to deal with concerns such as those expressed above will require more than retraining personnel or transferring them to different organizational slots; we are advocating far more than the replacement of a principal or a ruling faculty administrative body by several students. An exchange of persons to fulfill already established roles or positions is a personnel move which does not constitute organizational change. Substituting one set of persons for another will accomplish little unless the intervening structure of representative politics and governance is changed. The replacement of a principal by six students does not automatically decrease the distance, or increase the dialogue, between the mass of students or faculty members and the decision-makers.

Some Examples of New Models

Several elaborate models of innovative organizational governance have been proposed by educators pursuing such issues (Robinson and Schoenfeld, 1970). One set of proposals deals with *representative bicameral systems.* Students and teaching faculty each elect representatives from among their numbers to compose two legislative or policy-making bodies. An executive or administrative committee implements policies and handles routine day-to-day matters. Babbidge (1969) suggests that such a model for higher education also include a final judicial authority residing with the board of trustees. John Adams High School, a public school in Portland, Oregon, is currently operating with a bicameral governance system.

Unicameral systems represent another basic model to broaden representation in school decision-making. These approaches invest the formal responsibilities of the principal and his staff in a single body composed of representatives from student, teacher, and administrative groups. In order to facilitate decision-making, this group is kept relatively small, or an executive committee is formed to handle details. Ramapo High School in Spring Valley, New York, is currently using this approach to governance (Sugarman, 1970).

"Town meetings" and similar face-to-face decision-making groups in which all members of the school subunit may participate (Mann, 1965; Raskin, 1968) represent a third, less formalized approach. The movement toward the decentralization of schools by unitizing, house plans, schools within schools, and educational parks tends to reduce the size of the learning unit and provide opportunity for town meeting participation. Although there is as yet no history of experience to evaluate these models, each attempts to deal with some of the generic issues raised earlier. Each broadens the representation of different interests within the school. Each model also encourages the surfacing of hidden conflicts in the formal decision-making mechanism. Although specific designs and models may vary, new structures should recognize and legitimize the endemic nature of differing interests, should provide appropriate organizational procedures for utilizing group differences and conflicts, and should be manned by individuals skilled in coping constructively with conflict and the need for change.

Some Problems with Participatory Structures

Research evidence bearing upon the "participation hypothesis" (Verba, 1961), is relevant to understanding the problems involved in new and more participatory forms of school governance. We generally assume that involvement in decision-making leads to decreased alienation from the organization and to increased satisfaction with both the process and the outcome of decisions. However, such consequences are more or less likely under varying circumstances and with varying organizational structures. We describe some attenuating conditions below to illustrate some of the complexities with which the advocates of increased student involvement must deal.

The first few problems in making participatory structures successful stem from potential dissatisfaction with the *outcome* of decisions made.

1. The *costs* involved in participating in the decision-making process can be too great and are not worth the actual benefits. For example, members of a fact-finding committee on student dress regulations may come to feel that the long weekly meetings of the group require more time than they expected, that the goal of establishing new policy is not being achieved, and that the testimony obtained is not worth the energy invested.

2. The *quality of the decision* can be impaired by increased participation. Decisions can be impaired because (a) the necessary resources are absent or scarce, (b) resources are *too* plentiful to be used efficiently, or (c) some are scarce while others are too plentiful.

3. Participation can bring to the surface *latent conflicts* that are relevant to the group but which cannot be utilized or handled constructively, and therefore immobilize the decision-making process.

The remaining conditions reflect some dissatisfaction with the *process* itself.

4. The *scope of participation may not match expectations.* For example, the principal who discusses with his teachers ways of implementing a new curriculum may find them angry that they were not involved in deciding the shape of the new curriculum in the first place.

5. Participants find they *lack the skills or values* for effective participation or have difficulty making decisions. This results in frustration, feelings of inadequacy, and decreased self-esteem.

6. Finally, an individual may find that participation does not meet his own *personal and interpersonal needs.*

New governance structures will require major elements of time, energy, and training to work effectively. One solution is to set aside an hour a day, and several additional hours a week, for students or faculty to meet in small cell groups or assemblies. At these times they can consider the political and educational decisions that must be (or have been) made for the school that week, and provide support and commitments for policy suggestions. Moreover, representatives can then transmit their feelings, findings, and decisions to their constituents, and receive feedback, suggestions and pressure from them. This time should be scheduled during the school day and not in stolen hours at night or on weekends. Only with continuing, legitimate, planned opportunities for political conversation and activity will new structures succeed despite lack of time, low energy, other priorities, traditional professional role definitions, political opposition, and the like. These problems are typical of the stumbling blocks in the movement from traditional to innovative forms of school power and governance. Effective training programs and strategies for organization development may help ease this process. We now turn to this topic.

Strategies for OD Through Student Retraining

The best of recent innovative OD projects in schools (Miles and Lake, 1967; COPED, 1967; Schmuck, Runkel and Langmeyer, 1969; and Schaible and Piotrowsky, 1970) do use interventions that change organizational structures and improve organizational skills of participation. New communication structures, rather than communication skills alone, are the focus of this recent work. Some of these efforts have also dealt with the problem of power, although it is approached cautiously and with an assumption of rational benevolence at the top of the hierarchy. Benevolence, like trust, is an important component of authority, but it cannot be *assumed* out of the context of the self-interest of an authority regarding goals, control, and stability.

None of these recent efforts, however, deals with students, student interests, and student power in more than minimal terms. Change efforts have focused almost entirely on adult administrators and teachers; any effort to train students in these areas is relatively new. Both because they are clients, and are seen as an immature and oppressed group, students generally have not been treated as part of the resources available to a system. Thus, we find few OD examples in which students are trained in new ways of relating to or altering the social system of the school.

Perhaps the key questions to be raised in the training of students cut across all of the particular skills or functions discussed above. One vital question is whether students should be trained primarily for *collaboration* with other parties in the school or for *advocacy* of their own interests. This issue cuts to the heart of one's diagnosis of the nature and ills of the educational bureaucracy. On the one hand, students may be envisioned as one of several collaborating parties in the school. In this context there would be a high priority on creating trust and positive forms of interaction among students, teachers, and administrators. This is in fact the primary choice made in most OD strategies.

An alternate perspective is to argue that collaboration is extremely difficult, if not impossible; the very structure of relations between adults and students in schools makes them natural opponents. The kinds of trust required for reciprocal pay-off simply may not exist at present, even if they may have at some point in history. In this context, it would be most important for the previously impotent majority to advance its own cause, and to let those in power figure out how to accommodate students' interests as well as advancing their own. This approach places the major burden of accommodation and system integration on those who have legitimate power and the historic obligation to seek integration, rather than on those out of power who seek redress and change in their roles. The extent to which these perspectives (collaboration and advocacy) may or may not be in conflict is simply not clear to us at present.

A second vital question is whether students seeking redress and change in the school should organize advocate groups solely among other *students* or among sympathetic and committed *non-students* as well. On one hand, the argument can be made that only students can be straightforward and reliable with one another, and that role group interests are so unique that they ought not to be contaminated. On the other hand, it is argued that various categories of oppressed people—students, faculty, and community—have enough in common to form intense coalitions. Advocate groups formed on the basis of common values rather than roles may cut across role group lines, making future system integration easier. Practical data on the relative ease of organizing efforts and the tested depth of commitment may be the only means for resolving this strategic dilemma.

These two questions each focus attention on the dilemma of system integration and subgroup interests. In brief, the conflicts attendant on and generated by subgroup interests must co-exist with efforts to integrate the system.[3] We are not urging interest group advocacy at the price of disintegration and chaos. However, neither are we encouraging (in the manner of much educational literature) system integration at the price of mere superficial consensus and the repression of subgroup interests. The tension between these issues is the central theoretical dilemma in the discussion of the change strategies that follow.

The retraining strategies discussed below have typically not been followed through to the actual implementation of new governance structures. It is our view, however, that they hold considerable promise for such implementation, and more real promise than most traditional organizational renewal strategies.

Training for Understanding and Collaboration

A prime focus of some efforts to train students for new roles in schools is *preparation for collaborative problem-solving* with other role-takers in the school district. This focus generally assumes that an overarching consensus of interests does (or can) exist among the various parties in schools and that areas of dissensus can be given lower priority or made subordinate to areas of consensus. Further, it assumes that building on areas of agreement is a useful way to integrate an organization. In this context an emphasis is placed on understanding of others as a prerequisite for work and collaboration in the conduct of school life.

The concept of collaboration seems to have several other implications as it is generally practiced. In our view, collaboration does not occur merely among people with like views; we use the term explicitly for situations in which people work together even though they have quite differing views. If people who did differ now come to total agreement, we will not call this collaboration either. The basis for meaningful collaboration must be built from assumptions and experiences of difference, as well as explorations of commonness. Respect for and maintenance of differences is clearly vital. This requires, in some cases, resistance to premature collaboration which denies or overwhelms differences or conflicts among subgroups.

Illustration 1: Training for Cross-Status Problem-Solving. One effort to train students for collaborative roles occurred in a summer program in an Illinois high school. Thirty-five students and faculty members were self-selected to constitute several cross-status problem-solving teams. In order to develop cross-status groupings that could work efficiently, all participants had to learn to work together as a cohesive and collaborative unit. They began their summer activities with a two-day workshop focusing on interpersonal sensitivity and group dynamics. In small group meetings, students and faculty discussed their relationships with one

[3]Coser (1967) makes this point well in criticizing both establishment-oriented consensus theories and conceptual trends toward societal anarchy.

another and their general concerns about interpersonal and group relations in school. Several other sessions were held in which participants were stimulated to identify and to resolve conflicts between different school groups. Sometimes the group of thirty-five persons was divided into student groups and adult groups, and sometimes they met in cross-status learning units.

Illustration 2: Training for Cross-Status Problem-Solving. Guskin and Guskin (1970) describe a similar effort in a Southwestern high school; forty students, twelve teachers, and the principal met together every day for three weeks during the summer. The focus of this program was also on developing a cadre of students skilled in group problem-solving procedures. The report indicates that consultants to the school tried

... to build a feeling of concern, and to create the necessary interpersonal relationships among workshop members that could support the later development of specific tactics for change. Attention was given to the development of skills in group organization, discussion leadership and political management.

Sessions of this sort may be effective mechanisms whereby persons learn how to cross status lines and develop cooperation and collaboration across previously impermeable boundaries separating persons from one another. At times, however, it has become important to recognize and deal with the natural desire for *separateness* with which persons come to such groups. Occasional separation of members into homogeneous role groupings or status groupings has proven effective in helping to create the articulation and understanding of differences so necessary for intergroup collaboration.

Illustration 3: Training for Cross-Status Perception Clarification. In a New Jersey high school workshop, student and teacher groups were separated. Each group was asked to develop a list of the ways in which they perceived members of the other group. The lists so created follow:

How Students Perceive Teachers
Unaware, think they are correct because they are older, putting on a big show, some making honest effort, think they are more mature because they are older, less outspoken, passive when the principal is there, take things personally, don't really listen, are prejudiced, some willing to listen even when they don't agree, curious about students' views.

How Teachers Perceive Students
Cherish individuality, hopelessness, confusion, self-confidence, frustration, sensitivity, eagerness, resistance to seeing both sides of the question, clannish, irresponsible, candid, bored, angry at inequities, powerless, flexible, racially polarized.

After the separate groups of students and adults shared their perceptions of one another, they attempted to explain the meaning of these perceptions to the other group. This design stressed the non-rational perceptions and stereotypes which people of differing status had of one another. The examination and clarification of mutual misperceptions is a necessary precursor of serious and honest collaboration.

These training programs appeared to be quite successful at the time. Cadres of students and teachers did learn to work together and developed provocative plans for school change. During the course of the year, however, the groups fell apart, and teachers and students ceased collaborating. The pressures to separate overcame the interpersonal bonds created in the training sessions. It appeared that the OD consultants had underestimated the time and energy it would take to maintain the openness of collaboration under normal school pressures.

In the development of such collaboration, it is crucial to stress the need for honesty and reciprocity across status groupings. All too often, dishonest collaboration develops: it involves one group's "dancing to another's tune" (e.g., students adjusting to administrators' priorities). Of course, such manipulation, conscious or otherwise, will not succeed for long. Students quickly reassert those differences or cite evidence of pseudo-collaboration which they have experienced. One junior high school student expressed her frustration to us in the following terms:

> We set up and approved this new constitution for the student government and it doesn't include an administration veto over our activities. But our advisor, who was mainly responsible in setting it up, only wants us to talk about certain things that won't rock the boat. We all know that he really controls it. So what good was the whole business?

One of the prime hazards of training for collaboration is that it may co-opt students into ignoring their needs and doing the bidding of the school administration. Students who are duped or seduced into collaboration and trust, and who find the trust unwarranted, will create far greater havoc and destruction for the school than if such "collaboration" had never occurred. An antidote to this danger may be provided by use of the following approaches to student training.

Training for Self-Interest Advocacy

A second major focus of training for students involves *preparing them to identify, develop, organize, and prosecute their own special interests.* If students are not able to look after their own interests, who then will protect or advance them? One traditional assumption is that trained educational professionals will act in their clients' best interests. But, as we have seen, this is a forlorn hope. Professionals now constitute a separate class in our society and schools; as such they have their own vested interests to protect and cannot be depended on to protect anyone who comes into conflict with them.

Rational conflict between students and adults having different goals and status is quite natural. Such conflict requires that each group seek the adjudication and prosecution of its own interests. The prosecution of one's self-interest does not necessarily exclude collaboration with other or opposing groups, but, it does suggest the necessity for careful consideration of the time and place for collaboration. The critical issue here is to treat both advocacy and collaboration as means to an end such as quality education, improved schooling, or greater learning. The collaborative stance described above comes close to urging collaboration as an end—as a desired style regardless of other organizational consequences. But for students, the outcome of the educational process is crucial, and preferred organizational and interpersonal styles must be judged by whether they lead to maximum learning, the basic purpose of school.

Needed Outcomes. The development of advocacy-oriented programs requires the separate training of students for different purposes in different ways with potentially different ends—in comparison to what might be needed for other members of the educational system. Students must be trained to identify their common interests, to organize peers around those interests, and to understand their opponents' positions and likely responses. They will also need to learn how to establish conditions for collaboration, to set terms and limits for negotiation and compromise, to decide when and whom to press in confrontation situations, to distinguish between "good" and "bad" principals, and to begin the establishment of institutional agreements for continued student participation in decision-making and curriculum reform.

As students learn more about the strange and often invisible workings of the school district and its personnel they will be able to reduce the non-rational, or stereotypic and ignorant, components of their conflicts with the school. Rather, rational conflicts around different structures of interest, privilege, and reward can receive fuller attention. With these ideas and skills, students will be able to develop action strategies that advance their unique interests.

Students are already learning informally, on their own, how to organize in their own self-interest and in support of their definitions of quality education. Our basic concern here is whether organizational change programs can help them do this in more disciplined and effective ways.[4]

One of the major results of such a training program should be the students' increased understanding of *how to influence other persons* in the school district. When students' interests have become clearly identified, and when students have become organized as a potent political force in their own right, they are more likely to be heard and others are more likely to respond to their concerns. As they understand the system better, students can exert leverage more judiciously and effectively. Sometimes rational discussion brings about rapid and effective adult responses; at other times a meaningful response can be secured only by dynamic political confrontation.

There is no implication here that students need to develop hatred or antagonism toward people with different interests—people we call opponents. Opponents do not have to be conceived of as enemies in a hostile interpersonal sense. In fact, we are concerned that people exercise compassion and respect for their role opponents, but that does not mean they should take those opponents as benevolent partners in a complex and partisan political enterprise. In American society, separateness and conflict seem to be feared greatly; it is understandable how opposition may become hostility or be interpreted as such. Particularly when individuals have been taught to fear such authorities as parents and teachers, they may have a personal need to escalate emotions in order to overcome fears and confront the authority figure at hand. Responses by authorities to these perceived attacks often further escalate the interaction. As part of the training program all parties must be helped to *avoid irrational attacks and defenses*. Probably the greatest help should be available to those whose historic interests and privileges are most threatened by student initiative and organization for change.

Another outcome of advocacy-oriented student groups should be more honest and effective forms of *collaboration* and *negotiation for change*. Students

---

[4]In implementing this approach, we have found that highly trained student consultants have to be responsible for conducting the actual interventions with student groups. Adult professional consultants seldom "put their bodies on the line" and lack credibility in the actual politics of school life. However, opportunities to work with and learn from adult consultants, removed from their local school setting, can give high school students and recent graduates a chance to develop the techniques and strategies needed to train fellow students in advocacy and change.

and adult educators generally have not dealt with one another in the context of equal power to affect outcomes, or equal vulnerability to each other's influence. One purpose of developing students' self-interest and political strength may be to equalize (at least temporarily) the balance of power so that true collaboration and negotiation can begin. Otherwise, negotiation among members of unequal power remains negotiation by dint of the superior group's altruism and sufferance, not because of functional necessity or the necessity for system survival. The *recognition of students as a legitimate and necessary political force* and the treatment of their demands as legitimate political and educational priorities are also key outcomes of any program preparing students for their role in school change.

Illustration 1: Training for Conflict Utilization. In one school in the West it became clear that school administrators were rejecting student-initiated conversations and suggestions for change. As a result, students were at the point of rioting and leaving school. A team of external consultants received administrative permission to work with the students in the midst of impending disorder. The consultants' entry into this highly politicized situation required the establishment of a relationship with the mistrustful and aggressive student groups. As the consultants presented their ideological and political credentials, they also presented to students some alternative images of influence and protest.

After several such entry and testing sessions, student leaders agreed to attend a series of training events. The training staff included two adults but was composed mainly of specially prepared older students from other school districts. Training in the outcomes discussed above was conducted solely for students and dealt with the district from their point of view, with their goals and needs in mind. A prime instructional procedure was the use of role-playing or simulation exercises in which students tested their skills and strategies in mock situations.

Skill training in negotiation and compromise, as well as confrontation and escalation with educators, was necessary. So, too, was practice in organizing a disciplined group of supporters. In the context of these sessions, student leaders considered anew their goals and their relations to larger groups of their peers.

As one result, large groups of students were organized in a disciplined, highly focused class boycott and potential school shutdown. Student leaders were then asked to join district administrators in direct negotiations, and larger groups of students waited on the results of these sessions. Changes that met student demands came about through students' patient and non-violent, but militant and hard-headed, advocacy of their own interests. A student organization was developed which proved to last over a period of time. Throughout the school year, students continued to mobilize strength and unity when it was required. The disciplined and non-violent nature of their subsequent protests prevented over-reactions from local administrators, police officers, and parents. This school now faces the challenge of institutionalizing this organizational revolution in a new governance form, one like the models of innovative governance discussed in the prior section.

Illustration 2: Training for Student-Administrator Confrontation. In another advocacy-oriented project, students from several high schools were trained to be consultants to a group of administrators concerned with problems of disruption, desegregation, and decentralization. The students identified their interests and concerns in these areas, with considerable anger about the ways they were treated in school. In planning their consultation with the group of administrators, the students initially discussed strategies of confrontation that included revenge and punishment. As they discussed the probable reaction of administrators to such approaches, they were able to put some additional perspective into their planning.

Even so, at the meeting itself, they threatened and distanced many administrators present. Their articulate analyses and unique perspectives on school problems were not heard and could not be used until each group was able to work through some of its feelings about the new role and power relationships being exemplified. While several consultants worked directly with the students, another tried to help the administrators. In this instance, part of the consultants' advocacy strategy involved opening up adults to the students' positions. The adult who worked with administrators was a partisan link: not a representative of students or a promoter of collaboration, but an advocate seeking to "soften up" the targets of change. He aided them in understanding students' positions, in examining and minimizing their defenses, and in beginning to make relevant responses. Since student militancy generally is likely to threaten educators, linkage to them in an organizational change program may help reduce some of the non-rational components of escalation.

Comments. Students who take leadership in organizing and representing their role group's interests must be carefully prepared so they will not be co-opted as tools of adult interests, just because they are negotiators or act in liaison with the adult establishment. Similarly, adults who wish to negotiate with students in good faith must take care not to put students in the co-opted position, a position that renders them impotent to themselves, their constituencies, *and* their opponents. Preparation of both students and adults for such negotiation and collaboration is undoubtedly a necessary part of the development of advocates.

It should be emphasized that a student advocacy approach can be practiced in its "pure" form only if students are considered the clients of the OD consultants. If administrators or "the district" is seen as the client, compromises will constantly be made to serve this end; there is no initial guarantee that "system" interests, especially as defined by administrators, are the same as or represent student interests. (Later, when student needs are articulated and integrated into a systemic picture, "system" and student interests are likely to be closer.) If, on the other hand, students request, pay for, or convince consultants to volunteer their services, they are the only group to whom the consultants are responsible. Students are more likely to be real clients as the sophistication of consultants, student groups, and community groups grows, and as the understanding grows that all parties to a conflict need expert help.

Training for Value-Homogeneous Groups

Up to this point, we have been considering change strategies that primarily involve working with separate or partially separate student groups on the basis of their role in school. This rests on the sound assumption, given our present educational structure, that there are significant common interests within role groups and significant differences between them.

Another strategy of organizational renewal may require the grouping of individuals from various parts of the district who share a common set of values or goals. This cross-role cadre then can be trained to operate as value advocates, much as the "role advocates" were trained in the previous section. It should be recognized that it is not easy to identify specific and common value positions in American education. The rhetoric of educational values and goals is so encompassing that it makes asserting and clarifying specific issues quite difficult. Therefore, organization and proselytization on this basis is harder than on the visible basis of role groupings.

Illustration: Training for a Value-Homogeneous Group. In a Northwestern high school a training program was initiated at the request of several students and a few teachers deeply committed to the concept of "shared power." They did not know exactly what this term meant to them, but they did want to provide students, especially, and teachers with more potent influence and authority in school affairs. Very careful screening of participants was undertaken to insure value-commonality about desired changes in power relations. Each member of an initial informal discussion group of eight spoke to three or four trusted colleagues, and the target population was gradually built to around seventy (thirty-five students, twenty-five teachers, two administrators, and eight parents).

This group met together for several retreats and working sessions with outside OD consultants. The initial training task focused on clarification of both role-related and "value-centric" issues. This was done by generating discussion around value issues in groups separated by role. Some examples of issues raised include:

Students have significant skill and expertise to add to school decisions.

Shared power should mean student, administrative, and community involvement in decisions about teacher recruiting, hiring, evaluation, and firing.

People in different groups should talk with one another honestly and openly.

It was discovered quickly that there were value and strategy differences within the role groups, but within much narrower limits than would have occurred in a randomly selected group. In the student group, particularly, the hope of potent outcomes caused other barriers to be crossed. As white and black students started to disagree about some racial issues, one black student, a Black Panther member, said, "Let's stop bickering about this; if we can get together on the other issues that's good enough."

Discussions in cross-role groups followed. In these groups, it became essential for persons to be sure about the positions of others, especially those others occupying different roles. Teachers inquired in depth in order to understand students' feelings about unfair and arbitrary discipline and bad teaching; then they were called on to share views about their own vulnerability to student evaluation of instruction. One of the most important events was an open discussion of others in similar roles who were not in attendance. For instance, students truly began to trust teachers' commitments when teachers talked openly about other teachers and their positions on issues, and likely ways of influencing or subverting them. Such honesty was evidence of willingness to break with one's role group and to place greater loyalty in the cross-role value group than in the professional role group.

This value-homogeneous group continued to meet throughout a year (sometimes with the blessings of the school administration) in order to develop plans for change and strategies to implement their plans.

One immediate outcome was the establishment of a student and faculty group that reviewed all key issues in the school and the principal's decisions, and advised him on policy matters. The student-faculty cadre was committed to the right to veto the principal's decisions but decided to build toward that end rather than raise it as a condition of their existence. Clear commitments were made by the administration to work toward that end.

A second outcome was establishment of a special class, for members of the cadre and a slowly increasing interest group, on educational issues and school decision-making. This official class was taught by the student and teacher members, with occasional visitors from outside groups and agencies.

A third outcome was the development of plans to organize a constitutional convention, with documents spelling out a new governance structure to be approved school-wide and city-wide. A position was taken by student and faculty members of the cadre and a negotiated agreement was finally made with key local administrators. The basic element of the negotiated agreement was as follows:

It is proposed that the secondary schools accept a *shared power concept* for decision-making to enhance the teaching-learning process at the building level. Power shall be shared by the students, community members, teachers and administrators in their respective schools as they participate in policy-making decisions pertaining to *any* aspect of the school. Representation of constituent groups shall be proportional to the population of the respective constituent groups, with the exception of the community, whose members will be decided by the constitutional committee. Implementation in each building shall be carried out by a constitutional committee elected by constituent groups of each school. The constitutional committee is to be selected in each school building, with the object to create, ratify, and present to the Board a constitution.

The principal's veto power in all areas will be relinquished as the shared power group becomes the recognized and accountable decision-making body of the school.

This statement reflects the slowly developing agreement to establish a local veto power as procedures become clearer and more implementable. In working toward all these outcomes the cadre met often and was instrumental in obtaining local and federal funds to sponsor planning sessions, workshops, and consultancies.

Comments. It is especially important in value-homogeneous groups for members from different role groups to recognize and deal with their own differences and goals. Given the tendency of such cadres to be organized against the larger "system," to mobilize around common conceptions of system injustices and brutality, internal differences are often initially masked or ignored in the pursuit of common goals. The focus of all energy outward is heightened by the magnitude of the task such cadres undertake, and the fear of consequences if they are not successful. However, the same intergenerational and cross-role issues mentioned in the earlier strategies apply here. Respect, honesty, and reciprocity must characterize relationships within the cadre. Given the threat of outside forces on the cadre, it is even more likely that student members of such cadres will be co-opted by outsiders if attention to internal processes is neglected.

The ability of such a cadre to resist splintering or inappropriate fraction, while at the same time respecting tolerable differences within, is a crucial issue.

Similarly, it is vital to sustain internal integrity while not alienating non-cadre collaborators or targets of change. In many schools where cadres have worked well internally they have done so at the cost of productive links to the outside. Although one excellent defense against outside pressure is to wall it off, internal secretiveness and "in-groupness" often alienate persons not in the group. To the extent that this reaction is based on real differences in values, it is quite appropriate, but it may be a strategic "red herring" and a tactical error if resistance is the reaction of outsiders.

People who decide to work together toward a specific end must know where each other stands, be able to count on one another, and be able to stand up together under pressure. There will be efforts made to break apart a cohesive team that threatens others' interests: adult educators may be tantalized by offers to be advisors to the superintendent or to be district specialists on community affairs; and students may be offered select seats on faculty committees. Such efforts to co-opt leading individuals with unique rewards and privileges must be placed in proper context. If the overriding issue is the attainment of collective power by new groups, then positions on a committee or new roles for radical advocates are mere tokens. Individuals recruited into an effective cadre must be prepared for the seductions of personal influence and gain.

The value-homogeneous group strategy differs from the collaboration model of OD in that there is no assumption that the cadre should necessarily include the legitimate or formal authority figures in the district. A simple collaborative model usually requires such involvement of top influentials.

Also, this strategy clearly assumes that the group so formed will reflect a much narrower range of value positions on the control and distribution of resources than is present in the larger school system. During different stages of the change process, the value-homogeneous model of change may utilize aspects of both the collaborative and advocacy orientations described earlier in its dealings with other groups in the school district.

In general, the major advantage of the collaborative approach is that it links students and student needs immediately to other parts of the district. Its major disadvantage lies in encouraging premature collaboration that obviates differences and conflict. This is especially true given the presence of skilled traditional practitioners of such collaboration.

The major advantage of role advocacy is precisely its mobilization of students' unique interests and their organization into a potent and disciplined subgroup. Its major disadvantages are potential escalation into chaos and difficulty in reintegration.

The value-homogeneous approach has the advantage of linking students and committed members of other groups in an enterprise with philosophic overtones. Its disadvantages lie in the difficulty of identifying and maintaining real collaboration via a value framework.

Some Risks and Benefits in Advocating Changed Decision-Making Structures

The strategies of change discussed here can bring many advantages to the school. Governance, the instructional process, and political participation should all be affected positively in ways described earlier. But advocates of these processes also run some risks; we speak in detail of these here to give a realistic view of school resistance to such strategies and thus to protect advocates and schools from naive notions of immediate reform.

Some Typical Risks. Regardless of the strategy or approach used, attempts to suggest change in educators' norms regarding professional sanctity and security, principals' legal responsibilities, and student roles are likely to create considerable public and professional resistance. Persons advocating such restructuring will be asked, induced, and sometimes coerced to change their behavior and conform to prior standards. Colleagues may snicker, jeer openly, or otherwise try to dissuade individuals involved in change processes. In some schools, teachers who have advocated such changes have suffered disciplinary action or have had their contracts terminated. Students have discovered notations about political conduct on their records, faced suspension, or found their own peers deriding the "non-coolness" of trying to change things. Some of these responses may be especially painful for students requiring a good record for college or for the immediate job market. School officials may also encourage students' parents to act as a pressure to prevent efforts at serious change.

Beyond interpersonal pressures and the invocation of traditional norms, there are also potential legal constraints which can be used against cadres attempting meaningful change in non-traditional ways. A small group of people may be seen as a "conspiracy" with the intent to create disruption. They may be charged with contention or disturbing the peace. The adults may be seen as contributing to the delinquency of minors. Some federal research and scholarship agencies have already agreed that funds may not be used for persons convicted for participation in some form of educational disorder or disruption.

Administrators typically are reluctant to have people they see as agitators organize students. The natural tendency of administrators is to avoid risk and reduce any tension in the school, not only because of their personal predilections, but also because of the pressure exerted on them by the superintendent's office, the school board, and the community. In crisis situations particularly, the options that principals feel are available to them are extremely limited: "tunnel vision" sets in.

Finally, the immediate effect of the approaches to change which we have described may be to intensify and polarize conflict, because of the increased coherence and articulation of the student groups. Furthermore, advocacy for this or any other segment of the school community may seriously antagonize other elements in the school and increase the scope and intensity of the conflict. However, the self-interests of various groups do exist, whether expressed openly or covertly; this approach can help to bring hidden tensions and conflicts into the open.

Each of the members of an advocate group or cadre faces somewhat different pressures. However, all can expect to be pressured not to hang together, not to truly focus on the dramatic changes we have described, and not to take the personal risks discussed here. One of the things group members may do to help each other is to examine and share the pressures that each member faces. Time must be found to allow for the sharing and potential resolution of such feelings; otherwise, dysfunctional anxieties or righteous indignation may result. Internal support also can be provided by assiduous attention to the dynamics of group and interpersonal processes.

Benefits. There are a number of benefits that may accrue to people committed to change processes like those we describe. First, their schools may avoid the risk of continuing school crisis and disorder. Student requests and demands for involvement and power in school decision-making, and educators' resistance and reluctance to meet those demands form a central focus of contention in schools across the nation. In numerous cases this has led to escalated confrontation and crisis. Crisis and confrontation are in themselves neither good nor bad; the question is whether they lead to improvement of the quality of life, in school and out. We believe that strategies using the power-conflict model of OD can do so.

If students are able to create and participate in new governance structures which represent their interests—and the competing interests of other school groups—our belief, supported by much practical experience, is that the living and learning processes in such schools will be more humane, more creative, and closer to national educational goals. It is not simply that the students' sense of control over their fate, so closely allied to other educational outcomes, increases. It is that the educational activities which ensue are better ones.

A final benefit may sound apocalyptic. Though it is clear, as we have said, that change agents and advocates face risks in trying to improve the quality of life in schools, it is even clearer that *not* to risk improvement attempts will lead to even greater risks and perhaps to disaster. The absence of imaginative and just change may very well result in more numerous and extreme short-term crises and the eventual collapse of our public educational system as we now know it. The renovation and restructuring of systems of power will not totally rejuvenate our schools nor guarantee correction of a series of other injustices. But it is one reform that holds large promise for a more adequate future in our schools.

Concluding Comments

Can important changes in schools be generated and implemented without some alteration in the allocation and distribution of power? Our conclusion is: No. In particular, the redistribution of power to people now impotent in role, style, and training will be required for meaningful response to student initiatives and organization. The creation of new internal decision-making structures which reflect and take advantage of new forms of power and newly trained individuals within the school promises higher quality in schools. We believe that long-range designs for change or organizational restructuring that do not stress such participation in school decision-making are bound to fail.

It is important to recognize that people entrusted with the management of schools have become a separate class (with special interests of their own) which may not always act in the best interest of the clients of the educational process. Regardless of their race, age, status, or skill, clients must be provided with the training requisite for full participation in society at large.

Programs to train students for self-governance or for active roles in school renewal must generate skills both in self-advocacy and collaboration with others. Traditional training activities have focused too much on collaborative styles, to the point where collaboration is viewed as an end rather than a means. The endemic nature of role-related and value-centric conflicts in schools requires that each group, and especially students, develop a means of articulating and presenting its own views.

Advocacy and collaboration are not exclusive; rather, they are each essential components of political change, of change in decision-making structures. Collaboration as a *sine qua non* neglects the interests of impotent groups; advocacy alone fails to provide for systemic integration. Advocacy that leads to collaboration and negotiation among differing but respected opponents is most likely to rejuvenate our schools in directions more satisfying to the people who live, work, and learn in them.

References

Argyris, C. 1964. *Integrating the individual and the organization.* New York: Wiley.
Babbidge, H. D. Jr. 1969. *Eighth annual faculty convocation.* Storrs, Connecticut: University of Connecticut.
Bennis, W. 1970. A funny thing happened on the way to the future. *American Psychologist* 25:595-608.
Buchanan, P. 1967. Crucial issues in organization development. In *Change in school systems,* ed. G. Watson. Washington, D.C.: National Training Laboratories.
____, 1969. Laboratory training and organizational development. *Administrative Science Quarterly* 14:466-80.
Campbell, A. 1968. Who governs the schools? *Saturday Review,* December 21, 1968, pp. 50-52, 63-65.
Chesler, M.A. 1969. Student and administrative crises. *Educational Leadership* 27:34-42.
____, and Arnstein, F. 1970. The school consultant: change agent or defender of the status quo? *Integrated Education* 8:19-25.
Coleman, J., et al. 1966. *Equality of educational opportunity.* Washington, D.C.: United States Government Printing Office.
Cooperative Project for Educational Development (COPED). 1970. Final Report, USOE Contract OEG 3-8-080069-0043 (010) Project #8-0069. Washington, D.C.: U.S. Office of Education.
Coser, L. 1956. *The functions of social conflict.* Glencoe, Illinois: Free Press.
____. 1967. *Continuities in the study of social conflict.* New York: Free Press.
Dahl, R. 1967. *Pluralist democracy in "the US"; conflict and consent.* Chicago: Rand McNally.
Duggal, S. 1969. *Relationship between school unrest, student participation in school management, and dogmatism and pupil control ideology of staff in high schools.* Unpublished dissertation, University of Michigan.
Fantini, M. D., and Young, M. A. 1970. *Designing education for tomorrow's cities.* New York: Holt, Rinehart and Winston.
Gamson, W. 1968. *Power and discontent.* Homewood, Illinois: Dorsey.
Guskin, A., and Guskin, S. 1970. *A social psychology of education.* Reading, Massachusetts: Addison-Wesley.
____, and Ross, R. In press. Advocacy and democracy: the long view. *Journal of American Orthopsychiatric Association.*
Haug, M., and Sussman, M. 1969. Professional autonomy and the revolt of the client. *Social Problems* 17: 153-61.
Janowitz, M. 1969. *Institution building in urban education.* New York: Russell Sage Foundation.
Katz, D., and Kahn, R. 1966. *The social psychology of organizations.* New York: Wiley.
Kvaraceus, W. 1965. Negro youth and school adaptation. In *Negro self-concept,* ed. W. Kvaraceus, et al. New York: McGraw-Hill.
Laue, J. 1968. Power, conflict and social change. In *Riots and rebellion; civil violence in the urban community,* eds. Masotti and Bower. Beverly Hills: Sage Publications. Pp. 85-96.
Leavitt, H. J. 1965. Applied organizational change in industry: structural, technological, and humanistic approaches. In *Handbook of organizations,* ed. J. G. March. Chicago: Rand McNally. Pp. 1144-1170.
Likert, R. 1961. *New patterns of management.* New York: McGraw-Hill.
Mann, E. 1965. A new school for the ghetto. *Our generation* 5:67-73.

McGregor, D. 1960. *The human side of enterprise.* New York: McGraw-Hill.

Miles, M., and Lake, D. 1967. Self-renewal in school systems, a strategy for planned change. In *Concepts for social change,* ed. G. Watson. Washington, D.C.: National Training Laboratories.

Perlmutter, H. V. 1965. *On the theory and practice of social architecture.* London: Tavistock Publications.

Polk, B. 1968. *Sense of internal control in a non-alienative environment: a flexible-modular school.* Unpublished dissertation, University of Michigan.

Raskin, M. 1968. Political socialization in the schools. *Harvard Educational Review* 38:550-53.

Reeves, Donald. 1970. A student voice on policy, a short history of the student bill of rights. New York City. Mimeographed (2 pp.)

Robinson, L., and Schoenfeld, J. 1970. *Student participation in academic governance.* Washington, D.C.: ERIC   Clearinghouse on Higher Education. Pp. 1-3.

Schaible, L., and Piotrowsky, L. 1970. Ann Arbor public school project. Terminal Report, USOE Contract Grant OEG-0-9-324128-2008(725). Ann Arbor, Michigan: University of Michigan.

Schmuck, R.; Runkel, P.; and Langmeyer, D. 1969. Improving organizational problem-solving in a school faculty. *Journal of Applied Behavioral Science* 5:455-82.

Smelser, N. 1963. *Theory of collective behavior.* New York: Free Press.

Sugarman, A. 1970. Students take over at Ramapo Senior High. *Inside Education,* February, p. 9.

Verba, S. 1961. *Small groups and political behavior.* Princeton, New Jersey: Princeton University Press.

Wittes, S. 1970. *Power and people: high schools in crisis.* Ann Arbor, Michigan: Institute for Social Research.

10

DEVELOPING TEAMS OF ORGANIZATIONAL SPECIALISTS *

Richard A. Schmuck

No American school district, no matter how well adapted to its current community, can stay the same and still remain adaptive in the long run. A district that hopes to have a positive impact must be able to change its modes of operating continuously as it finds itself becoming less effective in coping with its changing environment. Consequently, the need for continuous training in OD in schools is paramount.

Too often innovative programs in schools initiated by outsiders or through outside funds stop or are dissipated when the outsiders or funds are removed. The termination of such projects occurs especially when the new projects make it necessary to establish delicate new role relations or new ways of group problem-solving. When innovations such as program planning and budgeting or the multi-unit school are attempted, for examples, they depend heavily on the actions of a coordinated team.

It is not practical to have outside organizational consultants continuously present in a school district. A special team of inside specialists is needed to replace the outside consultants after completion of their project. This chapter describes how one school district was helped to develop such an inside cadre of organizational specialists. The OD strategy described here should be compared especially with the one employed in Chapter 8.

Organizational specialists competent to carry out OD training are urgently needed in many school districts. Outside organization development consultants are not sufficient. A team of internal specialists is important so that the training first introduced into the district from the outside later can become part of the internal structure, thereby serving as a mechanism for continuous organizational problem-solving. Rarely have school districts employed specialists who would attempt to improve the communication patterns as well as group processes and

* The contents of this chapter were drawn from three technical reports published by the Center for the Advanced Study of Educational Administration, University of Oregon, Eugene, Oregon: R. Schmuck, P. Runkel, and D. Langmeyer, *Theory to Guide Organizational Training in Schools,* 1969; D. Langmeyer, R. Schmuck, and P. Runkel, *Technology for Organizational Training in Schools,* 1969; and R. Schmuck, C. Blondino, and P. Runkel, *Organizational Specialists in a School District,* 1970. Special acknowledgement is granted to Philip J. Runkel who collaborated in developing the contents of this chapter.

organizational procedures that affect everyone. This chapter describes one experience in developing a team of organizational specialists in a school district. First, let us turn to the organizational theory behind this project.

Organizational Theory

Schools are open, living systems, contained within, but constantly influencing and being influenced by the community. They are complex organizations stabilized by role expectations and interpersonal norms. Faculty members behave predictably largely because they adhere to shared expectations for what is appropriate in the school. Norms are compelling stabilizers because individuals monitor one another's behavior. It is the strength of this shared feeling that makes a school organization so resistant to modification but at the same time offers it a tool for planned change. If change in schools is to be viable, changes in interpersonal expectations must be shared so that each person knows that his colleagues have changed their expectations in the same way that he has changed his own.

Put in a different way, schools are more than the sum of their individual members and curriculum materials. The staff has characteristics quite different from those of its individual members. These can be referred to as the school's systemic characteristics. Effective management of the school is evidenced when greater production occurs than would be expected from a simple summing up of individual resources. As an open system, the organization's efficiency is measured by how completely resources are used in developing its products. A school's efficiency is defined as the degree to which resources, such as the capabilities and attitudes of students and staff, as well as the quality of curriculum materials, are optimally integrated and processed to produce the desired products: namely, capable, competent, responsible, and happy persons.

Postulates

Four postulates are basic to this theory of school organizations.

1. Schools are made up of components (e.g., people and curriculum) which are organized into *subsystems* by means of communication, decision-making, job allocation, and program evaluation. Some important subsystems take the form of classrooms, departmental groups, curriculum committees, building groups, and administrative cabinets.

2. Schools are goal-directed. The subsystems are organized presumably to achieve the system's goals and they are organized with functional differences. For example, the superintendents' administrative committee may forecast about the future in order to accommodate changing times; classroom teachers may diagnose the learning needs of their students; and curriculum committees may scan the outside world for new ideas and practices.

3. Schools display some degrees of openness and adaptability, and to a certain degree, schools are always changing (although at times I feel not enough or not in the right ways). Schools are constantly mapping part of their environmental variety into their internal organization. Strain within schools occurs when one

subsystem (such as the curriculum division) brings into the school district new practices and another subsystem (such as a building staff) is mostly closed to the new practice. Locations in the school district that manifest openness to the outside environment are administrative cabinets in relation to the school board, curriculum committees in relation to outside innovations, and teachers' professional organizations in relation to other similar organizations in the community. Such subsystems often are in conflict with other subsystems less directly related to the outside environment.

4. Schools are constituted with many resources within their subsystems that are not being used at any one time. This repertoire for adaptation can be referred to as a *variety pool*. While the variety pool will inevitably include a number of processes which are irrelevant or even deleterious in relation to its goals, a district, to be adaptive, must seek, support, and facilitate the emergence of whatever resources exist for maximizing its educative functions.

Organization Development

These postulates help move us toward an orientation for OD in schools. First, training interventions will be more effective if they deal with subsystems and not just randomly selected components. Further, the total school takes its shape from the ways the functional subsystems connect their efforts to one another. For this reason, OD efforts should focus on relationships within and between subsystems. Second, training interventions should confront the school with discrepancies between striving for goals and actual goal achievement. Since the goals of a school district lie in its interaction with its environment, an intervention in a district should be designed to affect the interresponsiveness of the system with its community. Third, interventions should be aimed at making every subsystem in the school more open to the influences of every other subsystem. From the point of view of this theory, increased openness is especially appropriate, on the one hand, in relationships between subsystems that are closer to the boundaries of the whole system (such as the curriculum division) and, on the other hand, in relations between the subsystems that are closer to the inner core of the system (such as classrooms).

Finally, interventions in OD should help the school define its variety pool by identifying system-wide resources and should help the district to build communication connections between subsystems. In this way, interventions often lead to the creation of new or *ad hoc* subsystems that exist only long enough to mobilize resources for certain isolated and irregular problems. Interventions quite often lead to the formation of problem-solving groups that did not exist in the formal structure of the school before the intervention. If school organizations are to be truly adaptive, they must be able to form new subsystems, change them, or dispose of them as needed.

Norms and Roles

When the organizational condition of a school district is diagnosed, repeated use should be made of the concepts *norm* and *role*. Norms provide the school organization with its structure and coherence. Members of a staff behave in patterned and predictable ways because their behaviors are guided by common expectations, attitudes, and understandings. Norms are especially serviceable and tenacious when individual staff members intrinsically value the normative behavior in the school or when they perceive such behavior as instrumental in reaching other valued goals. In any case, norms are strong stabilizers of organizational behavior.

Roles are the groups of functions that individual staff members perform as part of their positions in the organization. These sets of functions or working activities are patterned and regular primarily because they are guided by organizational norms. Administrators, teachers, and students behave in predictable ways because each expects the other to do so.

Role-taking is done as part of an interaction with other role-takers. If it is said that an organizational member is performing poorly in a given role, what is meant is that the interaction between him and his role reciprocators is producing a breakdown within the subsystem. In this sense, the point of any intervention for improving a subsystem is not a *person* but rather *the interaction patterns linking role reciprocators.* It would be a psychologist's fallacy, for example, to focus on the internal dynamics of only one role-taker, no matter how significant he may be within the organization.

Any attempt to intervene into a school must include new ways of carrying out interpersonal interaction; further, these new procedures should be entered into by the actual role reciprocators who make the school run. Norms and roles cannot be changed in a vacuum. Changes in organizational norms and roles are most efficiently brought into being and made stable by asking staff members to behave in new ways in their actual work-group setting while, at the same time, other role-takers observe these new behaviors. Norms will not be altered unless other relevant role-takers are allowed to see that their colleagues actually accept the new patterns of behavior in the setting of the school.

Personality

Many subsystems in school districts call for staff members to interact daily in mutual interdependence and reciprocity. These subsystems, especially when they are face-to-face and intimate, require more detailed norms than does the district at large. The norms of such subsystems center on methods for work, interpersonal values, and social-emotional customs. Each face-to-face work group rewards certain manners of speech, behaviors, gestures, etc., and not others; it also approves certain topics for discussion and not others.

In these groups, individual differences in personality become important: sometimes crucially so. Especially important are emotional predispositions and interpersonal competencies or skills. Alteration of some interpersonal patterns can be guided by formal changes, but sometimes patterns of interpersonal interactions that deeply involve the egos of the participants can be changed only through the same process by which they are maintained—through new one-to-one actions supported by other members of the subsystem and legitimized through the formation of new intra-group norms.

Because man's rational and emotional sides are inextricably mingled, an organizational training intervention can be successful only if it takes adequate account of man's emotional nature. Research evidence shows that men invest emotion in at least three domains: (1) *striving toward achievement,* also labeled curiosity, exploration, or activity, (2) *affiliation,* also delineated by some as the interpersonal dimension of love, indifference, and hostility, and (3) *influence or power,* also described as the dimension of dominance-submission.

All interpersonal relations and the motivations concomitant with them can be construed as having achievement, affiliation, and influence components. Emotional experiences can become problems when any one of these motivational states is frustrated. Typical emotions noted in observations of schools resulting from frustrations of these motivations are feelings of inferiority, worthlessness, being "put down," loneliness, betrayal, lack of interest, and dullness. These feelings, in turn, prevent staff members from making maximum use of their potentials as role-takers. Although it seems impossible to arrange human affairs to eliminate emotional frustrations, it does appear possible to bring about organizational norms and procedures in schools that will mobilize emotional states for productive ends and make it more likely that the work of the school will flow smoothly.

Feelings in the area of achievement can be harnessed productively when staff members have a clear conception of one another's goals. Ambiguity about expected outcomes is usually more emotionally frustrating than conflict over goals. In the latter instance, persons on a school staff can gain security by realizing where they stand in relations to others. Ambiguity, however, reduces the likelihood that feelings will be associated with a clear referent; consequently, the frustrated person cannot easily find a way out of his frustration. Affiliative feelings can be gratified through the building of a cohesive unit in which staff members find friendliness and the reciprocal exchange of support and warmth. Feelings related to power can be satisfied through an organization's allowance for influence at all levels. Such a dispersion of influence will facilitate the open expression of frustration over being placed in a submissive or dominated relation to others. (Then, too, some persons become anxious when they find themselves in a position of *dominance*.) All emotional states are potentially harnessed through taking a problem-solving orientation to organizational life in the schools.

Organizational Training

Organizational training seeks to increase the effectiveness of groups as task-oriented entities and tries to lead school personnel to function more effectively as components of working bodies carrying out the specific tasks of the school. The key to successful organizational training lies in a school's capacity to solve its own problems by using the resources already present. These resources include information about different curricula, willingness to take risks, and creativity in teaching. Staff resources are not simply ideas residing in a filing cabinet. Rather, resources are truly available only when a work group calls upon members for fresh ways of doing things, when each member feels unafraid in offering his own ideas for use, and when the norms of the group enable a new idea to be moved into action with reasonable speed and commitment. These capabilities are enhanced by (1) developing clear communication networks up, down, and laterally, (2) increasing understanding on the part of members of the district of the various educational goals in different parts of the district, (3) increasing understanding on the part of members of how people in different parts of the total school district affect one another, and (4) involving more personnel at all levels in decision-making.

Organizational training differs from the sort of help offered by a traditional management consulting firm. Traditional consultants work on problems as they are defined by the administrators of the organization. After interviews and observations are made, reports are issued that recommend solutions to the original problems. Rarely does a traditional consultant stay with an organization long enough to help it carry the recommendations into practice. Organizational training consultants, on the other hand, explore problems from the perspectives of all parts of the organization and include relevant parties within and without the organization in designing and implementing change. Frequent training sessions help the school personnel to carry out the changes they themselves designed.

Organizational training also differs from sensitivity training. Although organizational training makes use of the organization as its own laboratory for experiential or inductive learning techniques, laboratory groups are used in very different ways from sensitivity or T-groups. The targets of organizational training are the membership as a whole and as subgroups. The training seeks to change norms and the definitions of roles. It does not seek to change personalities, nor is it aimed at facilitating personal growth. I do not believe that the T-group is a helpful tool for refurbishing organizational life.

Naturally, deep feelings often arise from task-oriented activities. To the extent that such feelings inhibit a group from accomplishing its organizational tasks, skill in coping with them should be introduced during organizational training tasks. For example, it should be expected that resolutions to intergenerational and interracial power struggles require catharsis along with some skill in communicating clearly about feelings.

Training for Self-Renewal

The goal of organizational training for schools is self-renewal in organizations. A self-renewing school is able to adapt to current changes in its environment while still maintaining an effective educational program. For example, since one current tension revolves around intergenerational conflict, the self-renewing school of today will find ways to involve students in more decisions about the school's operation and what is to be taught in the classrooms.

Self-renewing organizations are adaptive in the long run; hence, they are not set in any single organizational structure or procedure. While there is typically some formal hierarchy, form follows function. People are organized into groups to solve specific problems; both the structure of the organization and the methods used in the groups change to suit the nature of the current problems. As examples, groups to modify curriculum may be highly structured, with a strict agenda, a designated leader to move the group along, and a well-defined method of voting to make decisions; while a long-range planning department, on the other hand, may be quite loosely organized, may permit ample latitude for dreaming, may allow considerable time for various experts to pool their points of view, and may insist that decisions finally be made through ballots submitted by community groups, parents, and students.

In self-renewing organizations, decisions are made by the persons who have the information. Instead of looking to those who have the legitimate authority, emphasis is placed on the best possible decision. Decision-making requires adequate information; all too often, those in authority lack information or have it in a distorted form. In a self-renewing school, for example, a group of students and parents may decide on dress codes; teachers and students may decide on classroom procedures; while some teachers, the principal, and the superintendent may decide on whether to engage in in-service leadership training for the principals.

A self-renewing organization has sensing processes and feedback mechanisms to tell when changes are needed. There is open communication among those in the school district and between the district and those in the city's environment on the question of when the school needs to change. A self-renewing organization manages itself according to specified goals accepted by its members. It has systematic methods (e.g., problem-solving techniques) for dealing with obstacles to reaching these goals. The goals, naturally, are open to change as the environment of the school district changes.

Finally, a self-renewing organization has a culture or climate which permits the processes mentioned above to take place. There is open, direct, and clear communication. Conflict is viewed as inevitable and natural and is brought out into the open so that it can be used to bring about creative change instead of impeding the work to be accomplished. Creativity, even wild dreaming, are encouraged. New ideas and new persons and groups are seen as additional resources rather than as troublemakers and threats.

The Intervention Process

Organizational training is a process for helping school organizations to become more self-renewing. The organizational trainer who intervenes in a school district should organize his work in three stages:

Stage 1: Improving Communication Skills. The trainer builds increased openness and ease of interpersonal communication among the district personnel by training them in such communication skills as paraphrasing, describing behavior, describing their own feelings, checking their perceptions of others' feelings, and giving and receiving feedback. This stage develops constructive openness, increasing confidence among the staff in the fact that communication with colleagues can be worthwhile.

Stage 2: Changing Norms. The trainer builds new norms that support helpfulness among the staff. Also, norms that support the surfacing of intergroup conflicts should be encouraged. The trainer can use the desires of professional personnel and their natural self-interest to ameliorate some of their actual problems and so provide a lever with which to change group norms. For example, the consultant can invite the educators to state some frustrations that they are encountering in their jobs and to practice a sequence of problem-solving steps to reduce these frustrations. Systematic problem-solving not only reduces frustrations but also yields the satisfaction of knowing that others value the contribution one has made to the solution. Changes in organizational norms of openness and candor occur when the consultant requires staff members to behave in new ways in their actual work groups, enabling their colleagues to observe the new patterns of behavior in the school setting.

Stage 3: Structural Change. The trainer builds new functions, roles, procedures, or policies. These new structures should become part of the basic fabric of the school district. They should be formal, institutionalized, and budgetarily supported. A cadre of organizational specialists inside a school district is one example of a new structure for organizational self-renewal.

Establishing Organizational Specialists

As part of a two-year intervention, consultants from the Center for the Advanced Study of Educational Administration (CASEA), led by Philip Runkel and me, established a cadre of organizational specialists in the school district at Kent, Washington. Consultants from outside the district launched the organizational training but later turned over the task of continued training in the skills of self-renewal to organizational specialists within the district.

Persons entering the cadre included a teacher, principal, counselor, curriculum specialist, and assistant superintendent; each performs only part time in the role of organizational specialist. The cadre is intended to function as an organizational substructure for self-renewal; it has connections with many other subsystems and can respond flexibly to organizational problems as they arise in the Kent district. The specialists do not relieve others of their problems nor solve problems for others. Rather, they enable others to solve problems more efficiently and effectively by improving certain group processes. In particular, the specialists can produce a lively ability for self-renewal by following these procedures:

1. Diagnosing the discrepancies that exist between the district's goals and its actual organizational performance.

2. Assessing the levels of role clarity in the district.

3. Checking on the flow of communication in the district.

4. Assessing the extent to which the district has a repertoire of interpersonal techniques that aid collaboration in small task groups.

5. Assessing the variety of human resources available for solving problems in the district.

6. Assessing the means by which the district selects some innovative activities to be maintained and others to be rejected.

7. Assessing the methods the district uses for institutionalizing innovations after they have been judged suitable and worth keeping.

In later sections of this chapter I will discuss the actions taken by the organizational specialists in Kent to implement these guides. The organizational training that was carried out by CASEA consultants to bring into being the cadre of organizational specialists is detailed below.

Interventions by CASEA Consultants

Organizational training events for several important parts of the Kent district were carried out by CASEA consultants for one year before the cadre of organizational specialists was started. Although most of the personnel were aware of the training, about 30 percent never were directly involved because of limited time and resources of the CASEA staff. These training events were designed to increase the communication and problem-solving skills of teams of personnel filling key positions in the district. The consultants' plan was to reveal the benefits of systematic training in communication skills and group problem-solving to teams of personnel in a variety of influential positions. One of the consultants' primary interests early in the project was to articulate the complex relationships that existed between staff and line personnel.

Stage 1: Training for Personnel with Line Functions. In April 1968, the consultants invited to the first training event selected influential personnel performing line functions in the district. The trainees included the superintendent and his cabinet, the elementary and secondary principals, and selected teachers who were leaders within the Kent Education Association. At least one teacher from every building attended the meeting, along with the key officers in the association.

The event lasted four days, but only the superintendent's cabinet was present all of the time. On the first day, before others arrived, the superintendent and his cabinet discussed ways in which communication was breaking down among them, the lack of clarity in their role definitions, the ambiguous norms that existed in the cabinet, and finally their strengths as a group.

On the second day, the principals joined the cabinet in a specially designed confrontation that brought into the open organizational problems seen by each group as involving the other. The surfaced problems were earmarked for future solution. First, the cabinet and principals were divided into three units: cabinet, elementary principals, and secondary principals. Next, each group met separately to consider helpful and unhelpful work-related behavior of the other two groups toward their own group. At the end of two hours, all agreed-upon actions of the other groups were written in large letters on sheets of newsprint. The session ended with a brief period of training in the communication skills of paraphrasing and behavior description.

Next, one group sat in a circle, surrounded by members of the other two groups. Participants sitting in the outer ring read aloud the descriptions they had written of the inside group. A member of the inner circle then paraphrased the description to make sure that his colleagues understood it. After all items describing the inside group were read, the remaining two groups took their turn in the center circle. During this step, group members in the inner circle who were receiving descriptions of their own group were *not* allowed to defend their group against the presumed allegations made by the others.

After this step, the three groups again met separately to find evidence that would support the descriptions they had received; they were instructed to recall examples of their own behavior that could have given the other group its impressions. The three groups then came together once again with one group forming an inner circle. Each inner group told the others of the evidence they had recalled to verify the perceptions of the others. Once again, the inner group was discouraged from defending itself; members were asked simply to describe the behavioral events they thought supported others' perceptions.

On the evening of the second day, teachers arrived to join the principals and cabinet and for four hours all of the key line personnel in the Kent district were together. A modified confrontation design was continued, culminating in a meeting in which the three groups indicated the organizational problems they thought existed in the Kent district. Discussion was lively, penetrating, and constructive; most personnel had never before confronted persons in other positions so openly with their perceptions of district problems. The principals went back to their buildings the next day, leaving time for teachers and cabinet to interact with one another. On the fourth day, the cabinet met alone to schedule some dates for problem-solving.

Stage 2: Training for Principals in Human Relations Skills. All principals were strongly urged to participate in a human relations laboratory in June 1968 that was designed and executed by the National Training Laboratories of the Northwest. In general, the training brought about increased skill in interpersonal relations and increased awareness of the effects of one's own responses on others (Thomas, 1970).

Stage 3: Organizational Training for Personnel with Staff Functions. Personnel in staff roles in the divisions of Student Personnel Services and Curriculum Development attended a three-day conference in September 1968; they were joined for one-half day by the principals.

The organizational training began with the staffs of Student Personnel and Curriculum divisions meeting separately to discuss the helps and hindrances that were occurring within each of their groups, with special attention to interpersonal processes within the groups. Specially chosen exercises made the interpersonal helps and hindrances easier to see. After this, the two groups, with the principals as a third group, participated in a period of confrontation. Just as in April, the confrontation unearthed a number of problems for systematic work. Finally, each group began a systematic process of problem-solving (see Chapter 3) and made plans to continue these efforts "back home."

Stage 4: Organizational Training for the Business Department. In November, 1968, the business personnel who had not yet been involved in the training were given two days of training in communication skills, group exercises, and problem-solving. The training was similar in spirit and design to the events with the line and staff personnel, except that no confrontations with other role groups took place.

Stage 5: Organizational Training for Selected School Staffs. From September 1968 to April 1969, the CASEA consultants worked with five different school staffs in the Kent district. These training events were aimed at introducing a large number of teachers to the benefits of organizational training and at reaching organizational subsystems within the district other than the administrative personnel. In general, these training events had small impact, especially as compared to the trainings with line and staff personnel. The chief effect was to increase the awareness of a number of personnel of the meaning and procedures of organizational training. Perhaps the most significant result of these interventions was that many of the volunteers to be trained as future organizational specialists came from the buildings in which some training took place.

Training the Organizational Specialists

In the spring of 1969, information was circulated throughout the district that a workshop would be held in June 1969 for Kent personnel who wished to become organizational specialists in the district. The mimeographed circular stated that the specialist would be knowledgeable and skillful in group processes. He would serve on committees to give feedback or as a trainer for special groups within the district. The consultants hoped that personnel from all hierarchical levels would volunteer to become organizational specialists.

The first step in establishing the role of organizational specialist in the district had been taken already when the school board approved the original project with the CASEA consultants. But it was necessary that the plan be supported with released time, a part-time coordinator, and the blessings of the district's administration. There were several tense moments at the end of the first year of organizational training when the teachers were negotiating for a new contract; early reports indicated that adequate financial support might not be available for the specialists. However, commitments for the project were high for both the teachers and the administrators, and the matter was resolved with ten days released time for each specialist during the school year and enough money for a coordinator to allocate three-tenths of his time to the project.

Applications were solicited from all professional members of the Kent district and twenty-three were selected. The recruits represented a wide cross-section of the district: teachers, counselors, elementary and secondary principals, specialists in curriculum and student personnel, and assistant superintendents who were members of the superintendent's cabinet.

The major training event for the specialists was a two-week workshop during June 1969. The goals of the first half of this workshop were to introduce the specialists to many of the skills, exercises, and procedures that the consultants had found useful in carrying out organizational training (Schmuck and Runkel, 1968). Other goals were to provide the specialists with an opportunity to explore the impact of their behavior on a group, to establish the cadre as a cohesive and supportive unit, and to give members practice in leading organizational training activities. Participants spent the first three days of the workshop in small groups experiencing many exercises, with each rotating to the role of co-trainer to get training experience. Each exercise was designed to make salient a certain type of group process such as interpersonal control, sharing of resources, or coordinating efforts and making certain "lessons" easy to comprehend. It was hoped that the specialists would learn how to use the exercises by experiencing them and examining their experiences.

During the last two days of the first week, participants were asked to design some exercises that would help strengthen their group as the cadre of organizational specialists. They carried out the exercises with their peers and engaged in critical discussion of them. The specialists reviewed and practiced the communicative skills of paraphrasing, describing behavior, describing their own feelings, and checking their individual perceptions of the feelings of others.

For the second week, the specialists divided into six subgroups; each subgroup was convened by a CASEA consultant. The entire group of specialists determined some potential target groups within the school district and each subgroup then chose one of these target groups for its work. Among the targeted groups were several schools that were changing their programs in the coming academic year, the principal and department heads at a senior high school, the elementary principals and counselors who were serving elementary youngsters, and a community advisory group made up of parents. The remainder of the second week was spent establishing goals for the training to be conducted with the target groups, gathering diagnostic data about them, analyzing the data to establish forces operating in the target groups, and designing training events. CASEA consultants worked closely with these subgroups, anticipating the follow-up help they would give to the specialists during the academic year.

CASEA consultants worked with the Kent specialists during the first two-thirds of the 1969-70 academic year, withdrawing in March 1970. Thus the training events that were engineered by the Kent specialists were observed and criticized by the outside consultants. This collaboration was part of a deliberate plan to support the development of training skills within the Kent cadre. Approximately ten different training events occurred with CASEA assistance. Most of these events were successful in raising interest in the district in improving communication, group processes, and organizational problem-solving.

Work of the Organizational Specialists

During the first year of operation, the organizational specialists focused primarily on four target groups: an elementary school staff moving toward a multi-unit structure, the superintendent and his cabinet, teachers interested in improving their communication skills, and a junior high school staff. Limited work was carried out with a group of parents and with a senior high school. Of the four primary interventions, three appeared to be successfully executed.

The most successful training was carried out at the elementary school that was moving toward a multi-unit organization. Several factors in this school were conducive to organizational training. The school had few walls; the newness and freedom of the physical plant encouraged the staff to be creative about teaching strategies. The principal had been trained as an organizational specialist; he felt secure with the training process and encouraged the more retiring staff members to become involved. A final indicator of potential success for the training was that some of the teachers aided the principal in selecting the particular specialists who were to work with the staff.

The first training with this school took place in August just before school began; it lasted for two days. The first day was spent in group exercises and in practicing communication skills. On the second day, the staff participated in group problem-solving, making plans to short-circuit organizational problems that might arise during the academic year. The specialists met again with the faculty for three half-day sessions during September, October, and November. (These sessions were easily arranged because the staff was double-shifting until Christmas.)

Assessment of the training indicated that the teachers thought that the specialists had developed a well-organized training design, that the teachers were experiencing clear communication with the principal, and that they were working smoothly and effectively in their teaching teams. Several teachers commented that they were gratified to see the specialists using the skills they were teaching.

A second successful intervention occurred when another team of specialists worked with the superintendent and his staff during cabinet meetings. Before any help from specialists was given, the superintendent and his staff generally agreed that communication at their cabinet meetings was poor. Participants seemed uncertain of their roles and hesitated to disagree at staff meetings with the superintendent even when debate might improve the group's decision-making. Few decisions were made at the meetings; cabinet members thought that decisions were being made on the outside in unknown ways. Other staff members in the district distrusted the lack of openness they perceived on the part of the cabinet. Much confusion and distrust persisted in the district.

In February 1970, the superintendent decided to open the cabinet meetings to broader participation. The group was renamed "staff" and several role groups (including principals and teachers) were invited to send representatives. In March, the superintendent and his staff agreed that one or two organizational specialists should attend staff meetings to serve as official observers of the communication processes.

As a result of feedback from the specialists at twelve weekly meetings, the following changes in group processes occurred:

1. The superintendent periodically stepped out of the role of "presenter." Presentations were made by a variety of participants.

2. The superintendent relinquished the role of convener (chairman or moderator) to participate more freely in the discussions.

3. Agreements were made by the group on procedures to help the meetings run smoothly. The superintendent (who had been expected to prescribe such procedural rules) acted merely as another member while these agreements were being reached.

4. Time at the end of the meeting was used to discuss (debrief) the group processes that occurred during that meeting. The specialists gave feedback during this time on their observations.

As a result of these changes, less adverse criticism of the meetings was made by participants and less distrust seemed to be manifested by others in the district toward the superintendent.

A third successful intervention was a two-course sequence prepared for interested teachers in the district. In the first course, entitled "Techniques in Communication," the communication skills of paraphrasing, behavior description, describing one's own feelings, and checking one's perception of others' feelings were taught. Also, the participants experienced several group exercises and learned how to carry out an organizational problem-solving sequence. The second course, entitled "Communications and Interpersonal Relations," was an advanced training experience in which the communication skills, exercises, and procedures were reviewed and related to group processes in the classroom. Students who successfully completed both courses and who were enthusiastic about them became candidates for the position of organizational specialist.

Although no intervention created a great deal of strain or adverse criticism, one can fairly be called unsuccessful. The negative experience took place in a training event designed for a junior high school. One of the organizational specialists had reported that some staff members in one of the junior high schools were seen by other faculty as failing to take their share of responsibility for encouraging students to behave properly in the halls. The resulting tension— so the specialists understood—had created several warring subgroups on the faculty; consequently, the faculty as a whole communicated and worked together very poorly. A team of specialists was assigned to the building and their conversations with the principal started during July 1969.

In November the specialists were taken aback to hear the teachers in the building state that the problem no longer existed. They discovered that during the summer the principal had taken steps to correct the lack of clarity about discipline in a way acceptable to most teachers. But the specialists did not learn of these steps until they had carried out several training sessions at the school. The specialists had intended the training to culminate in a problem-solving process to work on clarifying staff norms about disciplining students. The school staff was surprised that the consultants raised discipline as a problem soon after they had worked on it. The specialists were unsure about how to respond, imagining that some of the teachers were unrealistically defending the existing condition of the school. The resulting confusions were followed by antagonistic remarks toward the specialists and a demand that they stop the training until further notice.

By the end of February 1970, the CASEA consultants were giving no aid to the organizational specialists in Kent in selecting tasks, designing training, or carrying out the training. The specialists made the transition very smoothly. By the end of February, they had laid plans for work well into the summer. By the end of the summer they had conducted organizational training ranging from half a day to a full week with seven elementary schools, the superintendent and his immediate staff, the program specialists within the curriculum division, a group of principals, some groups of parents, and a group of eighty students in a "multi-ethnic camp." Moreover, they had laid plans for the following year that included some continued or advanced work and some new work.

Coordinator of the Organizational Specialists

A key role in helping the specialists to function effectively was carried out by the coordinator. Many of his duties were quite similar to those carried out by curriculum coordinators; he handled budget arrangements, stored relevant training materials in his office, kept careful records of the project, served as convener of the specialists' steering committee, and worked closely with colleges in the state of Washington to arrange for training courses with college credit.

Some of his other duties were unique in the district. Because the organizational specialists cut across all important jobs in the district and because they served the entire system, the coordinator reported directly to the superintendent. All projects were discussed with the superintendent before they were launched.

The coordinator served as an active link between the specialists and the rest of the district. When the coordinator received a request for specialists' services, he and the person or group requesting the service typically listed the particular specialists who would be mutually acceptable. Only those listed would then be asked about their availability. In relaying requests to the specialists, the coordinator ordered the requests so as to rotate the work fairly evenly; the object was to avoid developing an elite corps which might become the only group to take on difficult training tasks. As the project gained prestige and was recognized by other school districts as valuable, the coordinator processed all out-of-district requests for services with the steering committee.

Lessons for Other Districts

A cadre of organizational specialists in a school district is one way of developing the self-renewing character of the district. Especially when the specialists are drawn from different roles and hierarchical levels in a district, their work together can build useful techniques whereby intra-district communications are clarified and constructive attitudes are taken to problem-solving. The success of the specialists depends on their ability to open up communication and to improve problem-solving skills in ways that allow existing resources to be used. Certain preconditions for a successful cadre of organizational specialists can be sketched as a result of experiences in this project.

From the beginning of the project, all significant role groups within a district should be involved in defining objectives and delineating problems. Second, a vertically organized group of persons of high influence should attend a short training event in which organizational training techniques are demonstrated. The demonstration should explicitly reveal the differences between organizational training and sensitivity training (Schmuck, Runkel, and Langmeyer, 1969). Third, this high-influence group should form a steering committee for the project from one of its own subgroups. The steering committee should decide on a means of advertising and of selecting the recruits for the training. These recruits should represent most of the significant professional roles in the district. Fourth, the specialists should experience intensive initial training during two or three weeks in which they learn how to perform as group facilitators. Finally, the cadre of specialists should try out their training skills in the district under the guidance of outside consultants. The outsiders should withdraw after about six months of help.

Experiences in Kent indicate a number of strengths in this method. We can point to a number of features of the project that speeded and heightened the effectiveness of the cadre of organizational specialists in their work in the district. Members of the district were able to comprehend something of the probable role of the organizational specialist through actual participation in some of the training that had been conducted by the CASEA consultants. (Actually, almost everyone who applied for training as an organizational specialist had experienced the work of CASEA firsthand.) This fact minimized false anticipations on the part of applicants and gave the two-week training something of a head start.

Because of participation in CASEA-led events, some members of the district with whom the specialists had to interact also had some familiarity with the kind of work the specialists would be doing. The superintendent, for example, knew what the specialists were talking about when they proposed to help with the processes during his staff meetings. Principals of schools knew what they were contracting for when they asked for help from the specialists. This familiarity lessened the likelihood of crossed signals, misapplications, and disappointments. The familiarity with the specialists' sort of work on the part of others in the district also resulted in a high level of confidence and support from others. The superintendent supported the work by allowing one of the curriculum specialists in the district to spend some time as coordinator of the cadre. He also supported the specialists by releasing ten days a year to each for his work as a specialist. The local education association, along with a newly formed group of principals, also supported efforts of the specialists in various ways.

The jobs represented among the specialists made available to them a wide variety of resources. These resources included intimate knowledge of particular schools, liaison with the local education association, and easy access to the superintendent.

The specialists were soon recognized as available to any segment of the district. No doubt this occurred because the wide range of jobs among the specialists prevented their being looked on as an adjunct of any one school or division, and also because they sought out, for their early projects, work that would take them into various segments of the district.

A norm was established early that maintained respect for diversity among the specialists. As early as the end of February, the steering committee of the organizational specialists (OS's) had stated that a member of the district could participate in the work of the Kent OS's in several ways: (1) as an occasional observer and reporter, (2) as an instructor in a course, (3) as an active member of a team of trainers in a particular intervention but not as a regular member of the OS's with duties to the OS's as a body, (4) as a regular member of the OS's, and (5) as a regular member with additional duty as a member of the steering committee. This tolerance of various roles within the OS's has enabled the OS's to make optimum use of the talents and time of each person who works with them. Moreover, the gradation of responsibility among the roles provides a natural channel for developing new members of the body as a whole.

My theory of OD leads me to believe that a key cause of the successful functioning of the OS's was their image not merely as a list of individuals but as a team or subsystem within the district, with a group identity as clear as that of a school or central office division. This subsystem character was produced among the OS's by giving them tasks during training that increased their interdependence and their readiness to call upon one another for help with the expectation of receiving it. The subsystem character, in turn, made it easy for the OS's to allocate duties, establish and disband subteams, and call upon the resources of one another on short notice.

As it evolved, the steering committee's success heightened the team-like feelings among the specialists. Members of the steering committee were selected from those specialists who wished to serve. Communication to all specialists was accomplished by the coordinator sending out minutes of all meetings. Each of the steering committee members has felt obliged to also communicate the results of meetings to those specialists with whom he has regular contact.

The theory also leads me to believe that the effectiveness of the OS's is enhanced by the strategy of conducting training for OD not merely with individuals, but with the groups through which people carry out their actual jobs (faculties of departments or schools, a planning committee consisting of department heads, and members of a central office division). The OS's do not look upon the courses they conduct in communicative skills as ends in themselves, but rather as preparation for later work with those same people in their natural work groups. The policy of training work groups minimizes the problem of transferring training. Informal reports of the work done with the faculties of seven elementary schools in August 1970 indicate that this strategy is working out successfully.

An OS is prohibited from working in that role within his home office or building. The Assistant Superintendent for Curriculum Development does not conduct organizational training among his own curriculum consultants, and the principal or teacher does not train faculty in his own building. This policy gives each OS the advantage of being an "outsider": trainees are more willing to expose their interpersonal stresses than they would otherwise be.

Finally, the development of systematic procedures of self-renewal represents another strength of the OS group. The in-service training needs of the specialists were listed by the steering committee. Next, a few training sessions were held for the specialists, with several more scheduled in the future. Plans were made to introduce interested staff members into the cadre of specialists, and these have begun to be implemented.

The project also suffered some weaknesses. In the early part of the project, sites for interventions were picked mostly by the OS's; they did not arise at the initiative of the people occupying those sites. An example of the result of this procedure occurred at the junior high school mentioned earlier. Aside from the fact that the OS's used out-of-date diagnostic information, many teachers in the building felt that the help of the OS's was being imposed upon them. This feeling would have been lessened or absent had the school invited the OS's to work with them. One way OS's can give a school the opportunity to invite them in (and increase the likelihood of such an invitation) is to make opportunities for the faculty to discuss its own problems within itself, with the OS's serving as little more than conveners of the discussions until an opportunity arises to offer their other skills.

A second weakness, with psychological effects similar to those of the first, was the perception on the part of many of the Kent staff that the specialists were part of the outside CASEA consultant group rather than an integral part of the district. We believe this perception was intensified among those personnel who never actually participated in any of the organizational training as a result of certain fears many of them formed about what the CASEA consultants—and consequently the OS's—might ask them to do. The most prominent fear was that of self-disclosure and the release of strong emotion that many people associate with "sensitivity training." We believe this misapprehension was strengthened by the principals' attendance at the Human Relations Laboratory in June 1968. That event consisted mostly of experience in T-groups, with personal rather than organizational development as the goal. Some principals communicated the belief to teachers that the training done by the CASEA consultants and OS's would be similar to their T-group experience. The CASEA consultants, especially, should have devoted more time to demonstrating the nature of the projected organizational training to interested teachers in the district.

The entire project gained new strength as groups within the district began to ask for training. After some six months of experience with organizational train-ing, the specialists let it be known that they would respond to invitations but would no longer attempt to initiate interventions. Invitations were more numerous than the OS's could accept. All those interventions listed earlier as having taken place after February 1970 as well as a number of smaller activities were the result of invitations.

The most serious threat to the project related to the professional expectations and workloads of the specialists. The Kent district already was involved in several change-oriented programs when the organizational specialist program was introduced. Many of the first cadre of specialists were committed to other programs considered beneficial, and there were several persons in conflict over which of the projects should receive highest priority. Seventeen of the original twenty-three specialists gave this project high priority, but only by spending on it considerable time beyond that anticipated. Other districts should seek clear commitments from their specialists with the understanding that some extra time will be required to make the project successful.

School districts should proceed carefully when developing a cadre of organizational specialists. The district should involve representatives of all ranks and types of jobs in the early phases, demonstrate repeatedly the nature of organizational training in various segments of the district, and wait for subgroups in the district to ask for help.

Administrators and influential teachers should be encouraged to support the project in concrete ways: payment for training events, the offer of secretarial services, and the offer of space for meetings and storage of training supplies, for example. Since most organizational specialists will be expending a great deal of extra time and energy in the project, the fragile relationship between the district and the project must be carefully nurtured. If these guidelines are followed, a school district will find that the development of a cadre of specialists in organizational training can be a relatively inexpensive way of refurbishing ineffective group processes and of bringing about a greater capacity for self-renewal.

References

Schmuck, R., and Runkel, P. 1968. *A preliminary manual for organizational training in schools.* Eugene, Oregon: Center for the Advanced Study of Educational Administration.

——; Runkel, P.; and Langmeyer, D. 1969. *Theory to guide organizational training in schools.* Technical Report No. 3. Eugene, Oregon: Center for the Advanced Study of Educational Administration.

Thomas, T. A. 1970. *Changes in elementary school principals as a result of laboratory training.* Technical Report No. 5, Eugene, Oregon: Center for the Advanced Study of Educational Administration.

11

NEEDS AND PROSPECTS

Richard A. Schmuck and Matthew B. Miles

Organization development in schools is brand new—less than a decade old. Within that period, very little formal research has been accomplished on its processes or effects. The literature that reports systematic evaluative data of OD interventions in school districts, aside from the studies in this book, is sparse and largely descriptive or speculative. Although many behavioral scientists have had experience with OD in schools, few have managed and evaluated a complete and sustained program of interventions. To our knowledge, among those who have implemented full OD programs in schools, only the authors in this book have carried out systematic research on their training efforts. As the reader can easily notice, the foregoing OD projects—even though they are sophisticated, considering the short history of such research—leave many questions unanswered. They not only suggest issues requiring more research, but also present a wide range of needs and prospects for more sophisticated projects.

Need for More Complete and Formal Research on OD Interventions in Schools

This is the first and perhaps most demanding need, especially if this new domain of planned change is to meet its claim to be science-based. Most OD practitioners are not researchers; they do not systematically evaluate the outcomes of interventions except in informal ways. Most OD consultants collect information from clients in the manner of an "artistic clinician." That is to say, as a competent consultant, the OD trainer collects data about his intervention in order to become alert to the responses and needs of his clients. He makes use of such information in designing future training sessions and may feed some of the data back as part of the training design (as discussed in Chapter 6). However, OD trainers seldom collect data to test their theory of organizational change, to evaluate outcomes after their intervention, or to compare what occurs in an OD-influenced school with other schools receiving different inputs. Unfortunately the "disinterested research function" has seldom been included in school OD projects.

Benedict et al. (1967) developed a carefully worked out research design for OD in schools that we encourage others to try. The "clinical-experimental" model, as they have labeled it, requires a separation between the consulting and research functions. Their design involves making theory-based predictions (facilitated by a "research observer" who collects data from consultants as they diagnose and plan), describing interventions with care, and using an extended experimental-control design to rule out the effects of change due to instrument sensitization or test-treatment interaction.

Within the macro-structure of this "clinical-experimental" design, we recommend that increased emphasis be given to documenting the flow of intervention events. More attention should be placed on the collection of organic data, i.e., rich, detailed, sequential information about occurrences during the training period and between training events. Also, evaluations assessing the effects of subparts of interventions are needed. Such questions as these might be focused on: What happens during and after each separate exercise or procedure at an OD laboratory event? What of relevance occurs between training episodes? Can organizational growth during OD be graphically and quantitatively described? What do local change teams or internal OD specialists (as in Chapter 10) do—in detail—as they carry out their roles?

Along this line, more vigorous use should be made of systematic observation, post-meeting reaction forms, tape-recording, and video-taping during interventions. Participants might be asked to keep brief written logs regularly or to speak periodically into cassette tapes about their perceptions of and attitudes toward OD events. Such reports could be guided by a "self-interview" set of explicit questions.

But even more important, OD researchers in schools should be creating more unobtrusive measures (see Webb, Campbell, Schwartz, and Sechrest, 1966): content analyses of agenda items or minutes for departmental, school faculty, and board meetings; observations of seating arrangements, including the closeness and distance of selected role-takers; analyses of absence rates; examinations of budgets; and content analyses of such items as newspaper clippings and the public speeches of the superintendent. An imaginative example comes from Warren Bennis, who wanted a measure of his visibility in the industrial organization with which he was consulting. He had his secretary telephone the firm and ask for "Dr. Bennis" at times when he was serving as a consultant, and record whether or not he was known, by whom, the time it took for him to be reached, and similar information.

Some OD projects—like those presented in this book—do provide for the collection and analysis of data to demonstrate whether primary objectives are achieved, but future projects should make use of more precise methods to study the effects of OD training more penetratingly. One of the best such orientations is the multi-trait, multi-method matrix of Campbell and Fiske (1959). In this approach, each of an array of variables is measured by two or more independent measurement procedures. Campbell and Fiske argue that close allegiance to a belief in the operational definition of variables has encouraged social scientists to depend unwisely on single classes of measurement, usually the most highly reactive procedures, such as interviews or questionnaires. Thus, apparent "results" may be no more than a generalized response to the mode of data collection being used, rather than an indicator of changes on the specific variables of real interest.

Research on OD in schools has been a case in point. Few studies that we know of have employed multiple independent methods for getting at a complex array of outcomes.[1] As Campbell and Fiske recommend, once a hypothesis has been confirmed by two or more independent measurement processes, the uncertainty of interpretation is much reduced. Multiple measures of self-renewing processes, e.g., interview, questionnaire, observation, content analysis, etc., would represent a leap forward for the future development of OD in schools.

Need for Clearer Theory About OD in Schools

Not enough OD practitioners in schools have been explicit about their postulates, assumptions, and hypotheses. Logical connections among actual data, the diagnoses made about an organization, the interventions proposed, and their short- and long-range consequences are seldom drawn out in complete enough detail. For example, OD practitioners have rarely been explicit about how a particular training event is meant to influence the organizational normative structure while at the same time changing interpersonal relations in a subgroup. As Lake and Callahan point out in Chapter 7, little theory has been explicated to guide such matters as entry, contract building, and sequencing. We also need much better conceptualization of the nature and functioning of long-term sequential strategies that will lead to the viable institutionalization of OD functions within school districts.

One way of sharpening up the theory of organization development in schools would be to include a "research observer" in the inside/outside consultants' design and planning meetings. (See Benedict et al., 1967, for a specific example.) This procedure allows the consultants to deliberate creatively and spontaneously while at the same time making provision for the systematic documentation of OD theory. The research observer raises questions to the consultants while they are working. He might ask about the diagnostic information that has led the trainers to propose a specific intervention or might ask for the specific data on which the diagnosis was based. He might also query the trainers concerning the assumptions about organizations or interpersonal relations that undergird their action plans. If this function is to contribute to the development of clearer theory, the consultants must have confidence and trust in the research observer and must plan the method by which they will respond to his role. Observer questions which are answered inadequately or vaguely by the consultants should be retained for further clarification and development.

Need to "Demystify" OD Technology

One issue that has tended to slow down the large-scale diffusion of OD in schools—and elsewhere, for that matter—has been the lack of clearly delineated, operational descriptions of the methods of intervention. OD consulting has been

---

[1] For two exceptions, see Beckhard and Lake (in press) and Schmuck and Runkel (1969). For a useful collection of instruments, see Fox, Jung, Ritvo, Schmuck, and Van Egmond (1970) and Lake, Miles, and Earle (1971).

carried out, in the main, by adept "artists" who remain vague about their skills or describe them only sketchily. Little concern has been shown for careful descriptions of the *what* and *how* of OD. (See Schein, 1969, for a notable exception in the area of process consultation.)

We think that OD consultants in schools should describe their techniques much more explicitly. Detailed descriptions are needed so that other less experienced consultants and internal specialists can use them, experimental replications of techniques can be carried out, and creative adaptations can be made for future designs. We think that enough is known now about successful techniques in such areas as clarifying communication, uncovering conflicts, feeding data back, improving group procedures, solving problems, and making decisions that a sizeable array of packages could be constructed.[2]

Even though many well-worked-out techniques are ready for description and dissemination, attention should be given to more careful reporting on the usual effects of each technique. We need more research studies reporting on how different sequences affect participants, what makes for effective start-up experiences, the way in which to end training experiences effectively, the way in which "ripple effects" move outward from a focal group into the surrounding organization, and so on.

Need to Broaden the Scope of OD Models

More effort should go into understanding the basic assumptions behind OD training and in exploring alternative models of the nature of man, organizations, society, and change. Some current models that we find interesting are:

Trust-Truth Model

Most OD projects in schools have been guided by a set of assumptions involving *trust* and *truth*. Such a "tender" model states that shared expectations involving trust, warmth, and supportiveness are formed as the members of a working team gain confidence and skill in communicating clearly and openly. These norms and skills, in turn, support collaborative problem-solving and the rational use of information in making decisions. This model assumes, along with McGregor (1967), that the work of schools is carried on through interpersonal interactions and that heightening abilities for problem-solving must commence with new norms for interpersonal openness and helpfulness.

Even though the trust-truth model has represented the primary guide for OD in schools, it has by no means been fully developed and researched. For example, one recent development, Jack Gibb's TORI processes (1966), needs exploration in educational settings. The TORI technology involves training groups of one hundred or so people in interpersonal sensitivities and skills that allow them to merge easily into a supportive community. Although the training

---

[2]For current developments in the packaging of OD techniques the interested reader should contact the NTL Institute for Applied Behavioral Science, 1201 N.E. 16th Street, Washington, D.C.; the Northwest Regional Educational Laboratory, 400 Lindsay Building, 710 S.W. Second Avenue, Portland, Oregon; or the Center for the Advanced Study of Educational Administration, Hendricks Hall, University of Oregon, Eugene, Oregon.

is largely unstructured and free-flowing, some of the techniques may be transferred via videotapes or movies.

Gibb's approach to training and other similar approaches that use "soft" intervention modes to put emphasis on personal and interpersonal growth differ significantly from the more structured techniques of most past OD training in schools. The success of Gibb's techniques, however, leads us to wonder about creative integrations of more unstructured, existential approaches with traditional OD. Such integration could be rather helpful, we suspect, in humanizing school cultures.[3]

This integration is interesting from at least two points of view. It would seem that the rigidities and coerciveness of large urban schools might be broken open and freed up by an OD strategy that included personally freeing and expressive activities. Conversely, dysfunctional aspects do exist in the permissive and open climates of many current "free schools." Such aspects might be reduced by an existential design that leads into structured OD components.

Power-Conflict Model

Although conflict is often surfaced and used in the trust-truth model, it has not been employed deliberately as a lever for change. Generally the trust-truth model has called for inter-group conflicts to be managed through collaborative problem-solving. We agree with Chesler and Lohman (Chapter 9) that much more research should be done on the effects of deliberately bringing conflict into the open; training groups to fight for their interests (especially "under-privileged" groups such as students, teacher aides, and substitutes); and building new organizational power structures, roles, norms, and procedures through negotiation. In the immediate future, especially, we believe that research is needed on the effects of OD trainers' advocacy of the interests of students or community groups in relation to the school. Study of the results of such confrontations—if well executed—could lead to stronger, more viable schools.[4]

Product-Accountability Model

The first two models emphasize human organizational processes as initial points of leverage for change. A third model—not tested in OD programs yet—is based on the assumption that schools can and should be held accountable for their products.

OD work with this model would commence by collecting data on such aspects as the reading performance or other achievements of students, their job performance after graduation, attitudes toward future learning, tendencies toward "pro-activeness" (as opposed to passivity), creativity, collaborative skills, and other similar items. These data would, in turn, be fed back to students, teachers, administrators, and parents as leverage points for heightening tension

[3] For interesting approaches that touch on using more personally freeing interventions in schools, see Leonard (1968), Kohl (1969), and Schmuck and Schmuck (1971). The importance of personal growth laboratories in creating viable models of a new culture has been thoughtfully discussed by Shepard (1970).

[4] For an interesting approach to the use of conflict to improve interpersonal relations, see Bach and Wyden (1969).

and interest, inducing increased communication across roles, and stimulating redesign of the school environment.

Such a strategy could also include deliberate attempts to change classroom cultures. We included in Chapter 2 several studies of changing the classroom behavior of teachers, but we believe that much more attention should be given to this problem in future OD designs. With students and classroom cultures as a focus, OD in schools should move more in the direction of employing an accountability model for leverage.[5]

Techno-Structural Model

In the OD cube in Chapter 1, we described the "hardest" of the intervention modes as techno-structural. Using such an approach, the OD intervener would lead participants into experimental redesign of some part of the school. This might include changes in the design or utilization of buildings; changes through alterations in scheduling, flow of students, and groupings of students; and changes through new types of staffing patterns (differentiated staffing) and teaching structures (multi-unit school). Work on the last of these is currently being carried out at the Center for the Advanced Study of Educational Administration (Schmuck and Runkel, 1969).

Need to Make OD Useful for More Types of Schools and Populations

Most successful OD interventions in schools have apparently taken place in conventional suburban or small city districts with fairly substantial economic and attitudinal support for schools. The thrust for the future should turn, we feel, toward large, urban school districts where the majority of American youngsters are educated, and "alternative-culture" schools aiming at the creation of highly individualized, open learning environments.

Derr (1970) describes an unsuccessful OD intervention in a large city; his analysis sheds light on some of the difficulties of executing OD in large urban districts. He pointed to (1) difficulties in negotiating a satisfactory entry and contract, (2) the insulation of the large and complex district from demands of community groups—especially underprivileged groups, (3) rigid bureaucratic patterns with associated norms working against openness, risk-taking, and innovation, and (4) the unwillingness of power-holders to share decision-making with others in the district.

Here are several assertions which bear on the desirability of doing OD in urban schools. First, urban schools must respond soon to the voices of all their clientele if present conflicts are not to erupt into unproductive violence. Second, some activist groups are bringing strong pressure on urban schools in order to reform them radically; some educators react to the threat in defensive and reactionary ways. This "backlash" reaction does not help matters. Third, it seems clear from our experience that professional personnel now in urban

---

[5]Feedback from students to teachers can be very powerful—i.e., can lead to changes in teachers' behavior. For research evidence see Gage, Runkel, and Chatterjee (1963) and Tuckman and Oliver (1968). For a medley of instruments to use with students for feedback to teachers, see Fox, Luszki, and Schmuck (1966).

schools can learn to accept and work with organizational and curricular innovations, even to the extent of sharing power with students and parents. Fourth, the current behavioral science and technology of organization development—as guided by the four models described above—can, we believe, make it possible for educators, students, and parents to learn new ways of working together (even when conflict is very great) to make changes in city schools.

We also believe that OD efforts during the next few years should be directed toward the rapidly burgeoning "free school" movement, devoted to the creation of small schools with humanistic, organic, open, permissive, "counter-culture" norms. (It is a charming comment on the rapid and radical development of free schools that a recent issue of *Big Rock Candy Mountain*[6] listed such books as Holt's *How Children Fail* (1964), Leonard's *Education and Ecstasy* (1968), and Gross and Gross's *Radical School Reform* (1969) under the heading "Bronze Oldies.") Hundreds of free schools have developed within the past two years alone, and they represent an important (and largely untapped) client system for OD training.

While urban schools are largely conventional, rigidly bureaucratized, and replete with conflict, most "free schools" have open, permissive environments, often with norms in opposition to bureaucratization. Norms such as "one man, one vote," "do your own thing," and "let people be" also can lead to organizational problems; some free-school participants, for instance, have reported difficulty in making decisions jointly, building group agreements, dealing with interpersonal conflicts, being able to rely on one another, and, in general, maintaining effective organization without becoming repressive.

OD training will have to be stretched and readapted considerably to respond to these two quite different types of schools. Problems of access, entry, and contract-building are considerably different. Training designs useful in more bureaucratized schools (e.g., those focusing on improvement of line-staff relationships, improvement of professional meetings, and involvement of teachers in organizational decisions) seem far less relevant to the free school, where the central learning concerns may be for such issues as institutional survival, intellectual clarity about educational issues, methods of decision-making which are highly responsive to child and adult needs without becoming time-wasting, and the constructive management of virulent conflict. For both sorts of schools, we believe that much more creative intervention designs are needed for bringing students, parents, and community groups into active confrontation with the other stakeholders of the school (teachers, administrators, boards, and specialists).

Need for More Emphasis on Preparing OD Practitioners to Work Within Districts

More projects deliberately designed to establish groups of skilled OD trainers in

[6]*Big Rock Candy Mountain* (Portola Institute, 1115 Merrill St., Menlo Park, California 94025) a bimonthly resources catalog for "alternative culture" schools. See also the *New Schools Exchange Newsletter* (New Schools Exchange, 301 E. Canon Perdido Street, Santa Barbara, California 93101) for up-to-date information on this movement.

school districts are needed. Highly developed theories and techniques will have no viable impact unless they can be used on a continuous basis by local OD specialists. A collaborative project between the Center for the Advanced Study of Educational Administration and the Northwest Regional Educational Laboratory is now under way to study the problems involved in developing groups of internal trainers. Assuming that it is feasible to install such groups in many districts, we believe that each district group will gain legitimacy and influence as it is formally and regionally linked to other similar groups. Institutions oriented to improvement in schools, such as regional educational laboratories, state and county departments of education, and commercial agencies, could coordinate the district groups and periodically arrange for advanced training sessions to refurbish them.

Summary

If OD in schools is going to mature and blossom, the need is great for more adequate research; clearer theory; sharper descriptions of techniques; the use of more models, types of schools, and populations; and the development of teams of OD specialists within many school districts that are linked regionally. If these needs can be worked on promptly and vigorously, we are optimistic about the part that OD can play in humanizing and rebuilding the American school.

References

Bach, G., and Wyden, P. 1969. *The intimate enemy*. New York: William Morrow.
Beckhard, R., and Lake, D. G. In press. Short and long-range effects of a team development effort. In *Strategies of social intervention: a behavioral science analysis,* eds. H. A. Hornstein, B. A. Benedict, W. W. Burke, R. Lewicki, and M. G. Hornstein. New York: Free Press.
Benedict, B.; Calder, P.; Callahan, D.; Hornstein, H.; and Miles, M. 1967. The clinical-experimental approach to assessing organizational change efforts. *Journal of Applied Behavioral Science,* 3: 347-80.
Campbell, D., and Fiske, D. 1959. Convergent and discriminant validation by the multitrait-multimethod matrix. *Psychological Bulletin* 56:81-105.
Derr, B. 1970. Organization development in one large urban school system. *Education and Urban Society*. September.
Fox, R.; Jung, C.; Ritvo, M.; Schmuck, R.; and Van Egmond, E. 1970. *Diagnosing the professional climate of your school*. Portland, Oregon: Northwest Regional Educational Laboratory.
____; Luszki, M.; and Schmuck, R. 1966. *Diagnosing classroom learning environments*. Chicago: Science Research Associates.
Gage, N.; Runkel, P.; and Chatterjee, B. 1963. Changing teacher behavior through feedback from pupils: an application of equilibrium theory. In *Readings in the social psychology of education,* eds. W. W. Charters and N. Gage. Boston: Allyn and Bacon. Pp. 173-181.
Gibb, J., and Gibb, L. 1966. Emergence therapy: the TORI processes in an emergent group. In *Theories and methods of group psychotherapy and counseling,* ed. G. M. Gazda. New York: Charles C. Thomas.
Gross, R., and Gross, B. 1969. *Radical school reform*. New York: Simon and Schuster.
Holt, J. 1964. *How children fail*. New York: Dell.
Kohl, H. 1969. *The open classroom*. New York: Vintage Books.

Lake, D.; Miles, M.; and Earle, R. 1971. *Assessment of social functioning.* New York: Teachers College Press.

Leonard, G. 1968. *Education and ecstasy.* New York: Dell.

McGregor, D. 1967. *The professional manager.* New York: McGraw-Hill.

Schein, E. 1969. *Process consultation: its role in organization development.* Reading, Massachusetts: Addison-Wesley.

Schmuck, R., and Runkel, P. 1969. Improving organizational processes in unitized elementary schools. Proposal for Program 30 Project. Eugene, Oregon: Center for the Advanced Study of Educational Administration.

_____. 1971. *Group processes in the classroom.* Dubuque, Iowa: Wm. C. Brown.

Shepard, H. A. 1970. Personal growth laboratories: toward an alternative culture. *Journal of Applied Behavioral Science* 6:259-66.

Tuckman, B., and Oliver, W. 1968. Effectiveness of feedback to teachers as a function of source. *Journal of Educational Psychology,* 59:297-301.

Webb, E.; Campbell, D.; Schwartz, R.; and Sechrest, L. 1966. *Unobtrusive measures: nonreactive research in the social sciences.* Chicago: Rand McNally.

APPENDIX: STUDIES SINCE 1971

Following is an annotated bibliography of studies carried out on organization development in schools during the past five years. We are indebted to Philip J. Runkel for his assistance in compiling and annotating this bibliography.

Alschuler, A. Toward a self-renewing school. *Journal of Applied Behavioral Science*, 1972, *8*(5), 577–600.

This case study describes how OD strategies can be used to introduce psychological curricula in a community college. The author hypothesizes that the success of the intervention was due to the combination of three factors: favorable historical antecedents, the nature of the intervention, and continuous leadership by key administrators before and after the intervention. The interdependence of these three factors is analyzed.

Arends, R. I., & Phelps, J. H. *Establishing organizational specialists within school districts*. Eugene, Ore.: University of Oregon, 1973.

Describes in detail how two cadres of organizational specialists were established, their rationale, and the success of their work.

Arends, R. I., Phelps, J. H., & Schmuck, R. A. *Organization development: Building human systems in schools*. Eugene, Ore.: University of Oregon, 1973.

This 50-page booklet introduces the concepts and methods of organization development to school people who have no previous acquaintance with the topic. Organization development enables the school to monitor and respond to the environment and to find, maintain, and use the resources and ideas needed to respond. OD does this by improving the school's self-renewing capabilities: communication processes, problem-solving processes, decision-making procedures, meeting procedures, and potential for collaboration. The school becomes self-renewing by experiencing learning-by-doing in the task group, skill training, new procedures, survey feedback, and group and intergroup exercises.

Baldridge, J. V., & Deal, T. E. (Eds.). *Managing change in educational organizations*. Berkeley, Calif.: McCutchan Publishing, 1975.

A useful compendium of 26 studies and essays, this volume demonstrates that educational research and development on organizational processes have provided valuable assistance for school administrators wrestling with the problems involved in changing schools. Over half of the book's material comes from contributions of the Stanford and Oregon R & D centers.

Blumberg, A., & Schmuck, R. A. Barriers to training in organization development for schools. *Educational Technology*, 1972, *12*(10), 30–34.

Schools, like other organizations, are increasingly faced with the challenge of making more effective use of their human resources. Strategies to accomplish this vary from the additions of administrative or staff positions, through inservice training programs, to organization development training. The last of these, though the least frequent, appears to be on the increase and is the concern of this article. The intent is to discuss the meaning of organization development training, to indicate some barriers to effective training, and to make note of some ways in which consultants might proceed to overcome barriers.

Bowers, D. G. OD techniques and theory results in 23 organizations: The Michigan ICL study. *Journal of Applied Behavioral Science*, 1973, *9*(1), 21–43.

Bowers compares empirically the impact over time of four interventions—interpersonal process consultation, task process consultation, laboratory training (group development), and survey feedback—and two control conditions—data handback and no treatment—on a host of attitudinal variables. Survey feedback, interpersonal process consultation, and data handback led to positive changes on a majority of the dependent measures, while task process consultation led to no change, and laboratory training and no treatment led to negative changes. Further analysis indicated that changes in perceived organizational climate (human resources primacy, communication flow, motivational climate, decision-making practices, technological readiness and lower-level influence) influenced the impacts of the interventions; without positive climate changes none of the interventions had very positive effects, and with them even laboratory training helped. The only intervention that directly improved organizational climate, however, was survey feedback.

Derr, C. (Ed.). Symposium on OD in schools. *Education and Urban Society*, 1976, *8*(2).

The entire issue of this journal is devoted to OD in schools. It includes research articles and several constructive critiques. The most balanced article in terms of indicating pros and cons is Miles's "Diffusing OD in Schools: The Prospects."

Derr, C. B., & Demb, A. Entry and urban school systems: The context and culture of new markets. *Education and Urban Society*, 1974, *6*(2), 135–152.

Describes processes of entry and ten factors that militate against the acceptance of OD by large city schools: lack of supportive and compelling environmental forces; lack of adequate financing; lack of required interdependence; high value on autonomy; promotion from within; dearth of professional schools teaching OD; general skepticism or mistrust; management by crisis; extreme environmental vulnerability; and low accessibility of educational consultants.

Doll, R. C., Love, B. J., & Levine, D. U. Systems renewal in a big-city school district: The lessons of Louisville. *Phi Delta Kappan*, 1973, *54*(8), 524–534.

The authors' conclusions include: "2. The format for training and organizational development should be closely interwoven with the regular academic schedule. 3. Plans for bringing about change falter when resources . . . are not provided in sufficient quantity. . . . 4. Planning and evaluation procedures emphasizing formative evaluation, behavioral objectives, criterion-referenced testing . . . have not as yet been shown to have great utility . . . other than their obvious role in helping call attention to blatant problems in the schools." Contains a history of the change efforts and many useful comments.

Duffin, R., Falusi, A., & Lawrence, P. Organization development: Problems can only be solved from the inside. *School Progress*, 1972, *41*(10), 62–64.

Describes some benefits produced by OD in York County, Ontario, including more effective meetings of groups of administrators, better allocations of teacher-pupil ratios, more exact predictions of enrollments, saving money on surplus textbooks, joint decisions by principals on budget, and savings on noninstructional costs.

Feitler, F. C., & Lippitt, L. L. A multi-district organizational effort. *Educational Technology*, 1972, *12*(10), 34–38.

Describes some of the thinking and implementation that went into development of a 14-school change project, that has come to be known as the "Consortium of Schools."

The Southern Tier Office for Educational Planning began this endeavor in the spring of 1970. The purpose of the project was to provide training input through OD to a number of schools in a five-county region which would allow specific schools to determine for themselves the nature and kinds of organizational and program changes that were appropriate and critically needed. Through training in planning, interpersonal skills, and small-group leadership skills, schools have begun to move proactively toward self-determined goals and objectives.

Flynn, C. W. *The principal as an organizational consultant to his own school.* Unpublished doctoral dissertation, University of Oregon, 1971.

"This study [tells of my] attempt . . . to step out of my role as principal for one year . . . to serve as an organizational consultant to my own staff and student body.

"Though I concluded that it is possible for a principal to be effective as an organizational consultant to his own staff, he encounters built-in problems not faced by external change agents. An outside consultant team has greater potential for success."

Flynn, C. W. Management effectiveness by organizational development. *Bulletin of the National Association of Secondary-School Principals,* 1974, *58*(382), 135–141.

"Obviously a system . . . is not without its trials. It takes time for people to learn to work together effectively in . . . an organizational pattern. One of the biggest changes that must take place is in the administrator who heads the organization. He must learn to share power and to feel comfortable in doing so. He must trust others not to misuse power and he must believe that generally better decisions will be made by groups, the members of which often have key pieces to the puzzles. The payoff is usually in the clarity of understanding that people have of the decisions that have been made and their ability and willingness to cooperate in implementing them. Clearly one of the disadvantages is the amount of time that must be devoted to problem solving and decision making."

Fox, R. S., Schmuck, R. A., Van Egmond, E., Ritvo, M., & Jung, C. *Diagnosing Professional Climate of Schools.* Fairfax, Va.: NTL Learning Resources Corporation, 1973.

A collection of diagnostic instruments for measuring aspects of the school organization. The compendium includes 30 instruments on such topics as organizational problem solving, staff role responsibilities, staff behaviors and norms, the use (or nonuse) of staff resources, and levels of community involvement in the school. Several guides to diagnosis are offered which are helpful to the practicing OD consultant.

Friedlander, F., & Brown, L.D. Organization development. In *Annual Review of Psychology* (Vol. 25). Palo Alto, Calif.: Annual Reviews, 1974.

A thorough review of empirical work on organization development, this article includes summaries of work in industry, nonprofit organizations, and schools. It is an important reference, especially for people interested in carrying out research on OD in Schools.

Gentry, J. E. *Organizational training and its impact on the organizational development of a reconstituted school.* Unpublished doctoral dissertation, Auburn University, 1971.

This investigation sought to determine whether organizational training helps to develop internal communications and interpersonal relationships to the extent that it facilitates the desegregation process and at the same time aids the problem-solving process dealing with curricular, instructional, and organizational change. Organizational training workshops had a meaningful, immediate short-range impact on the principal and staff. Participants cited a feeling of excitement relative to the new school year. Anxiety about working in a bi-racial situation was reduced and there seemed to be a smooth transition into the bi-racial teaching situation.

Gross, N., Giacquinta, J. B., & Bernstein, M. *Implementing organizational innovations.* New York: Basic Books, 1971.

A telling account of an attempt to effect change in a school setting, with a searching analysis of factors which spelled success and failure. The study is replete with implications for the OD consultant.

Havelock, R. G. A critique: Has OD become a social technology? *Educational Technology,* 1972, *12*(10), 61–76.

The author compares organization development with five criteria that an innovation must meet if it would rate as a social technology.

Lake, D. G., Miles, M. B., & Earle, R. B. *Measuring human behavior.* New York: Teachers College Press, 1973.

A compendium of numerous instruments for empirical measurement, this book will be useful both to the OD consultant wanting to find ideas for diagnosis and to the OD research-evaluator looking for reliable and valid instruments for studying social behavior in schools.

Langmeyer, D., Schmuck, R. A., & Runkel, P. J. Technology for organizational training in schools. *Sociological Inquiry,* 1971, *41,* 193–204.

Describes an organizational training methodology in which the focus of intervention is on the organizational interactions of role occupants, not on personalities. The emphasis is on problem solving and/or communicative skills.

Lehman, L. Organizational change and the teacher. *Educational Technology,* 1972, *12*(10), 52–54.

"Many schools and school systems are currently considering various kinds of radical change: team teaching, open classrooms, participative decision making, parent and community involvement, curricular revision and new evaluation techniques, to mention a few. Some of them are turning to OD and other consultancy services for help. Dr. Martin Luther King Elementary School in Syracuse, New York, embarked on a curricular and organizational change program five years ago. For the first three years the staff worked with a team of OD consultants from Syracuse University. . . . What follows [is an account of] how this happened, . . . the master plan for change that was originally presented, and then, from [the] . . . point of view [of] . . . a teacher in the school, comment on what took place and [assessment of] . . . the successes and failings of the whole program."

Luke, R. A., Jr., & Mial, D. An emergent interuniversity consortium for educational change. *Journal of Applied Behavioral Science,* 1971, *7,* 194–214.

Describes the development of an interuniversity consortium, COPED (Cooperative Project for Educational Development), designed to develop and test strategies for planned change in educational systems. To maximize the resources available to client systems, it was decided to involve five universities, each with specialized resources and interests. It was acknowledged from the beginning that considerable energy would have to be devoted to such intraorganizational issues as power and influence, membership concerns, institutional and individual needs for autonomy, and consultant-client relationships. This report identifies the major organizational and interpersonal issues and describes how the consortium dealt with the issue of its own maintenance.

Margulies, N. Organizational development in a university setting: Some problems of initiating change. *Educational Technology,* 1972, *12*(10), 48–51.

This article focuses on a situation in which an effort was made to initiate an organization development program in a university setting. The specific "client" organization within that university was the College of Social Sciences. The impetus for engaging in organization development came from one of the department chairmen, who thought that the OD process and technology held some promise for assessing and dealing with the current problems of the College of Social Sciences.

Murray, D. G. *Organizational development training for adopting multi-unit structure: A comparative case study of two elementary schools.* Unpublished doctoral dissertation, University of Oregon, 1973.

The purpose of this study was to illuminate understanding of the processes of change toward the multiunit structure or organization in two schools that received organization development training. Two years after the training, interviews taken at each school disclosed wide differences in the collaboration among staff members and the form of unitized arrangements. One became a full-fledged multiunit school, with team teaching; the other went back to a more traditional, self-contained organizational arrangement. The reasons for these differences are explored, and a suggested sequencing of organizational training prior to attempted implementation is provided, as well as a checklist for researchers and practitioners to increase their awareness of possible difficulties encountered in this kind of attempt.

Murray, D. G., & Schmuck, R. A. The counselor-consultant as a specialist in organization development. *Elementary School Guidance and Counseling,* 1972, 7(2), 99–104.

Describes why and how school counselors should attempt to change their roles to act as OD consultants in schools and classrooms.

Nagle, J. M., & Balderson, J. H. *Group problem solving: The D-A-P approach.* Eugene, Oregon: University of Oregon, 1974.

Presents a systematic procedure for group problem solving, including phases for generating designative information (D), appraisive information (A), and prescriptive information (P). In other words, these phases are problem identification, plan development, and implementation. The booklet gives detailed sub-steps within each of the major phases.

Nelson, J. E., Schwartz, M., & Schmuck, R. A. *Collegial supervision: A sub-study of organization development in multi-unit schools.* Eugene, Ore.: University of Oregon, 1974.

Reports an experiment in aiding teachers to provide criticism and help for one another in improving their teaching. Results were mixed, but generally schools that received OD consultation showed more faculty sharing and collaboration compared to those that did not receive OD help.

Newell, T. Organization development in schools. *American Education,* 1973, 9(10), 28–32.

An assessment of the purpose, promise, and difficulties of OD in schools.

Owens, R. G., & Steinhoff, C. R. *Administering change in schools.* Englewood Cliffs, N. J.: Prentice-Hall, 1976.

Offers a concise introduction to crucial knowledge and concepts that underlie the best contemporary behavioral science approaches to the management of school change. Half the book delineates the theory and technology of OD.

Phelps, J. H., & Arends, R. I. *Helping parents and educators to solve school problems together: An application of organization development.* Eugene, Ore.: University of Oregon, 1973.

Story of an OD project to resolve conflicts between an elementary school staff and parents. A new decision-making structure was built, though it showed signs of weakening in the following year.

Pino, R., Emory, R., & Jung, C. *Preparing educational training consultants.* Portland, Ore.: Northwest Regional Educational Laboratory, 1973.

A packaged program for training OD consultants for schools and districts. It relates quite closely to the work on OD done at the University of Oregon. Makes use of *The Handbook of Organization Development in Schools.*

Poole, E. A. *A study of the effects of an organizational problem-solving intervention strategy on the development of self-renewing characteristics of a school faculty.* Unpublished doctoral dissertation, Indiana University, 1971.

This study is a description of a five-phase organization development intervention strategy and an attempt to determine the direct and indirect effects of an organizational skill-training program—emphasizing group communication, decision-making, and problem-solving skills—on the self-renewing characteristics of a school faculty. The intervention was successful in introducing communication and problem-solving skills into the daily activities of the school; however, the recognition and use of these skills was greater at the interpersonal level than the organizational level to move the school toward a state of self-renewal.

Porter, C. M., & Schmuck, R. A. *Psychological effects of training in organization development on school district personnel in key line positions (Technical Report No. 14).* Eugene, Ore.: University of Oregon, 1973.

The purpose of this study was to assess changes in attitude among an experimental group of key personnel from a school district that received organization development training and established its own cadre of organizational specialists. The study covers a period from

1968–1970, and takes a careful look at the ways an individual's perceptions of organizational tasks and role relationships might change as a result of OD training.

Runkel, P. J. *Conditions for success and failure of organizational development in schools.* Paper presented to the American Educational Research Association, Eugene, Oregon, 1974.

Evidence is presented on the importance of readiness to share the human resources in a school and readiness for collaboration. Additional important preconditions are listed.

Runkel, P. J. *Bibliography on organizational change in schools.* Eugene, Ore.: University of Oregon, 1974.

A compendium of 433 annotated citations, many of which relate directly to OD in schools. This appendix borrowed liberally from Runkel's work.

Runkel, P. J., & Schmuck, R. A. *Findings from the research and development program on strategies of organizational change at CEPM-CASEA. Eugene, Ore.: University of Oregon, 1974.*

Reviews seven years of research and development. Contains sections on entry, diagnosis, transition, maintenance, effects of OD, controversies, implications for further research, and references to program publications.

Runkel, P. J., Wyant, S. H., & Bell, W. E. *Organizational specialists in a school district: Four years of innovation (Technical Report, Vols. I, II, III).* Eugene, Ore.: University of Oregon, 1975.

This voluminous research report traces the ebb and flow of a major OD effort with an entire school district over a four-year period. The most important result of the effort for the district was an internal cadre of OD specialists made up of the educators themselves. Data indicate that these internal consultants were frequently more effective than outside experts in facilitating organizational improvement in local schools.

Saturen, S. L. *On the way to adaptability: Some conditions for organizational self-renewal in elementary schools.* Unpublished doctoral dissertation, University of Oregon, 1972.

The purpose of this study was to investigate empirically a theory about conditions antecedent to organizational adaptability. During the spring of 1968, 1969, or 1970, pretest measures were taken in thirty elementary schools of (1) whether teachers' expectations supported variety of expression (in particular, open communication of job-related emotions and disagreements), and (2) whether teachers' expectations supported collaboration. During the year following collection of the pretest measures, six of the thirty schools received training in organization development designed by staff members of CASEA to produce adaptability. Five types of post-measures were collected one or two years after the pretest and were assessed to indicate each school's ability to adapt. Over the several dependent variables, the results showed that some predictions were repeatedly confirmed whereas others were repeatedly contradicted.

Schmuck, R. A. Developing collaborative decision making: The importance of trusting, strong, and skillful leaders. *Educational Technology,* 1972, *12*(10), 43–47.

"We often consider administrators at the top of a school district's hierarchy to be the primary wielders of power, with teachers and students possessing decreasing amounts of power to determine what takes place in their schools. But many districts exist for which this picture is oversimplified. In particular, there are some districts in which much of the power thought to be traditionally held by the central office administrators is shared with principals, teachers, and students. I believe that such democratic structures are ideal outcomes for a program of organizational development in schools. . . . Although it does not develop easily, school district groups, building faculties, and classroom groups can be trained to make decisions efficiently, without the necessity for external pressure or surveillance."

Schmuck, R. A. *Incorporating survey feedback in OD interventions.* Paper presented to the American Educational Research Association, Eugene, Oregon, 1973.

Among the various macro-designs used in implementing OD consultation in schools are training, confrontation, process consultation, and data feedback. According to analysis by Bowers (see reference above), the last of these shows great promise in industry. This article describes how data feedback methods can be built into OD efforts with schools.

Schmuck, R. A. Bringing parents and students into school management: A new program of research and development on organization development. *Education and Urban Society,* 1974, 6(2), 205–221.

A proposed plan for building decision-making interfaces among parents, students, and educators. The steps on how OD consultation might be used to establish such structured changes are delineated.

Schmuck, R. A. How can schools accomplish humanistic change? *Educational Leadership,* March 1975, 32(6), 380–383.

Part of the answer lies in humanizing relationships among staff members in contrast to a sole focus on the classroom as a target for improvement.

Schmuck, R. A. & Runkel, P. J. Integrating organizational specialists into school districts. In W. W. Burke (Ed.), *Contemporary organization development: Conceptual orientations and interventions.* Arlington, Va.: NTL Institute for Applied Behavioral Science, 1972.

Benefits and difficulties in establishing and making use of a cadre of organizational specialists in a school district. Included is a brief report on the two cadres established so far by CASEA.

Schmuck, R. A., Arends, J. H. & Arends, R. I. *Tailoring OD interventions for schools.* Eugene, Ore.: University of Oregon, 1974.

Offers three guidelines for consultants that take into account special attributes of school organizations: (1) continually restate the goals of the consultation; (2) be prepared to undertake special procedures for increasing the readiness of the client organization; and (3) make it clear that successful OD requires sustained effort over many months. Two guidelines are based on the sequential and cyclic nature of OD: (4) carefully assess progress at each stage to ascertain how much of earlier stages needs to be recycled; and (5) be sure the macro-design includes micro-designs for recycling the processes of trust building, goal setting, and diagnostic information gathering. The dynamics of entry yield three guidelines: (6) establish a clear, supportive, and collaborative relationship with key authorities; (7) engage all participants in introductory demonstrations and contract building; and (8) clarify interpersonal perceptions, feelings, and motivations. Four guidelines are connected with diagnosis: (9) tell clients early that a formal diagnosis will precede training; (10) insist on collecting data on present conditions, including the state of any follow-up or lack of it on previous problem identifications; (11) use both formal and informal methods of data collection; and (12) use diagnostic data for feedback to clients and for further planning. Considerations in the design of interventions yield four guidelines: (13) do not let the consultants' personal motives, knowledge, or preferred skills outweigh the evidence on the kinds of activities and sequences that will best reach the goals of the intervention; (14) adapt the themes of training, data feedback, confrontation, and process consultation to the local situation; (15) build the macro-design to encompass the mode of intervention, the focus of attention, and diagnosed problems; and (16) phase the work to meet short-term and long-term intervention goals, and include time to renegotiate the plan when unexpected events occur.

Schmuck, R. A., Murray, D., Smith, M. A., Schwartz, M., & Runkel, M. *Consultation for innovative schools: OD for multiunit structures.* Eugene, Ore.: University of Oregon, 1975.

Describes the results of applying organization development in two different ways to help elementary schools adopt team-teaching and multiunit structure. In one strategy, labeled "OD," the entire staff of the school received training; in the other, labeled "GD," a small group from the staff received training. Training and consultation are described in detail. Researchers collected data from two OD schools, four GD schools, and two control schools. Data compare the nature of changes among the schools and the relations of the changes to goal clarity, readiness for change, satisfaction with job and with interpersonal relations, openness in communication, influence patterns, and norms for collaboration. Final chapter offers some indicators of readiness: emerging interdependence, principal's commitment to collaboration, staff consensus on the use of consultants, norm for openness and confrontation, norm for persistence on task, and norm for tolerating differences in educational philosophy. Chapter also lists recommendations for consultants.

Schmuck, R. A., Runkel, P. J., Saturen, S. L., Martell, R. T. & Derr, C. B. *Handbook of organization development in schools.* Palo Alto, Calif.: Mayfield Publishing (formerly National Press Books), 1972.

Written for the school consultants, administrators, organization curriculum specialists and counselors who are involved in the process of change in their schools. It is also useful to professors and students of educational administration, research and development centers in education, and regional laboratories. The authors have provided a collection of directions and specifications useful in the practical application of OD techniques. It is designed as a reference tool and as an action-oriented guide. The first two chapters explain the overall concepts necessary for planning intervention in schools and districts and set the framework for the rest of the *Handbook.* Exercises are described by which organizational members can examine their own communicative processes and learn some new methods of face-to-face communication. The authors offer some procedures for use in several situations that are likely to arise during an organization's actual work day. Finally, ways of building training episodes are described to help increase the flow and clarity of communication. The last two chapters discuss the design and evaluation of training programs.

Schwartz, M., Steefel, N., & Schmuck, R. A. *The development of educational teams.* Eugene, Ore.: University of Oregon, 1976.

An introduction to the trends toward teaming and functional interdependence in education and to how OD methods can be used in this context.

Simons, D. L. *Durability of organizational training for a school faculty.* Unpublished doctoral dissertation, University of Oregon, 1974.

Data were obtained one year and two years after the close of the intervention. Organizational changes that occurred were documented through questionnaires, interviews, and informal observation in the target and comparison schools.

Findings indicated that during the 1968–69 school year the trained staff members did maintain favorable perceptions about the continued use of training and about the persistence of outcomes of training. However, during the last post-test year and after a successor principal took over, a definite change in perception occurred. All but three of the eleven interview questions showed a strong shift toward unfavorable responses.

A new principal entering a school that has experienced organization development must receive training with the staff. This preparation is essential if a successor and trained staff are to work together successfully and maintain the training outcomes.

Smith, L. M., & Keith, P. M. *Anatomy of educational innovation: An organizational analysis of an elementary school.* New York: John Wiley, 1971.

An ecological study of attempted change in a single school with the process of change closely examined. The attempted organizational change was abandoned. Like the study cited earlier by Gross, et al., this one is replete with caveats and action implications for the OD consultant working in schools.

Smith, M. A. *A comparison of two elementary schools involved in a major organizational change, or you win a few; you lose a few.* Unpublished doctoral dissertation, University of Oregon, 1972.

"In 1970, in each of four 'group development' schools, a [presumed] subsystem (namely, a group consisting of the principal and six staff members), was trained in a 40-hour workshop and also received 40 hours of training during the following school year. Of these four schools, two changed to the multiunit structure and two did not. The central focus of this dissertation is to explore, through case histories, the two GD schools that differed in outcome yet seemed most similar at the beginning of training.

"The subsystem in the successful school differed from its counterpart in the unsuccessful school by clarifying its role as an interim group until a legitimate subsystem was chosen, and by setting up a method for changing and renewing the subsystem. . . . Recommendations involve ways of clarifying the innovation not only for members of the subsystem but also for all other staff; increasing the motivation of principal and staff to spend the time and effort required for implementation; and facilitating the continuing process of renewal and readjustment to establish the new roles, procedures, and goals that are required for the innovation to be effective and viable."

Starling, W. *An unsuccessful attempt to implement an educational innovation: A case study.* Unpublished doctoral dissertation, University of Oregon, 1973.

"The faculty [of an elementary school] was given the opportunity to move toward differentiated staffing in a multiunit structure after all but two of them voted to become involved in the project. The principal and four of the teachers received five days of training—resembling consultation in organization development—in communication skills, goal setting, decision making, and problem solving to facilitate this movement toward the new school structure. At the end of four months after the training, staff members were confused, unhappy, and voted to withdraw from the project. This case [has] special interest because of the current widespread acceptance of differentiated staffing and the proven effectiveness of the OD consultative change strategy with a host of other faculties."

Wyant, S. H. *Organizational development from the inside: A progress report on the first cadre of organizational specialists (Technical Report No. 12).* Eugene, Ore.: University of Oregon, 1972.

This document reports the experiences of organization development specialists and compares organization development with two other change strategies. Organization development aims to increase the effectiveness of task groups in schools by teaching them how to communicate clearly, use systematic methods to solve problems, draw out and use group members' information and resources, and build new norms and roles that support group processes. Organizational specialists in Kent, Washington, met with many difficulties because of budget and personnel constraints, but they did succeed in improving skills of district subsystems. When compared with innovative team and change-agent team strategies, the organization development strategy was the only one that could claim specific, long-range improvements in the school systems.

Wyant, S. H. *The effects of organization development training on communications in elementary schools.* Unpublished doctoral dissertation, University of Oregon, 1974.

The study focused on two types of schools: those that had received organization development training—here called "trained"—and those with team-teaching or multiunit organizational structures—here called "collaborative." It was predicted that schools that were both trained and collaborative would score highest on criterion tests of communication, that schools untrained but collaborative and schools trained but not collaborative would score next highest, and that schools both untrained and not collaborative would score lowest.

Effects of training appeared to be weak when all trained schools were considered together. Further analysis showed that small amounts of training have deleterious effect on communication whereas larger amounts of training facilitate communication.

One overall conclusion was that organization development training does have a positive effect on communication, provided that sufficient training is received. Another was that organizational structure also influences communication, but the effect is likely to diminish (in contrast to the effects of training) over time. The major recommendation of the study was that schools undertaking organization development training should ensure that sufficient training is obtained.

THE CONTRIBUTORS

The Editors

Matthew B. Miles grew up in small-town New England, and attended Antioch College, and Teachers College, Columbia University. He was on the psychology faculty at Teachers College from 1955 until 1971, when he joined the Program in Humanistic Education of the State University of New York at Albany. His primary field of interest has been, most generally, social psychology and education. The main focus of his work has been on the creation and study of change in persons, groups, and organizations. His primary reference group has been applied behavioral scientists sharing such interests (both in the U.S.A. and Europe), most of them affiliated with the National Training Laboratories, of which he is a Fellow. He is the editor of the *Journal of Applied Behavioral Science.*

He carried out some of the first systematic evaluation research on T-groups (1960); wrote *Learning to Work in Groups,* a guide to training methods (1959); and edited *Innovation in Education* (1964) and *Learning in Social Settings* (with W. W. Charters, Jr., 1970). His current work includes a book on the small group as a medium and target of change; a compendium of interpersonal and group-oriented research instruments; and an intensive study of the processes and effects of encounter groups. He has consulted with a wide range of educational, non-profit, and business organizations.

Though he is not ordinarily a political being, he spent a good portion of the summer of 1970 in organizing the American Educational Research Association membership to protest against the Indochina war, and helped create a group of researchers willing to volunteer their skills for work on crucial social issues.

In his spare time he likes to cook (and eat), is a good still photographer, drives a BMW 2002, and is trying to do better at keeping his weight on the downhill ski. At the time of editing this book he was 44, and was pleased to read that recurrent identity crises are the hallmark of the healthy man. He is married to Betty Miles, the author of children's books. They have three children, all old enough to know better about most things in life.

Richard A. Schmuck has been a social psychologist of education for nearly a decade. In college, he prepared to teach English in hopes of helping high school students explore their inner and interpersonal selves through literature. After practice teaching, he became interested in humanistic psychology and sociology. All his degrees, the B.A. in English literature (1958), the M.A. in psychology (1959), and the Ph.D. in social psychology (1962) were earned at the University of Michigan. His focus throughout graduate school was on discovering ways to make classrooms more open, informal, person-centered, and democratic.

From 1962 to 1967, he carried out action research on improving inter-personal relations in classrooms. He taught social psychology and did research at the Institute for Social Research at the University of Michigan and he taught educational psychology and carried out research in the Group Dynamics Center at Temple University. While in Philadelphia, he developed an interest in organization development after becoming frustrated in attempts to humanize urban classrooms. He realized that instructional innovations—especially those designed to bring teachers and students closer together as persons—were influenced greatly by the culture, group norms, and organizational procedures of the school and its district. Since 1967 he has done research and development on OD in schools at the Center for the Advanced Study of Educational Adminis-tration at the University of Oregon, where he is professor of educational psychology.

At 34, he is one of the youngest Fellows of the National Training Laboratories. He is the author (or co-author) of more than sixty publications, including four books. The fourth, *Group Processes in the Classroom* (1971), was written with his wife, Patricia, who also is an educator and author. They are preparing another manuscript on schools.

He jogs four miles a day through wooded hills around Eugene, Oregon, plays "tackle me up" football with his son, Allen, farms thirteen apple trees at the foot of Mt. Hood, and reads poems to his daughter, Julie, as well as occasionally writing one himself.

The Authors

Ronald C. Bigelow began his career as a junior high school science teacher, after receiving his bachelor's degree in general science from the University of Oregon. After three years of teaching and directing curriculum development activities, he received a National Science Foundation Fellowship to complete his master's degree, again in general science, at Oregon State University. On returning to the public schools, he became the vice principal of a junior high school, where he began learning firsthand the problems of making an organization run. During this period he participated in several human relations training workshops. The obvious applicability of some of the workshop techniques he experienced to some of the management problems he faced daily led him to return to graduate school so that he could prepare himself to apply these techniques systematically to an organizational setting.

He completed his Ph.D. in education at the University of Oregon in 1969, under the guidance of Richard Schmuck and Philip Runkel. Following that he was an assistant professor of education at the University of Utah, and is now with the Peace Corps. His interest is still with the application of small group techniques to subjects ranging from organizational management to cross-cultural adjustment.

He is married, has three children, and resides in Washington, D.C. His wife, Lynne, is active in group work, having co-trained with Ron in both cross-cultural adjustment and OD work.

Daniel M. Callahan received a Ph.D. in social psychology from Teachers College, Columbia University in 1968. While there he studied and worked closely with Matthew Miles on two projects: Organization Development in Schools and the Cooperative Project for Educational Development (COPED). After his stay at Columbia, he went to the University of Minnesota as an assistant professor in the School Psychology Training Program. After two years of Minnesota winters, he decided to return to the East, where he is now a program associate in the Program in Humanistic Education of the State University of New York at Albany.

His major professional interests are research and practice on organization development in educational institutions. He holds membership in the National Training Laboratories, the American Educational Research Association, the American Psychological Association, and the Society of Sigma Xi.

Mark A. Chesler is a project director with the Educational Change Team, a group of scholars and activists at the University of Michigan working on issues of school conflict and change. He has developed short- and long-range change programs with several school districts that are trying to cope with racism and student unrest. He is also concerned with the ideologies and practices of professionals in the field of applied behavioral science.

He received his Ph.D. in social psychology from the University of Michigan in 1966, and has taught in the Sociology Department and the School of Education since then. He has written in the areas of racism, school roles and structures, and change strategies and processes, and is the co-author (with J. Winter and J. Rabow) of *Vital Problems for American Society* (1968) and (with R. Schmuck and R. Lippitt) of *Problem Solving to Improve Classroom Learning* (1966).

He and his wife, Joan, live with their two daughters, Naomi and Deborah, in Ann Arbor, Michigan. He thinks that schools will have to change soon for these little humans to grow into their potential as big humans.

Richard Diller received his Ph.D. in psychology from the University of Oregon in 1971. He started his career with five years as a Presbyterian pastor. His degrees were the B.A. from the University of California at Berkeley (1956) and the B.D. from Princeton Theological Seminary (1959). While serving the church he became interested in group work, took courses at Fresno State, and later enrolled in social psychology at Oregon. He is developing a unique blend as a professional psychologist, including experimental techniques and consulting skills.

His experimental work on social judgment has been carried out with Robyn Dawes at the Oregon Research Institute. At the same time he has been working with Fred Fosmire, Philip Runkel and Richard Schmuck on OD in schools.

He, his wife and their three children enjoy sailing and hiking.

Fred Fosmire is a professor in the Department of Psychology at the University of Oregon, an associate of the National Training Laboratories, and a clinical diplomate of the American Board of Examiners in Professional Psychology. He received his Ph.D. from the University of Texas in 1952. Although he was first a clinical and personality psychologist, he now works in social psychology and group processes. His current research focuses on developing tasks that will help groups learn about themselves.

Married with four children, he is turned on both by his family and by a variety of vocational activities, including consulting and teaching. He also gets involved in such recreational activities as dirt-bike riding, hiking, whitewater boating, skin diving, fly fishing, and squash.

Max R. Goodson is Professor of Educational Policy Studies at the University of Wisconsin. He has held several key positions in educational administration. He was Dean of the School of Education, Boston University (1957-1962) and Co-Director of the Wisconsin Research and Development Center for Cognitive Learning at the University of Wisconsin (1965-1967). He also was editor-in-chief for the Boston publishing house of Ginn and Company (1962-1965).

He has been a busy consultant, author, and educational researcher. Like Richard Schmuck and Matthew Miles, he is a Fellow of the National Training Laboratories. His many publications include *Formal Organizations in the School System* (1969, a book quite relevant to organization development in schools), "Dialogue on Higher Education," and "Normative Instruction in the Elementary School." His current research is on the future of schooling in America, with particular emphasis on the role played by values in relation to change.

Warren O. Hagstrom, a sociologist, is a Fellow of the American Sociological Association. His first two degrees were received at the University of Minnesota (1952 and 1954); he earned the Ph.D. at the University of California at Berkeley (1963). Currently, he is professor of sociology at the University of Wisconsin.

He performed an important role in the Cooperative Project for Educational Development described in Chapter 1. He served on the research committee, contributing significantly to research design and to the development of instruments. His research interests continue to be mostly in the sociology of education. However, he also has strong interests in the sociology of science and of occupations and professions. His published work includes *The Scientific Community* (1967), an important analysis of the sociology of scientists, and the provocative "What is the Meaning of Santa Claus?" (1966).

Carolin Keutzer has a Ph.D. in psychology from the University of Oregon, and she holds a joint appointment in that department and in the University's counseling center. She is very active professionally—conducting research, teaching, counseling, consulting, and serving professional organizations—as well as being a wife and mother.

She and her husband both are artists on water skis, and she is in addition an accomplished organist, pianist, and painter.

Dale Lake earned the Doctor of Education degree in social psychology from Teachers College, Columbia University, in 1967. His doctoral dissertation was honored with the distinguished Creative Talent Award from the American Institute of Research. His most recent book is *Perceiving and Behaving,* published by Teachers College Press, 1970.

His most important current project involves the development of a unique and innovative organization that embodies what he views as the best principles of both community and bureaucracy in one organization. He hopes that the thirty people at the Program in Humanistic Education of the State University of New York at Albany have discovered a way to experiment with the processes of their work-flow so that they are, in Warren Bennis's words, "moving beyond bureaucracy."

Daniel Langmeyer is a social psychologist and is an assistant professor at the University of Cincinnati and a research coordinator in that university's Community Psychology Institute.

He completed his B.S. in psychology at Brooklyn College and did his graduate work in social psychology at the University of Oregon, where he studied with Richard Schmuck, Philip Runkel, and Fred Fosmire. As a research assistant affiliated with the Center for the Advanced Study of Educational Administration at the University of Oregon, he was introduced to the techniques and mysteries of organization development in schools. After receiving the Ph.D. (1968), he remained at CASEA as a visiting research associate for one year. It was then that he collaborated with Schmuck and Runkel in the research reported in Chapter 3.

Since leaving Oregon he has participated in the behavioral science intern program sponsored by the National Training Laboratories and has become a professional member of that organization. In his work at the University of Cincinnati, he has developed action research programs focused primarily on public schools and on teacher training programs. Dan likes to think of himself as both an experimentalist and an applied behavioral scientist, although for the moment, at least, he cannot find time to devote to the small group laboratory.

John E. Lohman is a project director with the Educational Change Team at the University of Michigan. He and his wife, Anita, are responsible for a project in which they are developing simulation exercises to study how individuals and groups cope with conflict. They plan to use these exercises to increase people's skills in dealing with conflict situations.

He received his Ph.D. (1969) in social psychology from the University of Michigan. His thesis dealt with the social-psychological and educational aspects of children's relationships with older and younger peers. He is a co-author (with R. Lippitt, R. Fox, and L. Schaible) of *The Teacher's Role in Social Science Investigation* (1969), as well as a social science curriculum for upper elementary school students.

He has a B.S. (1961) in chemistry from Cal Tech, and is interested in hiking, camping, music, and designing creative living arrangements. He has consulted with numerous school districts and has worked with student, teacher, administrator, and community groups in problems of organizational change, with particular focus on sharing power in the governance of schools.

Charles T. McElvaney became interested in organization development interventions after he was involved in the project reported by Miles and him in Chapter 6. He started his professional life as a clinical psychologist after completing a V.A. training program near New York City. His degrees—all in psychology—were the B.A. from Upsala College (1949) and the M.A. (1952) and Ph.D. (1957), both from Teachers College, Columbia University.

During some of the time that he was working on his doctorate, as well as the year following, he was employed as school psychologist and director of guidance in the Bellevue, New Jersey, schools. From 1958 to 1970 he was the supervisor of special education—functioning as coordinator of psychological services—in the Allegheny County Schools, Pittsburgh, Pennsylvania. Following a post-doctoral intern program with the National Training Laboratories: Institute of Applied Behavioral Science (1966), he coordinated and conducted several training programs in group processes for school personnel in Allegheny County.

Currently he is supervisor of psychological services in Prince Georges County Schools, Upper Marlboro, Maryland, where he is managing an intensive program to prepare twenty staff members in the district (supervisors, principals, pupil personnel workers, counselors, and psychologists) to function as consultants. This internal cadre—similar to the one described in Chapter 10—will plan, design, and conduct OD programs within the district.

Philip Runkel took his bachelor's degree from a teacher's college with a major in mathematics in 1939. His doctorate in 1956 was in social psychology from the University of Michigan. In the interim, he taught geometry, general science, field astronomy, topographical computing, woodworking, mechanical drawing, and other subjects to various groups at various places. He also spent some years as an engineering draftsman in the Panama Canal Zone. At the University of Illinois, after 1955, he was at different times a member of the Bureau of Educational Research and Associate Director of the Office of Educational Testing. He came to Oregon and the Center for the Advanced Study of Educational Administration in 1964. He holds a patent on a circuit for theatrical switchboards and has edited a book on innovative college teaching, *The Changing College Classroom: Innovations in Teaching* (1969).

INDEX

Variety pool: in school subsystems, 215
Verbal communication skills: relevance to classroom of, 84
Veto power, 207
Vulnerability: in schools, 16

War, 18
Washington, 226
Weschler, I.R., 4
West Virginia Pulp and Paper Company, 4
Western Behavioral Sciences Institute, 21

Western Michigan University Student Opinion Questionnaire, 82
Whole staff participation: importance of in training, 65
Wisconsin Department of Public Instruction, 182
Work group: as focus of intervention, 92; training transfer and, 228

Year-trend, 99
Yeshiva University, 19